School, Home, Community **You and Your Health**

Julius B. Richmond, M.D.
Elenore T. Pounds, M.A.

In consultation with
Orvis A. Harrelson, M.D., M.P.H.
Gladys Gardner Jenkins, M.A.
Dieter H. Sussdorf, Ph.D.
Wallace Ann Wesley, Hs.D.

Scott, Foresman and Company
Glenview, Illinois

Dallas, Texas Palo Alto, California
Oakland, New Jersey Tucker, Georgia

Authors

Julius B. Richmond, M.D. Professor of Child Psychiatry and Human Development and Professor and Chairman, Department of Social and Preventive Medicine, Harvard Medical School; Director, Judge Baker Guidance Center; Chief of Psychiatric Service, Children's Hospital Medical Center, Boston, Massachusetts.

Elenore T. Pounds, M.A. Writer; lecturer; former Directing Editor of the Health and Personal Development Program; classroom teacher; coauthor of the *Health and Growth* Program; author of *Drugs and Your Safety* and other *Health Enrichment Booklets*.

Consultants

Orvis A. Harrelson, M.D., M.P.H. Corporate Medical Director, Weyerhauser Company, Tacoma, Washington; former Administrative Director of Health, Tacoma Public Schools, Tacoma, Washington.

Gladys Gardner Jenkins, M.A. Lecturer in Parent-Child-Teacher Relationships, University of Iowa, Iowa City, Iowa; former member, National Advisory Council on Child Growth and Human Development; author of *Helping Children Reach Their Potential;* coauthor of *These Are Your Children*.

Dieter H. Sussdorf, Ph.D. Associate Professor of Microbiology, Cornell University Graduate School of Medical Sciences, New York, New York; coauthor of *Methods in Immunology*.

Wallace Ann Wesley, Hs.D. Director, Department of Health Education, American Medical Association, Chicago, Illinois; former teacher at primary through college levels.

ISBN: 0-673-11006-0

345678910-RRC-858483828180797877

Content Specialists

Richard H. Blum, Ph.D. Consulting Professor, Department of Psychology and Director, Joint Program in Drugs, Crime, and Community Studies, Center for Interdisciplinary Research, Stanford University, Stanford, California.

Willie D. Ford, Ph.D. Professor, Nutrition and Home Economics, Grambling State University, Grambling, Louisiana; former Nutrition Specialist, U.S. Department of Agriculture, University of Nebraska, Lincoln, Nebraska.

Lucia Guzman, B.S. Assistant to the Dean for Student Affairs, University of Texas School of Allied Health Sciences, University of Texas Medical Branch, Galveston, Texas.

Barbara J. Kohuth, B.S. Environmental Health Educator; Head, Office of Environmental Education and Public Information, Cleveland Department of Public Health and Welfare, Cleveland, Ohio.

Boyd T. Marsh, M.A., B.S. Deputy Health Commissioner for Environmental Health, Cleveland Department of Public Health and Welfare, Cleveland, Ohio.

Norman H. Olsen, D.D.S. Chairman of the Department of Pedodontics and Dean of The Dental School, Northwestern University, Chicago, Illinois.

Marguerite Robinson, M.S. Consumer Specialist, Department of Health, Education, Welfare, Food and Drug Administration, Chicago, Illinois; Past President, Chicago Nutrition Association, Chicago, Illinois.

Joan Tillotson, Ph.D. Consultant in Movement Education, The University of North Carolina at Charlotte, Charlotte, North Carolina.

Wilma Yee, B.S., R.N. Public Health Nurse and School Nurse, Oakland Public Schools, Oakland, California.

The assistance of the National Safety Council, Chicago, Illinois, in reviewing the safety advice in this material is gratefully acknowledged.

Learner Feedback

Experimental versions of many of the lessons in the YOU AND YOUR HEALTH Program for grade five were used during the 1975–1976 school year with students at Arnold School, Torrance, California; Mayport Elementary School, Atlantic Beach, Florida; Timucuan School, Jacksonville, Florida; and Public School 276, Brooklyn, New York. The authors and editors of the program are grateful to the students and to the teachers in these schools for their comments and their suggestions.

Contents

1 Your Emotions

10 Preview It
11 What Kinds of Emotions Do People Have?
12 How Do You Show Emotions?
16 Enjoy It
17 Should You Try to Hide All Your Emotions?
19 How Can You Get Over Angry Feelings?
   Sum It Up.
21 What Can Help When Everything Goes Wrong?
23 What Can Help If You and Your Family Move?
   Sum It Up.
25 Health Around Us
26 What Can Help When You Feel Different?
   How Girls and Boys Grow Up. Sum It Up.
30 Enjoy It
31 Write It
32 **Things to Do. Special Research. Can You Show What You Know? Review It. Health Test for Chapter One. What Do You Think?**
37 School and Home

2 Your Senses and Your Brain

40 Preview It
41 How Many Senses Do You Have?
42 How Do You See?
   Light to See By. The Front of the Eye. The Eyeball. Inside the Eyeball. The Eyeball. The Eyes and the Brain. Seeing Near and Far. When Eyes Need Help. Sum It Up.
50 Enjoy It
51 How Do You Hear?
   How Sounds Get Started. The Outer Ear. The Middle Ear. The Inner Ear. Sum It Up. Another View of the Parts of the Ear.
58 Health Around Us
59 How Do You Taste and Smell Things?
   Four Main Tastes. How You Taste Things. Sense of Taste. How You Smell Things. Sum It Up. Sense of Smell.
65 Where Is Your Sense of Touch?
   Nerve Endings in Your Skin. A Greatly Enlarged View of the Skin.
68 What Does Your Brain Do?
   The Human Brain. The Cerebrum. Special Centers of the Brain. The Cerebellum. The Brain Stem. Sum It Up. The Brain.
74 Your Nervous System
75 A Pioneer in Medical Science
76 Write It
78 **Things to Do. Special Research. Can You Show What You Know? Review It. Health Test for Chapter Two. What Do You Think?**
83 School and Home

3 Your Skin, Hair, and Nails

86 Preview It
87 What Is the Epidermis?
A Closer Look at the Epidermis. Skin Color. Sum It Up.
90 What Is the Dermis?
Blood Vessels in the Skin. Sweat Glands. Oil Glands. A Fatty Layer. Ridges in the Skin. Sum It Up. The Skin Is More Than a Cover.
98 Enjoy It
99 How Does Your Skin Function?
The Skin and Body Temperature. The Skin as a Storehouse. The Skin Helps Remove Wastes. The Skin Helps Heal Small Cuts. The Skin and Vitamin D. Sum It Up.
101 How Can You Take Care of Your Skin?
Washing Your Hands and Face. Baths. Showers. "Stand-up" Baths. Shampooing Your Hair. Clothes to Suit the Weather. Avoiding Sunburn. Sum It Up.
104 How Do Your Hair and Nails Grow?
105 How Do You Take Care of Fingernails and Toenails?
106 Tell It
108 Write It
110 Health Around Us
111 **Things to Do. Special Research. Can You Show What You Know? Review It. Health Test for Chapter Three. What Do You Think?**
115 School and Home

4 Your Bones and Muscles

118 Preview It
119 What Is the Make-up of the Skeleton?
The Wonderfully Designed Skeleton. The Skull Bones. The Backbone. The Ribs. The Hipbones. The Hand Bones. The Foot Bones. The Leg Bones.
127 How Do Bones Fit Together?
Kinds of Joints. The Skeleton.
130 How Do Your Bones Look—Outside and Inside?
The Long Bones. The Flat Bones. Marrow. Sum It Up.
133 How Do Your Bones Grow?
Growth in Thickness and Length. Ligaments and Tendons. Sum It Up.
135 Health Around Us
136 What Do Skeletal Muscles Do?
Muscles of the Trunk. Arm and Leg Muscles.
138 What Are Voluntary and Involuntary Muscles?
Striped Muscles. Smooth Muscles. Heart Muscle. How You Can Build Strong Muscles. Sum It Up.
140 Picture Essay: Muscles—the Body's Movers
146 Write It
147 What Can You Do About Your Posture?
150 Enjoy It
152 **Things to Do. Can You Show What You Know? Review It. Health Test for Chapter Four. What Do You Think?**
157 School and Home

5 How Your Body Uses Food

160 Preview It
161 How Do Your Teeth Help You Eat?
163 How Do You Take Care of Your Teeth?
Sum It Up. Care of Your Teeth. Brushing. Another Way to Fight Plaque.
167 How Does the Food You Eat Get Digested?
Your Mouth Helps. Your Stomach Helps. Your Small Intestine Helps. The Liver and Gall Bladder. Your Large Intestine. Your Kidneys and Urinary Bladder. Sum It Up. The Kidney. How Food Is Digested: A Diagram.
180 A Pioneer in Medical Science
182 Health Around Us
183 How Does What You Eat Affect You?
You Are What You Eat. A Daily Food Guide. Using a Daily Food Guide. Vegetable-Fruit Group. Meat Group. Milk Group. Bread-Cereal Group. Sum It Up.
188 Enjoy It
189 Tell It
190 **Things to Do. More Things to Do. Special Research. Can You Show What You Know? Review It. Health Test for Chapter Five. What Do You Think?**
197 School and Home

6 Your Heart and Lungs

200 Preview It
201 How Does Your Circulatory System Work?
The Heart. Inside the Heart. The Blood Vessels. The Blood. Sum It Up.
208 Pioneers in Medical Science
209 Picture Essay: The Mighty Heart
212 Another Pioneer in Medical Science
213 Health Around Us
214 How Does Your Respiratory System Work?
Your Nose Helps. Your Lungs Get Air. How You Breathe. The Exchange in the Lungs. When You Need More Air. Your Voice Box. Sum It Up.
220 Picture Essay: Your Lungs
223 Health Around Us
224 Tell It
226 Write It
228 **Things to Do. Special Research. Can You Show What You Know? Review It. Health Test for Chapter Six. What Do You Think?**
233 School and Home

7 Your Questions About Safety, Drugs, and Smoking

236 Preview It

237 Could You Pass a Bicycle-Safety Test?
Bicycle-Safety Knowledge Test. Performance Tests. Test of Bicycle Mechanical Condition.

242 Safety Around Us

243 What Should You Do in Case of Fire?
A Fire in a House. A Fire in an Apartment.

246 Safety Around Us

247 What Causes Bumps and Falls?
Sum It Up.

249 What Should People Know About Drugs?
Side Effects. Alcohol Is a Drug. Alcoholics. Alcohol and Young People. Sum It Up.

254 Safety Around Us

255 What's the Harm in Smoking?
How Smoking Damages the Lungs. Smoking and Other Lung Diseases. Smoking and Heart Disease. Reasons for Smoking. Another Kind of Smoking: Marijuana. Sum It Up.

260 **Things to Do. Special Research. More Things to Do. Special Research. Can You Show What You Know? Review It. Health Test for Chapter Seven. What Do You Think?**

265 School and Home

266 Do You *Use* What You Know?

268 Books

269 Metric Chart

270 Glossary

279 Index

For the Teacher

287 About the Book

288 Acknowledgments

1 Your Emotions

If someone asked you why a chapter on feelings or emotions is in a book about health, what would you say?

What do you think your emotions might have to do with your health?

9

Preview It

Do you know that your emotions are a part of everything you do? Your feelings even affect the way your body works.

For example, suppose that you feel happy and relaxed. Your food is easier to digest. You sleep better too. Your heart does not have to work so hard. All the organs in your body function smoothly.

Suppose, on the other hand, that you feel worried. The worry may spoil your appetite. It may keep you from digesting your food well. The worry also may keep you from concentrating on your schoolwork.

You can see that it is important to know something about your emotions. It is important, too, to learn to deal with them. You want to deal with your emotions in ways that help you and do not hurt others.

Learning about your emotions can help you grow up to be a strong and healthy person.

Quickly look through this chapter. Locate seven big questions. What clues do the questions give you about what you will learn? What question interests you the most?

What Kinds of Emotions Do People Have?

Every human being has emotions. But not all people have the same ones at exactly the same time.

Anger is a word that expresses one emotion. What are some other emotions people may have?

You can see a list of some of these emotions on this page. What makes this an interesting list to look at? What words can you add to the list?

ANGER

HAPPiness

Love

FEAR

PRIDE

How Do You Show Emotions?

You show your emotions in many ways. For example, one way you can show them is with your whole body. Glance at the pictures below. What emotions do you think these young people show?

Ed

Gwen

Bruce

Look at the pictures on this page. What emotions are shown? How are emotions being expressed?

Another way you can express emotions is by the tone of your voice. Look at these words: *Never mind*. How would you say them to express anger? How would you say them to express kindness?

Sometimes you can show your emotions by the expressions on your face. For instance, look at the pictures on pages 14 and 15.

Ed

Sam

Tony

Beth

Sheila

What emotions are being expressed by the girl in these pictures? What do you notice about the eyes? the mouth?

Sadness **Happiness** **Fear**

What might cause a person to feel the emotions you see on these two pages?

Anger **Excitement** **Worry**

15

ENJOY IT

Sometimes you can express feelings in the pictures you draw or paint. That is what the artist Paul Klee has done here. The artist called this picture "Companions Hiking." How do you think the companions feel?

Paul Klee, "Companions Hiking," courtesy of Hermann and Margrit Rupf-Foundation, Museum of Fine Arts, Berne, Switzerland.

16

Should You Try to Hide All Your Emotions?

Tom's friend Joe has walked off with another boy. Tom feels left out and hurt. But he thinks, "I won't show how I feel. I won't tell *anyone* how I feel."

Do you think it is good to hide all your feelings? Why or why not?

Talk over your ideas. Then compare yours with the ones given on the next page.

When you think about hiding emotions, do you think of hiding unpleasant ones? Certainly most of us would not want to hide the pleasant ones. How would you feel if your parents and friends did not show their unpleasant and pleasant feelings for you? This could cause problems at times.

Suppose someone is bullying a small child. Or suppose you see someone mistreating an animal. It is natural to show that you are upset at such times. You might speak up and say "Stop teasing" or "Let that animal alone." Speaking up usually helps you feel better too.

Let's look at Tom's problem. He feels he is being treated unfairly or being left out. It is natural for him to be upset. Tom might take a second look. Sometimes there is just a misunderstanding. For example, even good friends have other friends too. So Tom's friend Joe may not have intended to hurt anyone's feelings.

If the hurt feelings don't go away soon, it may help to talk things over with someone. Tom might talk to somebody in his family. Or he might talk to his teacher or to his friend. Talking about how he feels may make him feel better. Maybe the other person can make a helpful suggestion.

What do you think Tom might do instead of feeling sorry for himself?

Something to Do

Do you think you are the only one who ever feels angry, left out, shy, or afraid?

You and others in your group might finish statements like these.

"Once I felt angry when . . ."
"Once I felt left out when . . ."
"Once I felt shy when . . ."
"Once I felt afraid when . . ."

Don't sign your papers. Just put them in a group scrapbook. Later, as you read the scrapbook, you will learn that you are not the only one who has these emotions. We all do.

How Can You Get Over Angry Feelings?

Ida is very angry. Her little brother has been getting into her things. She is thinking, "I'm so mad I don't know what to do. And I just can't stop being angry!"

What do you think she can do to get over her angry feelings?

Talk over your ideas. Then compare yours with the ones given on the next page.

What should you do about angry feelings that stay with you for a while? One thing you can do is let out these feelings. If feelings are locked up, you will feel mean and unhappy. Such feelings can also keep your body from working properly.

Sooner or later the feelings will come out anyway. Sometimes the feelings will be disguised. You may take out your feelings on some other person or thing. Angry feelings may come out in teasing or bullying small children or even animals. You are just getting rid of anger you feel toward someone else. Anger of this kind is sometimes called *displaced anger.*

Angry feelings that are bottled up inside you may come out in ways that cause pain. You may find that your head aches or your stomach hurts.

So, for these reasons, try to let out angry feelings by talking them out. This does not mean going around telling everyone about your feelings. But it does mean talking, if you can, to someone you trust. Often this person is a family member.

Suppose there is no one around to talk to when you feel like talking. There are other things that can help you through your angry period. Later you can talk over and think through your feelings.

Meanwhile, instead of taking out your angry feelings on someone, get busy doing something. Take a long walk. Play a strenuous game. Clean your room or some other part of the house. What else might you do?

Sum It Up

What would you think are disadvantages in trying to hide all your feelings?

What are some helpful ways of dealing with angry feelings?

Why are emotions discussed in a health book?

What Can Help When Everything Goes Wrong?

Rose is upset. She thinks her friends don't want her around. She quarreled with her sister before supper. Now she can't keep her mind on her homework.

What do you think might help a person when everything seems to go wrong?

Talk over your ideas. Then compare yours with the ones given on the next page.

21

There are ways to deal with upset feelings. These ways can make the feelings seem less bothersome. Many times it helps to try to think of a cause.

Thinking about *why* you feel as you do may be difficult at times. You may not want to admit to yourself what has caused your feelings. But it does help if you can discover what is behind them. Then it may be easier for you to deal with them.

Suppose you feel that others are leaving you out of things or do not want you around. Could it be that you are often cross or quarrelsome? Do you say mean things to others? Do you stay by yourself and wait for others to be friendly?

Often it helps to make some friendly moves of your own. Ask someone to play with you. Look for friends outside the group you think are not too friendly. Look around you too. Do you notice someone who seems left out? This person may be happy to have you for a friend.

If you frequently feel quarrelsome, stop and think. Ask yourself, "Is it because I always want my own way?" If so, try giving in now and then. If you give others their way at times, they are more likely to go along with you at other times.

When everything seems to go wrong, turn your attention to something pleasant for a while. But be sure to come back to your problem later when you feel calm. Then you will be able to work it out. Meanwhile, play a game. Watch a TV program that is interesting. Work on a hobby. What else might help until you feel ready to figure out what to do?

Books to Read

You could learn about emotions by reading books about boys and girls your age. Look in the library for books like these about young people who manage their feelings in various ways:

Canfield, Dorothy. *Understood Betsy* (Holt).

Cleaver, Vera and Bill. *Grover* (Lippincott).

Ney, John. *Ox* (Little).

Stolz, Mary. *A Wonderful, Terrible Time* (Harper).

What Can Help If You and Your Family Move?

Roberto has just moved. These thoughts keep running through his mind. "I've lost all my old friends. Things will never be the same. I'll probably hate my new school."

What might make Roberto feel better about moving to a new place?

Talk over your ideas. Then compare yours with the ones given on the next page.

Perhaps the first thing for Roberto to do is to accept the fact that he *has* moved. He can't go back to his former home. So he might as well start to look for good things about his new home.

Roberto knows it's important that his family stay together. So he has to think of them all helping when a parent's work brings him to some new place to live.

Roberto can remember, too, that he is not the only one who has had to move. Millions of boys and girls move every year. They find that the first few weeks may be difficult. But this period usually does not last long.

At school Roberto can help himself by making friendly moves toward others. Instead of staying off by himself, he can try to join in a conversation or a game. If he needs help, he should ask for it. Others are usually quite willing to show a newcomer how things are done.

Of course, there are things that Roberto's group at school can do to help. Some groups appoint a Special Friend. The person stays with a newcomer for the first week or so. The Special Friend sees that the newcomer is not left alone at lunchtime or on the playground.

Some groups have a Welcoming Committee. The committee members talk to the newcomer. They find out all about him or her. Then they share this information. They have a special group meeting to introduce the newcomer.

What might your group do to help a newcomer feel welcome?

Sum It Up

What can you do to help yourself when everything seems to go wrong?

What are two or three things that can help a boy or girl who has had to move to a new home?

HEALTH AROUND US

If you look around you, you will see people helping themselves. They are enjoying hobbies. Hobbies are things people do just for fun. The hobbies make them feel happy and relaxed.

The pictures here suggest some hobbies that boys and girls may have. What are the hobbies?

What is your hobby? Why do you like it?

What Can Help When You Feel Different?

Jack is the shortest boy in his group. He doesn't like it very much. He wishes he were tall like his friend Dave. Sometimes Jack thinks, "Why do I have to be so different? Is there anything I can do?"

What might help a person who worries about being different?

Talk over your ideas. Then compare yours with the ones given on the next page.

One thing we all need to keep in mind is that each person is unique. For example, nobody is exactly like you. No one has a voice just like yours. Nobody thinks just the way you do. No one looks exactly like you. Not even so-called identical twins are exactly alike.

Differences among people make life more interesting. Think what our world would be like if everyone looked alike, dressed alike, and had the same kind of abilities.

Each group that you belong to is interesting because of the many different persons in it.

Differences in height and weight among young people your age are usual. You have only to look around you to see that.

All through the growing-up years, each boy or girl grows in his or her own way. And each young person has a different pattern for growing.

Some boys and girls your age may not be growing very much for a time now. Others may be starting to "shoot up" tall and to gain weight.

Then, too, people have different body builds. Some boys and girls are small-boned. They do not weigh nearly as much as others their age who are large-boned. Some young people may be stockily built and may weigh more than others their age.

Perhaps you wonder, "Is there something special I can do to make myself grow as I should?" The best thing to do is to follow the rules for healthful living. What are they?

What Do You Think?

Tony, age 11, noted that his sister, age 10, was taller than he was.

"There must be something wrong with me," Tony thought.

Do you agree with Tony? Why or why not?

How Girls and Boys Grow Up

There is something important to know about girls. Sometime between the ages of nine or ten and thirteen, girls may make sudden and rather large gains in height and weight. Ten- and eleven-year-old girls have been known to grow four or five inches in one year. They may gain up to twenty pounds. Such changes are not unusual. These changes are known as the *growth spurt.*

Often these gains for girls are preceded or followed by periods of little or no change in height or weight. Girls don't usually keep the extra fat gained in a growth spurt. It is kept only if a girl has developed a pattern of overeating regularly. On the other hand, boys usually do not make these large height and weight gains in such short periods of time. Boys' gains are made more steadily over a longer period of years.

Until the age of nine or ten, boys may grow a little more in height than girls their age do. Then for a few years, the girls begin to shoot up. From ages ten to thirteen, some girls are taller than boys. By sixteen and one-half years, most girls have reached their adult height and build.

Later, boys begin to catch up. By age sixteen or so, many boys will be as tall or taller than the girls their age. Boys continue to grow in height until eighteen or even until their early twenties.

Not all parts of your body grow at the same time. And not all parts reach adult size at the same time. This unevenness of growth may cause a little awkwardness at times. Why do you think this happens?

Sum It Up

Make a list of facts about how boys and girls grow—facts you had not thought about before.

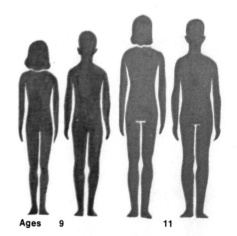

Ages   9   11

Until the age of nine or ten, boys may grow a little more in height than girls their age do. Then for a few years, the girls begin to shoot up. From ten to thirteen years, some girls are taller than boys.

ENJOY IT

Me

As long as I live
I shall always be
My Self—and no other,
Just me.

Like a tree.

Like a willow or elder,
An aspen, a thorn,
Or a cypress forlorn.

Like a flower
For its hour
A primrose, a pink
Or a violet—
Sunned by the sun
And with dewdrops wet.

Always just me.

Why are you glad to be "My Self—and no other"?
Can you make some changes in yourself? What
changes might you want to make?

WRITE IT

You have learned that you are unique. Nobody is just like you. Stop and think about some of the things that make you special. Then write about these things. Below you can see what some other students have written.

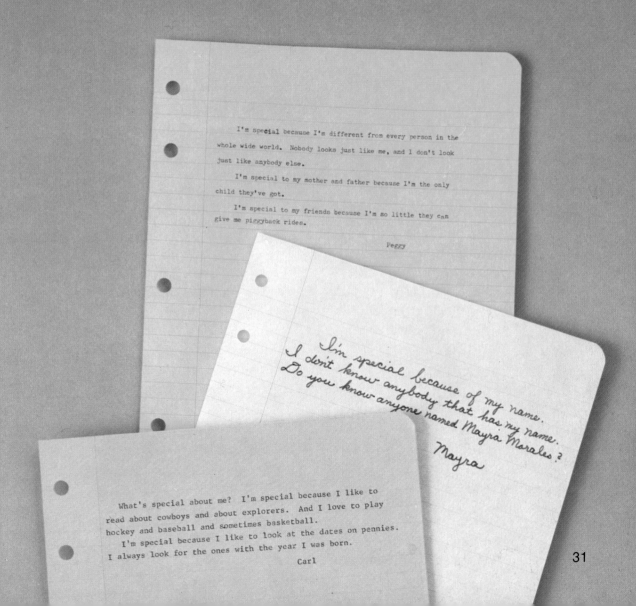

I'm special because I'm different from every person in the whole wide world. Nobody looks just like me, and I don't look just like anybody else.

I'm special to my mother and father because I'm the only child they've got.

I'm special to my friends because I'm so little they can give me piggyback rides.

Peggy

I'm special because of my name. I don't know anybody that has my name. Do you know anyone named Mayra Morales?

Mayra

What's special about me? I'm special because I like to read about cowboys and about explorers. And I love to play hockey and baseball and sometimes basketball.

I'm special because I like to look at the dates on pennies. I always look for the ones with the year I was born.

Carl

Things to Do

1. The word *sad* can be changed to *joy* by changing one letter at a time. Copy the puzzle below and finish it.

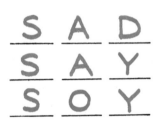

S A D
S A Y
S O Y
___ ___ ___

Now tell or write about a time when your sadness changed to joy.

2. Copy the words below. Beside each word, write a word that means just the opposite.

happy_____
love_____
nervous_____
fearless_____
interested_____
friendly_____

3. Copy this list of emotions. Find and correct the four spelling errors.

happy   nervus
angery   guilty
afrade   boored

4. Write a riddle about the good qualities of someone in your group. Be ready to read it aloud for others to guess. Later you might help make a *Riddles About Us* scrapbook. In it you could put all the different riddles.

5. Make a *Self-Portrait Exhibit* for your bulletin board. Each person can draw or paint a picture of himself or herself.

6. Did you know that there are often many different ways to deal with a situation? Some ways are better than other ways.

Here is a situation that may make boys and girls your age feel angry. *You want to play with friends but you have to go visiting with your family.*

Work together with others to act out some skits. In one skit, you may show your anger by words and by such actions as stamping your foot.

In another skit you might show anger by sulking and not talking.

In still another, you might decide to make the best of things and try to be pleasant.

Later, discuss everyone's ideas about behaving in these different ways. Maybe you can act out other ways too.

Special Research

Write a recommendation or an "advertisement" about a book you have read. Be sure to describe the problems or feelings of the main characters. Here are some examples.

I really liked the book called Roosevelt Grady. It gave me a good idea of what it would be like if you had to move all the time. Read to find out if Roosevelt Grady ever does get a permanent home. The author of this book is Louisa R. Shotwell.

Would you like to read about a girl who sometimes has trouble telling the truth? Then read the book Ellen Grae by Vera and Bill Cleaver.

33

Can You Show What You Know?[1]

Page numbers show you where to look back in the chapter for information, if you need it.

1. Tell what emotions have to do with a person's health. (10)
2. List six or eight different emotions that we all have at times. (11)
3. Mention two ways in which people may show their emotions. (13)
4. Suggest one disadvantage in always trying to hide one's emotions. (18)
5. Tell what is meant by displaced anger. (20)
6. Mention one thing that can help you get over angry feelings that stay with you for a while. (20)
7. Suggest something that may help you calm yourself when everything is going wrong. (22)
8. Mention one or two things that can help a person feel better about moving to a new place. (24)
9. Act out a way to make a newcomer feel welcome. (24)

[1]Behavioral objectives in the cognitive area are stated here directly to students themselves.

Review It

Page numbers show you where to look back in the chapter for information, if you need it.

1. Why is talking out problems a useful way for one to deal with upset feelings? (20)

2. What example can you give of someone taking out feelings on another person or thing? (20)

3. What can a feeling such as worry have to do with digesting food? (10)

4. What are some things that happy feelings can do to promote good health? (10)

5. If you wanted to show encouragement to someone, how would you do it? (13)

6. How would you explain this statement? "Each boy or girl has his or her own timetable for growth." (28)

7. What have you learned about how most girls grow from age ten to thirteen? (29)

8. What have you learned about how most boys grow from age ten to eighteen or twenty? (29)

9. What do you think is meant by "trying to make the best of it" in case your family has to move? (24)

10. What might help a person who frequently feels quarrelsome? (22)

11. What might make others want to leave someone out of things? (22)

12. What are hobbies? How might a hobby affect a person's feelings? (25)

13. What example can you give to support the statement "Each person is unique"? (28)

14. Why might a ten-year-old girl be taller than her twelve-year-old brother? (29)

15. How do individual differences help make life more interesting? (28)

16. What can help you through an angry period until you are able to talk out your feelings? (20)

Health Test for Chapter One

Copy each number on a piece of paper. After each number write the correct answer to the question, *true* or *false*. Rewrite each false statement to make it true.

1. Your emotions can affect the way your body works.

2. You should try to hide all of your emotions.

3. When you are happy and relaxed, you are likely to sleep better.

4. Not all humans have emotions.

5. You often show your emotions by the expressions on your face.

6. When you have angry feelings locked up inside you, you feel happy.

7. Having a temper tantrum is a good way to work through your angry feelings.

8. Angry feelings may be a cause for a person's headache.

9. It often helps if you think about why you are feeling hurt or left out.

10. If you have to move to a new place, it helps to try to accept the move instead of fussing about it.

11. Hobbies are relaxing.

12. Newcomers want to be left alone.

13. A person who keeps saying mean things to others may be left out.

14. You can express emotions by the tone of your voice.

15. A pat on the back is one way to express an emotion.

16. Differences in people make this a dull world.

17. All boys and girls your age are growing rapidly.

18. Boys may grow in height until they are thirty years old.

19. Some ten-year-old girls may make sudden and rather large gains in height or weight.

20. Learning about emotions can help you be a healthy person.

Number of Answers   20

Number Right   _____

Score (Number Right X 5)   _____

What Do You Think?

What is the most important thing you learned in this chapter? Write about it on a piece of paper.

SCHOOL & HOME

You have learned things in this chapter that can help you at home. What, for example, have you learned that can help when you have angry feelings? How could you help a younger child who feels left out of things?

You know that individuals differ too. But did you ever stop to think that homes differ? A home is where you live with people who care for you and give you things you need. People in each home have different ways of doing things. What food, for example, is a favorite in your home? What special way is used to celebrate a birthday in your home? What do you like to do for fun?

You have written about what is special about *you*. Now you might write about why your home is unique. What will you say?

2 Your Senses and Your Brain

How do your senses help make life interesting for you?

Why might it be said that "the brain is in charge of the senses"?

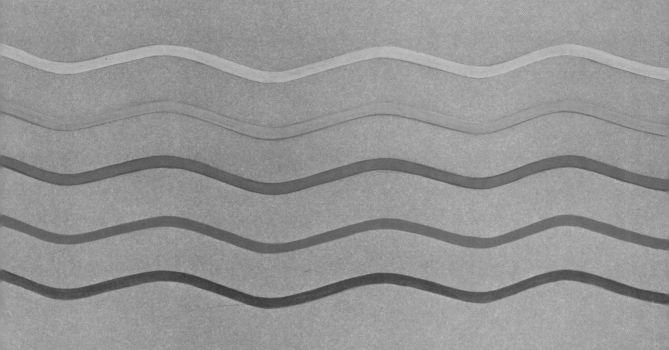

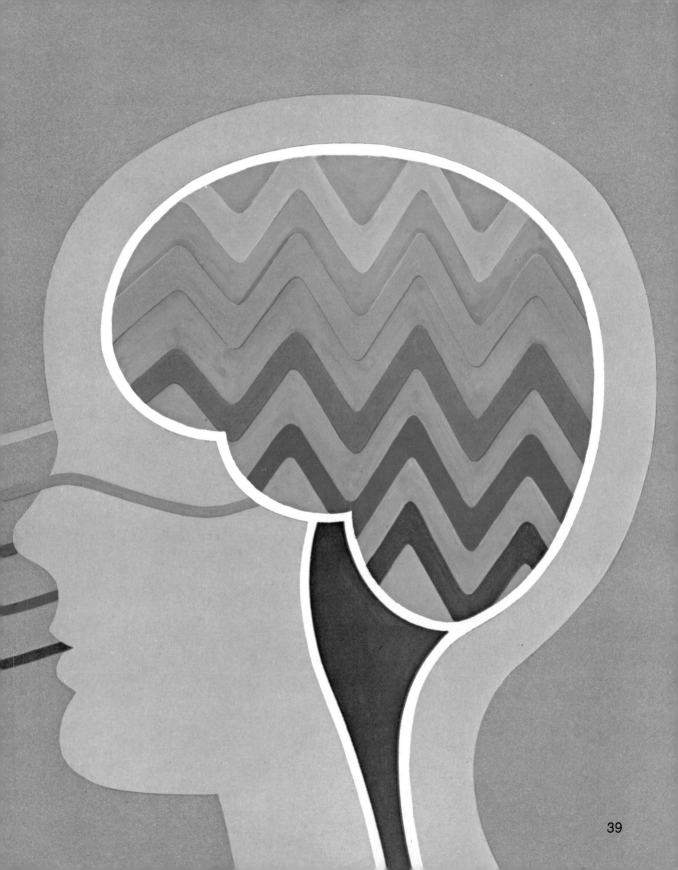

Preview It

You know about the five main senses. These are seeing, hearing, tasting, smelling, and touching.

Of which sense might it be said "only this one can conquer great distances"?

Which sense comes to mind when you hear the word *vibrations*?

Which sense is the "skin sense"?

There are other senses besides the five main senses. There is also the brain. Could you see, hear, touch, taste, or smell without it? Why or why not?

You will find answers to these questions in this chapter. Turn quickly through the chapter. Locate the six main questions in the chapter titles. Look for answers to the main questions as you study the chapter.

As you read to find out about your senses, look for information about the "deep senses." What do you think they are?

How Many Senses Do You Have?

Your five main senses help you know what is going on around you. Other senses help you as well. Deep within your body are some sensory *nerves.* They tell you of your body's needs. These *deep senses* tell you when you are hungry and when you have had too much to eat. They let you know when you are thirsty. These senses tell you when you need to go to the toilet. They let you know when you need to breathe more fresh air.

You have a *muscle sense* too. This sense helps you carry out movements without your eyes controlling them. For example, you can walk without having to watch your legs.

Your muscle sense helps you know about weight. If you lift several objects, your muscle sense tells you which one is heaviest.

If you want to know about left and right, your muscle sense and *sense of direction* are needed. Both help you know about up and down and backward and forward. These senses help you walk, ride a bicycle, and play games.

You also have a *sense of balance.* Some hollow loops called *semicircular canals* are in your inner ear. They help you keep your balance as you sit, stand, or walk.

Some things about the senses are not completely understood as yet. For instance, some people have "internal clocks." These people wake up just before the alarm clock goes off. Do you have an "internal clock"? What makes you think so?

Do You Know?

People differ in the way they sense things. For example, one scientist tried an experiment. He gave some boys and girls a harmless chemical to taste. To some it tasted salty. Others found it bitter. Such individual differences are to be expected. Why?

How Do You See?

Of all your senses, the sense of sight tells you the most about the world around you. Through your eyes you see people and things. You can read books and signs and learn from them. You can see things near you. Or you can see things like the sun and stars that are millions of miles away.

Light to See By

Your eyes need light to see. So you must know something about light to understand how you see.

Suppose you are in a completely dark room. Your eyes may be open but you do not see anything. Then suppose you turn on a flashlight. When the flashlight goes on, you may see a table nearby.

The light from your flashlight shines on the table. But it cannot go through the table. So the light bounces back from it. This light is *reflected light.*

Some of the reflected light goes into your eyes. Parts of your eye record the light message. Another eye part sends the message to your brain. Part of your brain tells you that you saw a table. Most things you see are by light that is reflected off objects. Can you name some other major sources of light?

The Front of the Eye

Now you know something about light. But you also need to learn something about your eyes.

There are parts of your eyes called *eyelids* and *eyelashes.* They help protect your eyes. How do you think they do this?

Books to Read

Look in the library for books like these that tell about the eyes.

Adler, Irving and Ruth. *Your Eyes* (John Day).

Bendick, Jeanne. *The Human Senses* (Watts).

Elgin, Kathleen. *The Human Body: The Eye* (Watts).

Your eyelids help protect your eyes by shutting quickly to keep out dust. Meanwhile, your eyelashes serve as screens against any other dirt.

The colored part of your eye is the *iris.* Study the pictures. Notice the little opening in the middle of the iris. This is the *pupil.*

The iris is really a ring of muscles. It acts quickly to change the size of the pupil in different lights. In this way the iris protects the sensitive back part of your eye from getting too much light.

Suppose you go into a brightly lit room. Those tiny muscles of the iris make the pupils smaller and less light gets in. Now suppose you go into a dark place. Those tiny muscles of the iris make your pupils larger. More light enters and you can see much better.

There is a cover over the pupil and the iris called the *cornea.* The cornea is colorless or transparent. This means you can see through it. The cornea also keeps bits of dust and dirt from going through the pupil of the eye.

Tear glands help keep the cornea clean. They are located above the outer corner of each eye. Liquid from these glands washes the eye's surface. Then the liquid drains into *ducts,* or tiny tubes. See the picture. These ducts empty into a larger duct which drains into the nose. That is why your nose runs when you cry.

When you blink, the eyelids spread tears over the front surface of the eye. The tears wash away dust and leave the cornea moist. There is a substance in tears that also helps destroy germs that may enter the eyes. How do you think this might help protect the eyes?

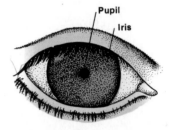

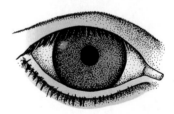

Which eye is in dim light?

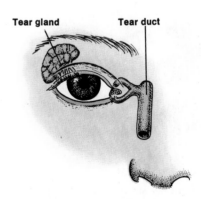

How do the tear glands help keep the eyes clean?

43

The Eyeball

If you could see the complete eye, known as the eyeball, it would look like the picture on page 45.

The outside of the eyeball has a strong white covering called the *sclera*. When you look in a mirror, you are seeing this covering or the whites of your eyes.

Inside the Eyeball

What is inside the eyeball? Look again at the picture at the right. Let's follow a ray of light as it goes into the eye.

First, the light easily passes through the colorless cover called the cornea. Next, the light goes through a clear watery liquid. Then the light passes on through the pupil and through the *lens.* This lens is a clear-looking part that can change in size to help you see better.

Light now moves on into another clear liquid. The dark lining of the eyeball makes it dark here. The liquid is jellylike. It fills the biggest part of the eyeball and keeps the eyeball round.

Finally, the light is focused on the *retina.* The retina is a thin filmlike tissue that lines the back of the eye. You can see a close-up view of a healthy retina on pages 46 and 47.

In the retina are some tiny cone-shaped parts of cells that respond to light. When a bright or colored light falls on the *cones,* they send messages about color to the brain. The retina also has many rod-shaped parts. These *rods* are in use only when you see black, white, and shades of gray.

Millions of other connecting parts of cells in the retina join the rods and cones. They also connect tiny thread like nerves. These tiny nerves come together to make the *optic nerve.* The optic nerve goes from the retina of each eye to the vision center on each side of the brain.

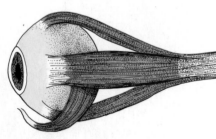

The eyeball is seen from the side, showing the muscles. These muscles can move your eyeballs up and down and sideways.

The Eyeball

What can you tell about some of the parts of the eye?

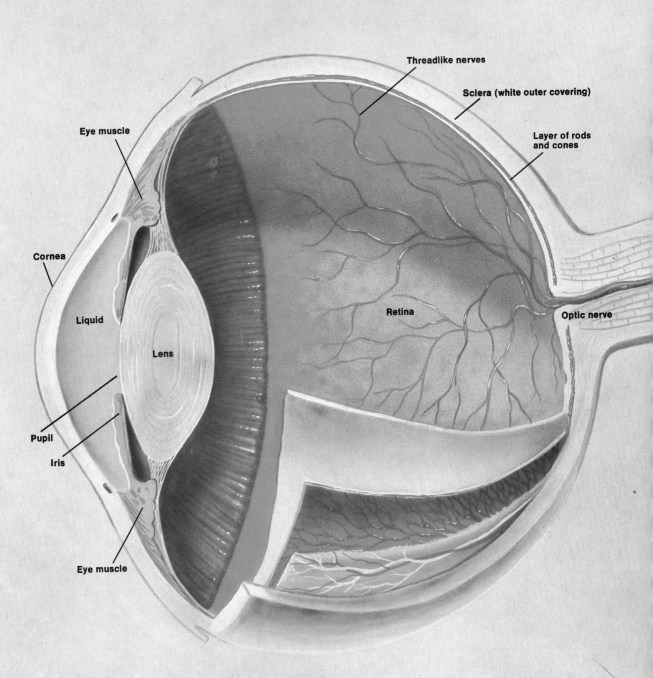

Threadlike nerves

Sclera (white outer covering)

Layer of rods and cones

Eye muscle

Cornea

Liquid

Lens

Retina

Optic nerve

Pupil

Iris

Eye muscle

On these two pages you can see a close-up of a healthy retina. (The light-colored spot is the beginning of the optic nerve.) The rods and cones lie in the deepest layer of the retina. Can you find them?

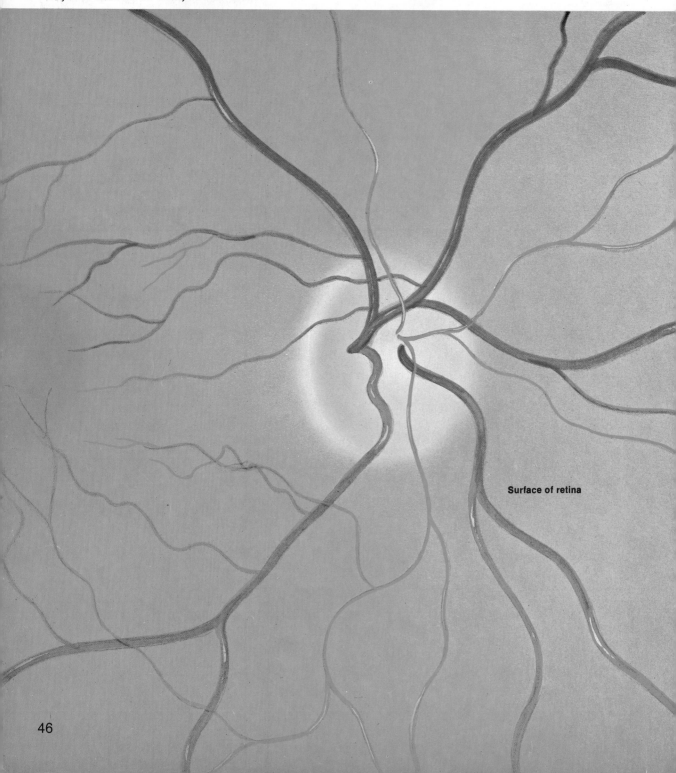

Surface of retina

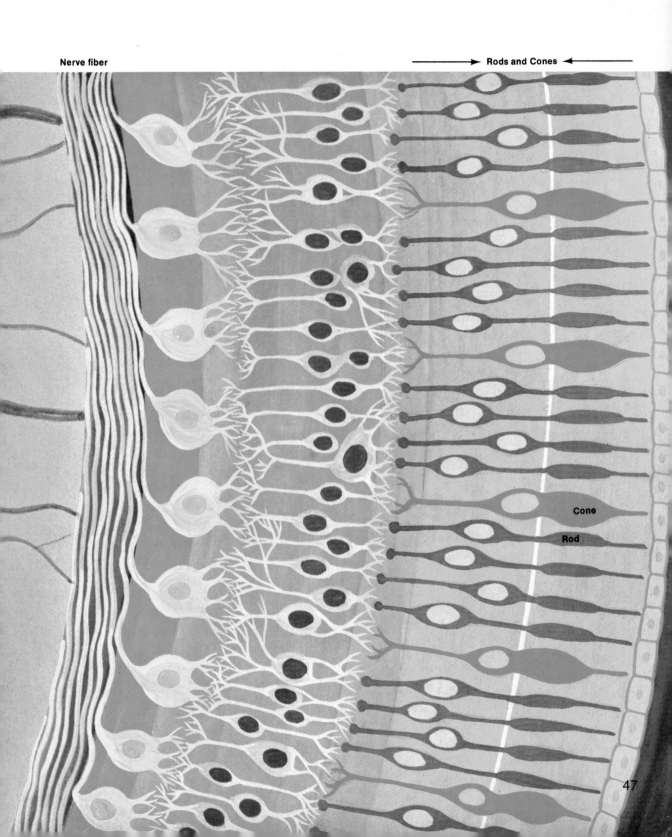

Cone

Rod

47

The Eyes and the Brain

When you look at something, the likeness or image is carried by rays of light through the pupils of each eye. The image goes on through the lens to the retina. Suppose you are looking at a tree. When the image of the tree goes to the retina, it is upside-down. See the diagram.

Since you have two eyes, you get one upside-down picture with each eye. The nerve cells of each retina send messages about these pictures to the brain.

When the messages reach the vision center in each side of your brain, the brain blends the pictures into one. The brain also makes the upside-down picture right-side up. The brain makes it clear that the picture is a tree.

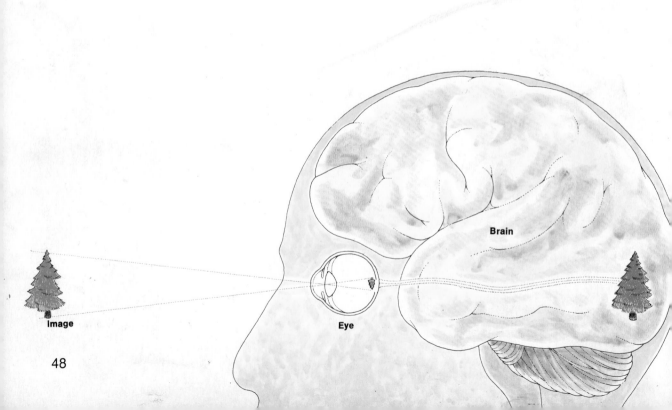

Image

Brain

Eye

48

Seeing Near and Far

The lens in each eye changes size to help you see better. It bends the light rays that come through it.

When you look at something far away, tiny muscles make the lens thinner. This thinner lens is the shape needed to slightly bend the light rays. The rays must come to a point, or *focus,* on the retina.

When you look at something nearby, tiny muscles make the lens thicker. A thicker lens is needed to bend light rays a lot more so that the object is in focus on the retina.

When Eyes Need Help

Sometimes the eyeball is too long from front to back. This causes light rays to focus in front of the retina. A person whose eyeball is like this is *near-sighted.* Nearby objects are easily seen while things far away are unclear.

Glasses or contact lenses can be made to help. These aids bend light rays so that a clear picture is formed on the retina. Things far away can now be seen more clearly.

An eyeball may be too short from front to back. This means a person is *farsighted.* Things far away are seen clearly. But the person does not see near-by very clearly. Nearby objects look blurred. The image is focused behind the retina in the far-sighted eye. How might glasses or contact lenses help a person with this problem?

Sum It Up

What does light have to do with seeing?

Why is it said that the eyes can "conquer great distance"?

What is meant by the "whites of your eyes"?

How do tears help the eyes?

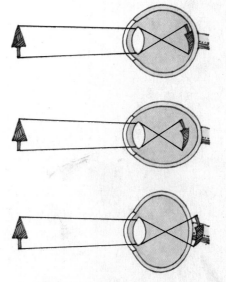

Which is the normal eye?
Which is the nearsighted eye?
Which is the farsighted eye?

ENJOY IT

It Is Not Far

Stars over snow,
    And in the west a planet
Swinging below a star—
    Look for a lovely thing and you will find it.
It is not far—
    It never will be far.

    What lovely thing have you seen lately?
    In what other ways does your sense of sight make
your life richer or more pleasant?

How Do You Hear?

Your sense of hearing helps you know what is happening in the world around you. You learn many things by listening to others. You hear beautiful music. You enjoy radio and television.

You are safer also because of your sense of hearing. You may hear a car honk at you. You can move quickly out of its way. You may hear the warning bell at a railroad crossing. You obey.

How Sounds Get Started

You know that you hear sounds. But do you know just what sounds are? Do you know how sounds get started?

Let's do a demonstration. Take a rubber band and stretch it between two fingers of the left hand. Pluck the band with a finger of your right hand. The rubber band moves back and forth very fast. Do you hear the sound it makes? All sounds are caused in the same way. There has to be something moving back and forth very fast to make a sound. This kind of motion is called *vibrating.*

When you talk, your vocal cords vibrate and make sounds. You cannot see the vocal cords vibrate. However, you can feel them. Just put your hand on your throat while you talk.

When anything vibrates, air is put into wavelike motions. These wavelike motions move out in all directions. The air moves like water does when you throw a stone into a pond.

Maybe these wavelike motions, called *sound,* enter your ear. The ear's structure helps funnel the sound deeper. What happens if the sound waves die out before they reach your ears? Would you hear the sound?

Sounds vary in loudness. If the vibrations that reach your ears are strong, the sounds you hear will be loud.

Sounds vary in pitch or tone. If the vibrations of air come very close together, the sound you hear will be very high. Some sounds are too high for the human ear to hear. Some animals, however, hear sounds that people cannot. These animals have a wider range of hearing.

Most sound waves travel through air. There are other ways, though, in which sounds can travel. Sounds can travel through liquids and through solids like wood, rock, and bone.

Now you know how sounds are made. So let's explore how your ears help you hear these sounds. First, you need to know about the three parts of the ear. These are *the outer ear, the middle ear,* and *the inner ear.*

The Outer Ear

The visible part of your ear is only the outer ear. This part is the curved flap on the outside of the head. It includes a short passageway that goes to the middle ear.

The curved flap of the outer ear is made mainly of *cartilage.* This material is harder than muscle but softer than bone. There is also some fat in the lower, rounded part of the ear. This part is the *lobe.* Can you feel the fat in the lobe of your ear?

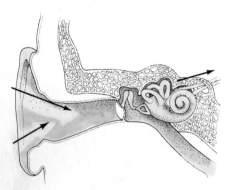

View of the middle and inner ear

The passageway from the outer ear to the eardrum is the *auditory canal*. Look at the picture on page 55. The first part of this canal is lined with hairs. It also has tiny glands that produce wax. The hairs and wax keep dust and insects from going to inner parts of the ear.

Sound waves that move into the outer ear continue along the auditory canal. Although the outer ear helps you hear, you could get along without it. The real hearing starts at the end of the canal. Here begins the middle ear.

The Middle Ear

The middle ear is a small cavity between the outer ear and the inner ear. See the picture on pages 56 and 57. This middle-ear cavity is separated from the outer ear by the *eardrum*. The eardrum stretches across the end of the auditory canal. This skinlike part looks like the covering of a drum. That is why it is called the eardrum.

The eardrum is attached to a chain of three little bones in the middle ear. This chain of bones extends across the middle-ear cavity to the inner ear.

When sounds strike the eardrum, it vibrates. The vibrations of the eardrum cause the bones in the middle ear to move. As these bones move, the vibrations are passed along. From the bones of the middle ear, the sound waves travel through the "second eardrum" or *oval window* to the inner ear.

Books to Read

You may want to look in the library for books about ears. Here are some books you may find.

Adler, Ruth and Irving. *Your Ears* (John Day).

Elgin, Kathleen. *The Human Body: The Ear* (Watts).

Zim, Herbert S. *Our Senses and How They Work* (Morrow).

There is also a tube going from the middle ear down into the throat. It is the *Eustachian tube.* Find it on the next page. This tube lets air in and out of the middle ear. The tube helps keep air pressure the same on both sides of the eardrum. Otherwise, you get an unpleasant feeling in the ear. You may know of this feeling while riding in airplanes or elevators.

The Inner Ear

The most important part of the ear is the snail-shaped part called the *cochlea.* Find where it is located in the inner ear on the next page.

Inside the snail-shaped cochlea are canals filled with liquid. There are also nerves attached to soft hair cells. When the last bone of the chain in the middle ear pushes on the oval window, the fluid in the inner ear vibrates.

The vibrating fluid pushes and pulls on the soft hair cells. The hair cells come together to form the hearing nerve, or the *auditory nerve.* The auditory nerve carries messages of sound to the hearing area on each side of the brain. The brain gives meaning to the sound messages. At that point you can hear.

You read about the semicircular canals earlier. They are also in the inner ear. They have nothing to do with hearing. They help you keep your balance. Can you find them on the next page?

Sum It Up

What are the three main parts of the ear?

How do sound waves travel through to the inner ear?

Tell what each of these parts of the ear does:

auditory nerve

bones of the middle ear

cochlea

eardrum

outer ear

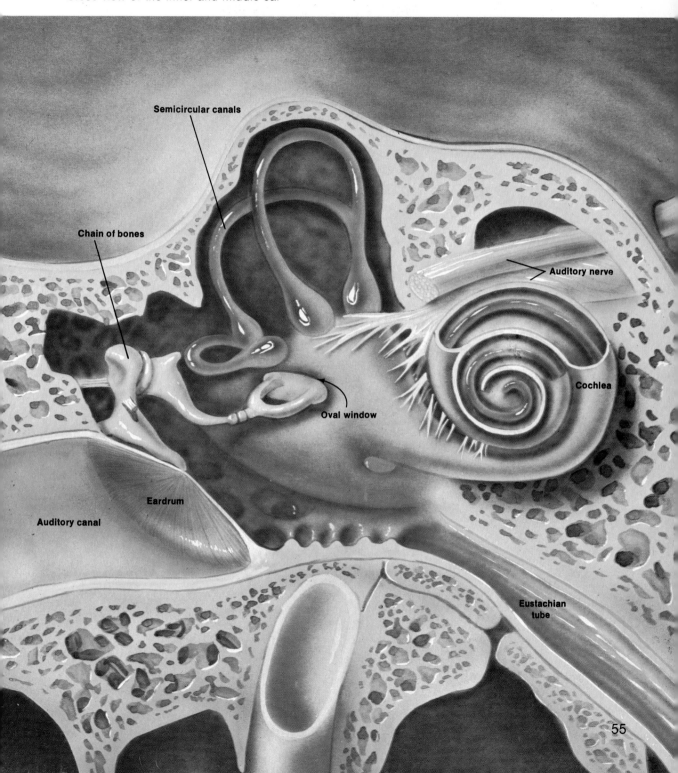

Semicircular canals

Chain of bones

Auditory nerve

Oval window

Cochlea

Eardrum

Auditory canal

Eustachian tube

55

Another View of the Parts of the Ear

Use the diagram to help you tell the story of how we hear. Follow the path that sound waves take through the ear. Then where do the messages go?

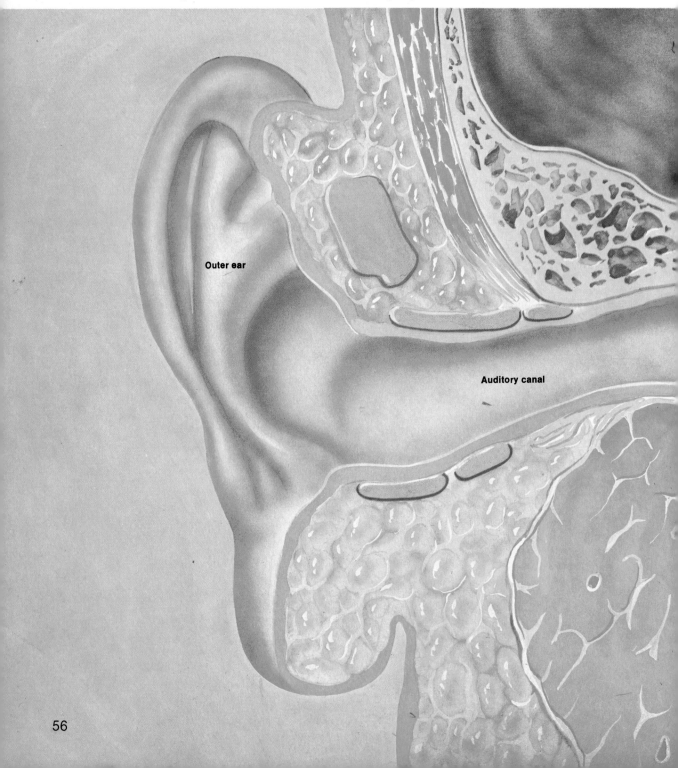

Outer ear

Auditory canal

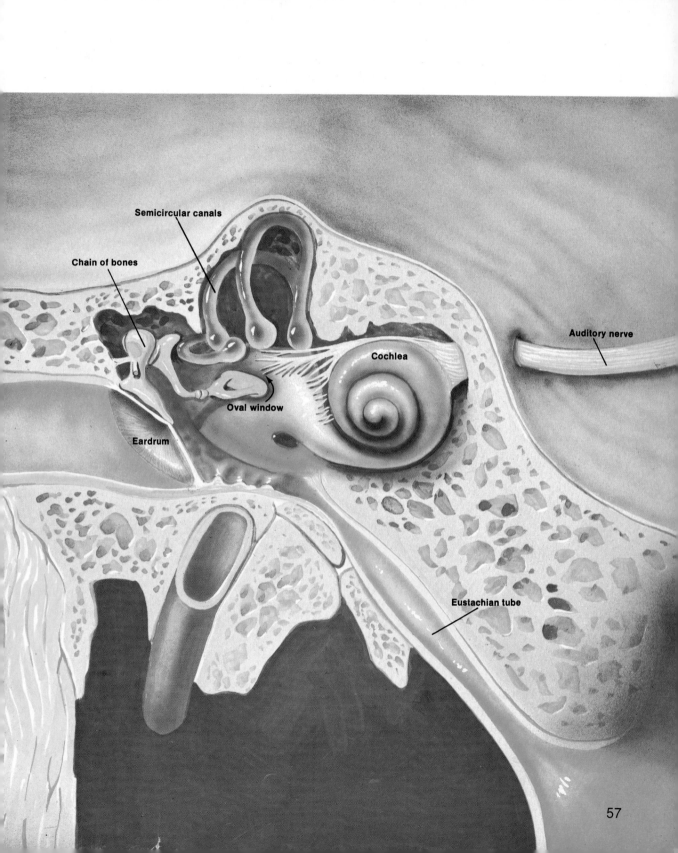

Semicircular canals

Chain of bones

Auditory nerve

Cochlea

Oval window

Eardrum

Eustachian tube

HEALTH AROUND US

Sometimes a disease or defect in some part of the ear keeps sound waves from traveling through the ear as they should. This may result in a slight or severe hearing loss. Living or working in a very noisy place over a long period of time can cause a hearing loss too.

An instrument known as an *audiometer* is used to test for a hearing loss. If a hearing loss is found early enough, steps can be taken to correct it or to keep it from getting worse.

Today there are various kinds of hearing aids for certain hearing problems. These aids can help people hear better. One kind of hearing aid makes the sound waves stronger as they go through the middle and inner ears.

Another kind is placed on the bone just behind the ear. Sound waves are picked up by this hearing aid and sent through the bone to the inner ear. There the sound waves start the liquid moving. This causes messages of sound to be sent to the brain. Then what happens?

How Do You Taste and Smell Things?

Without the senses of taste and smell, your life would not be nearly so pleasant. Most of the time these senses work together. Find out for yourself.

Shut your eyes and hold your nose. Then have someone feed you small bits of raw fruits and vegetables. Can you tell what foods you are eating when you can't smell as you taste them?

Of course, without thinking about it, you have done something like this before. You did it the last time you had a bad cold and your nose was "stopped up." How did food taste to you then?

Four Main Tastes

There are times when the senses of taste and smell do not work together. This happens when the four basic tastes do not depend on the sense of smell. You can taste these even when you cannot smell anything. Most other tastes are thought to result from a blending of these four tastes: sweet, salty, sour, bitter. Some research workers, however, think they are finding other basic tastes. One of them is a metallic taste.

Your sense of taste is found chiefly in tiny parts on the surface of your tongue. These tiny parts are *taste buds*. You will learn more about these taste buds later.

Some Things to Do

1. Here is something to try. It shows how the sense of smell helps you taste. Blindfold a classmate. Put a piece of sliced onion under his or her nose, but give a piece of carrot to eat instead. Ask how it tastes.

2. Look in the library for the book *Taste, Touch, and Smell* by Irving Adler (John Day).

On the tongue each of the four main tastes has a center. In each center, things are tasted more strongly than in other places. For example, candy tastes sweeter on the tip of the tongue than on other places. Look at the "map." Where are salty things tasted most strongly?

As you eat, however, you taste with your whole tongue. So you do not have to worry about pushing foods to a certain part of the tongue to taste them.

How You Taste Things

To taste things, you must mix the food you eat with liquid called *saliva*. Then certain parts of your tongue pick up the messages of taste. The messages are sent by nerves to the taste area on each side of your brain.

Suppose you dry the tip of your tongue with a paper towel. Then put a little sugar on the tip of your tongue. Will you taste the sugar? No, you won't taste the sweetness until saliva starts to dissolve the sugar. This is because sugar is a chemical. The foods you eat are chemicals. These chemicals must be dissolved before you taste anything. They are dissolved in water or in the saliva in your mouth.

To bring out the flavor, you must chew food well mixing it thoroughly with saliva. This helps make the food taste better.

If you look at your tongue in a mirror, you will see little bumps on it. These bumps are *papillae.* Inside the papillae are the taste buds. The papillae at the back of your tongue are the biggest ones. Some of them have as many as 200 taste buds in them. There are about 9000 taste buds on your tongue.

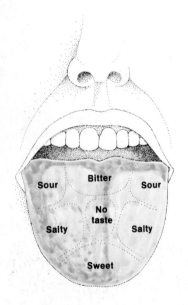

Look at the picture. You can see how taste buds look under a microscope. First locate the tiny hairlike parts found in the taste cell that is labeled. Tiny hairlike parts come out of openings in each taste bud. They look like little pits on the tongue. These parts are stimulated by chemicals which are the food you eat. Their message is carried through the taste cell to the nerve thread.

Now find the nerve thread at the bottom of the taste bud. It gathers together with other nerve threads into a large nerve. This large nerve carries all these taste messages to the taste area on each side of the brain. The brain then interprets the messages. Until then, you do not know what it is you are tasting.

Your tongue does other things besides sensing taste. The tongue also senses the hot and cold, the roughness and smoothness, the hardness and softness of what you eat. For example, it isn't only the taste of ice cream that you enjoy. What else do you enjoy about it?

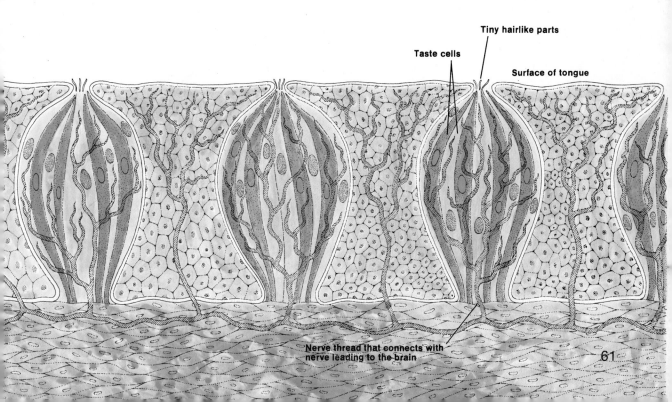

Tiny hairlike parts

Taste cells

Surface of tongue

Nerve thread that connects with nerve leading to the brain

Sense of Taste

Here you see a cut-away view of the tongue and the taste nerves. What must happen to the food you eat before you can taste it?

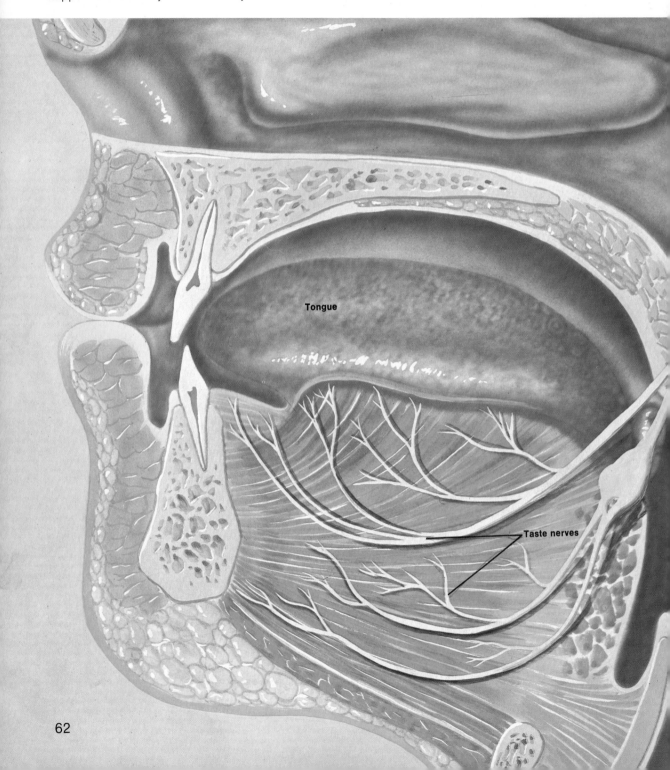

Tongue

Taste nerves

How You Smell Things

Foods are made up of chemicals. These chemicals make it possible for you to taste and smell things. That is why the senses of taste and smell are called the "chemical senses."

Let's see what happens when you smell a flower. The flower has certain chemicals in it. Some of these chemicals keep breaking away in the form of gases. These gases mix with the gases in the air and come into your nose.

The chemicals dissolve in the moist lining of your nose. From there they reach the nerve endings, or smelling cells. The cells are in the upper part of your nose. These nerve endings join the large *olfactory nerve.* The nerve carries the message to the smelling center on each side of your brain. The brain interprets what it is you are smelling. See the picture. Also find the smelling cells and olfactory nerve on page 64.

Individuals react differently to things they taste. They differ in how they react to things they smell. For example, some flowers smell more fragrant to certain people than to others. A few people cannot smell a flower at all. When the smelling cells in the nose become used to one particular odor, the nerve cells stop sending messages about that odor. How do you think this could be dangerous?

Sum It Up

Why are the senses of taste and smell said to go together?

What happens before you *taste* a piece of apple?

Which senses are the "chemical senses"? Why are they called that?

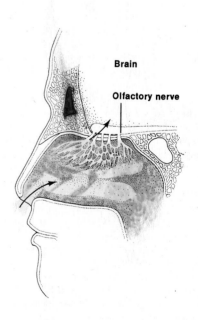

Brain

Olfactory nerve

Sense of Smell

Here you see a cut-away view of the inside of the nose. What happens to help you smell something like a hamburger cooking?

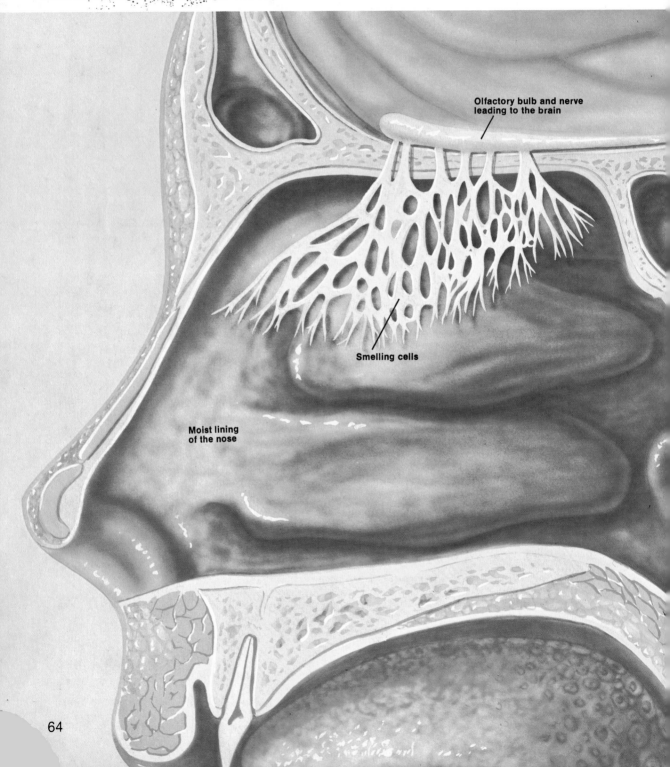

Olfactory bulb and nerve leading to the brain

Smelling cells

Moist lining of the nose

Where Is Your Sense of Touch?

You get many sensations through the skin. So another good name for the sense of touch is the *skin sense.* The five special skin senses are *touch, pressure, heat, cold,* and *pain.* Each has different nerve endings.

Touch and pressure are responsible for helping you know if things are rough, smooth, hard, or soft. Pain, itch, and tickle sensations are received by the nerve endings for pain. Heat and cold each have separate nerve endings.

Nerve Endings in Your Skin

To understand how you feel things, you need to know about the nerve endings in your skin.

The outer part of your skin is the *epidermis.* It is made up of layers. The topmost part is mostly dried cells that are dead. These cells are constantly being rubbed off. The lower part of the epidermis has live growing cells in it. As these cells grow and form new cells, they push upward to the topmost part of the epidermis. There are no nerve endings in the outer part of the epidermis.

Under the epidermis is the true skin, or *dermis.* In the dermis are many blood vessels and many different nerve endings.

Each tiny hair growing in the skin has a nerve around it. There are other kinds of nerve endings in the dermis too. These nerve endings send messages to the brain. The messages are about things that touch the skin. They tell whether things are hot or cold, smooth or rough, soft or hard, and so on. Special nerve endings also send messages of pain to the brain. Look at the picture on the next two pages. What does it show?

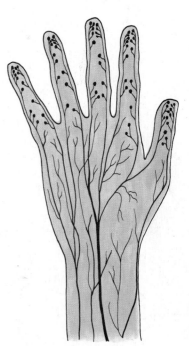

This picture shows nerve endings in the fingers. Why are your fingers particularly helpful in telling whether things are hot or cold, smooth or rough, and so on?

A Greatly Enlarged View of the Skin

This key will help you find the nerve endings in the diagram: A. deep pressure, B. pressure, C. heat, D. touch, E. light touch, F. cold, G. pain.

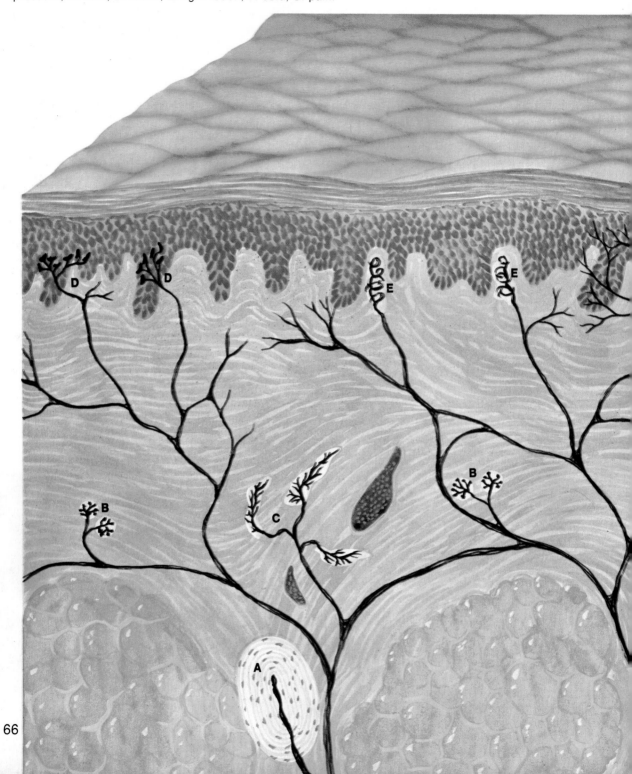

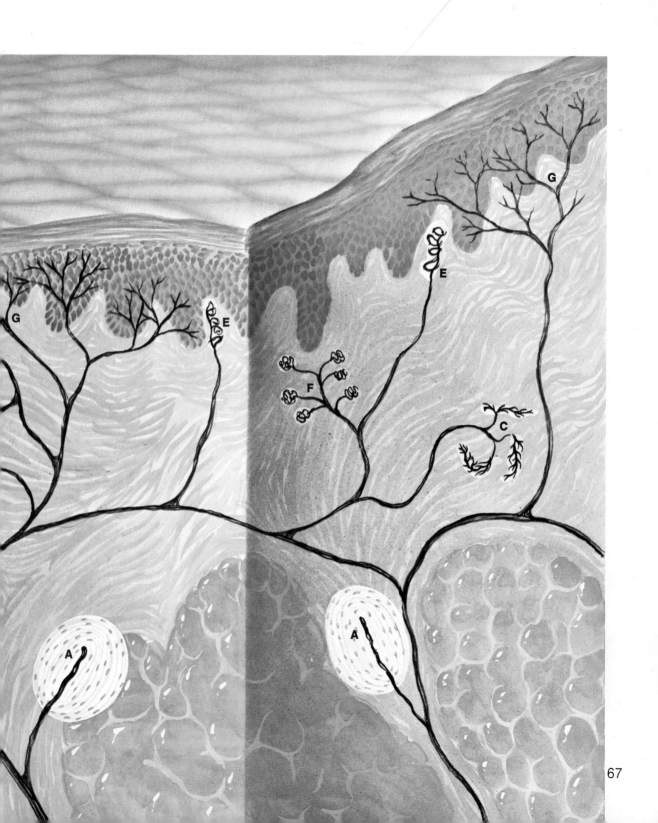

What Does Your Brain Do?

Your senses are very important to you. But they would not be much help without nerves to carry messages to your brain. Nor would the senses be much use without the brain. The brain tells you what the messages mean.

Your brain receives messages that are brought to it over the *sensory nerves.* The brain interprets these messages. It decides what to do about them. If action is needed, the brain sends messages to the muscles over the *motor nerves.* Then the muscles move as instructed.

Did you know that your brain almost reached its full size by the time you were five years old? It will continue to grow very slowly until you are about twenty years old. However, you can grow in learning how to use your brain all your life.

At full size your brain will weigh a little more than one kilogram. Very smart people may have small, average-sized, or large brains.

What does the brain look like? It is a soft, spongy mass of tissue. It is protected on the outside by the bones of the head, or *skull.* Between the skull and the brain there are three softer covers, or *membranes.* See the picture at the left. Between the first and the second membranes, there is a fluid. The third or outer membrane covers the other two membranes.

Your brain has three main parts. These are the *cerebrum,* the *cerebellum,* and the *brain stem.* The lowest part of the brain stem is the *medulla oblongata.* It is connected to the *spinal cord.* Each part of the brain is connected by nerves with all other parts. See the picture on page 69.

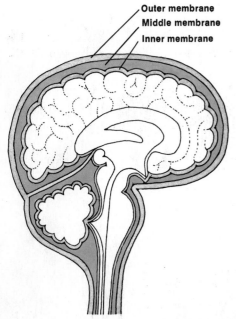

Outer membrane
Middle membrane
Inner membrane

In what ways is the brain protected?

The Human Brain

Notice the size and shape of the cerebrum, the cerebellum, and the brain stem. Do you think the brain has symmetry?

The Brain (from the front)

Cerebrum

Cerebellum

Brain stem

(Medulla oblongata)

Spinal cord

The Cerebrum

The cerebrum is the largest part of the brain. It has a grayish-pink cover called the *cerebral cortex.* The cerebral cortex has deep wrinkles in it. The wrinkles give more room for brain cells than a smooth cover would. Under the grayish-pink cover the cerebrum is white. The white parts are the nerves. These nerves carry messages to and from all parts of the body.

The cerebrum is divided into two parts or halves, left and right. The right side of your brain controls the motion in the left side of your face and body. The left side of your brain controls the motion in the right side of your face and body. See the picture on this page. The two halves of the cerebrum are connected by a band of nerves that joins them near the bottom. In each half of the cerebrum there are special centers on the cortex. For example, there are centers for messages of hearing, seeing, touching, tasting, and smelling. These messages come from the main sense organs. There is a speech center too.

Messages from the eyes travel over the optic nerve to the seeing, or vision, center on each side of the cerebrum. Where do messages from the ears go?

You can see the special center for each of the five senses in the picture on the next page. You can also see the motor center. From the motor center, messages are sent out to the muscles in your body. The messages tell the muscles how to move.

Scientists over the years have done much work to find these special centers in the cerebral cortex. Scientists learned most of this information by studying people with brain injuries.

Right side of brain   **Left side of brain**

Left side of brain controls right side of body   **Right side of brain controls left side of body**

Special Centers of the Brain

The cerebrum is the biggest part of the brain. Notice the wrinkled cover called the cerebral cortex. Can you find the special center for each of the five main senses?

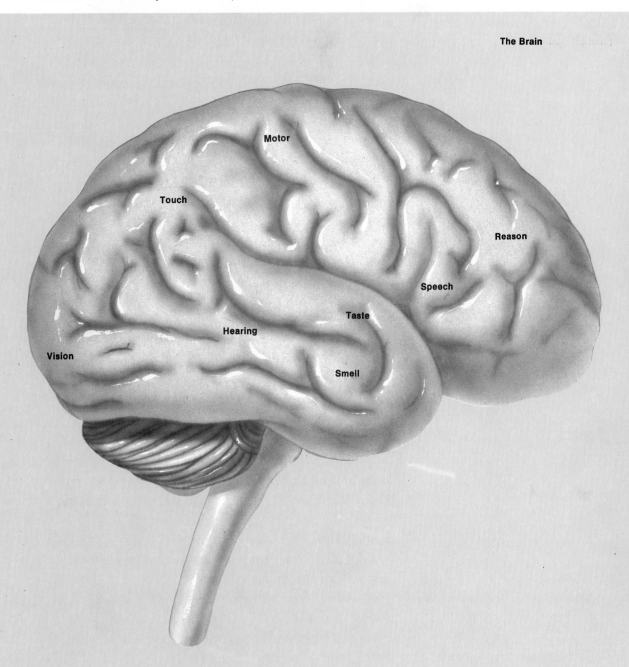

The Brain

Motor

Touch

Reason

Speech

Taste

Hearing

Vision

Smell

However, there are many sections of the brain that we still do not know much about. Brain scientists are not exactly sure where thinking, reasoning, and remembering take place. Most believe that thinking occurs in the forward part of the cerebrum. The cerebrum helps you learn, remember, forget, talk, and write. It helps you feel emotions such as those of fear and joy.

The Cerebellum

The cerebellum is divided into two halves that are connected by nerves. The cerebellum sees that your muscles work together. In that way, you are able to walk, run, and play games. The cerebellum also receives messages from the semicircular canals and helps you keep your balance.

After you decide to move, the cerebellum takes over and keeps you moving. This leaves your mind free to think about other things.

The Brain Stem

Look again at the brain stem on the next page. This column of nerve tissue connects the cerebrum with the spinal cord. Nerves on their way to and from the higher centers of the brain pass through the brain stem.

The lowest part of the brain stem is the *medulla oblongata.* It helps control such things as breathing, body temperature, food digestion, and blood circulation. Why are all these things important to you?

Sum It Up

What does the brain do when it receives messages from the sense organs?

What are the three main parts of the brain? What does each part do?

About how much does the brain weigh?

How is the brain protected?

What do we know for sure about the brain?

Books to Read

Cosgrove, Margaret. *The Wonders Inside You* (Dodd).

Elgin, Kathleen. *The Human Body: The Brain* (Watts).

Perera, Gretchen and Thomas. *Your Brain Power* (Coward).

Showers, Paul. *Use Your Brain* (Crowell).

The Brain

Here you can see the left half of the brain—with part of the cerebellum cut away to show the gray and whitish matter inside it.

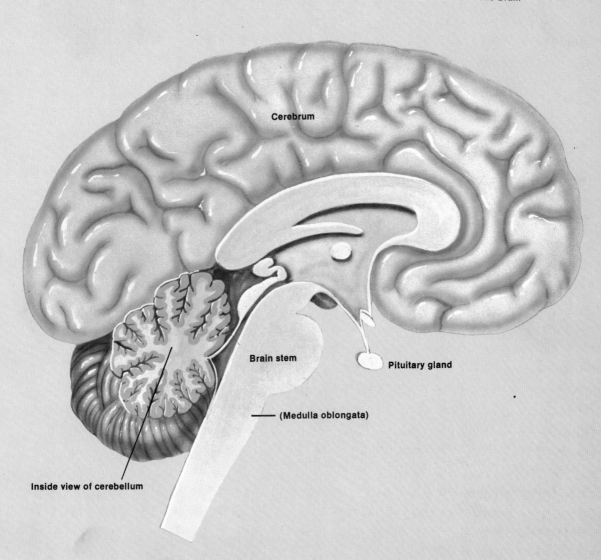

Cerebrum

Brain stem

Pituitary gland

(Medulla oblongata)

Inside view of cerebellum

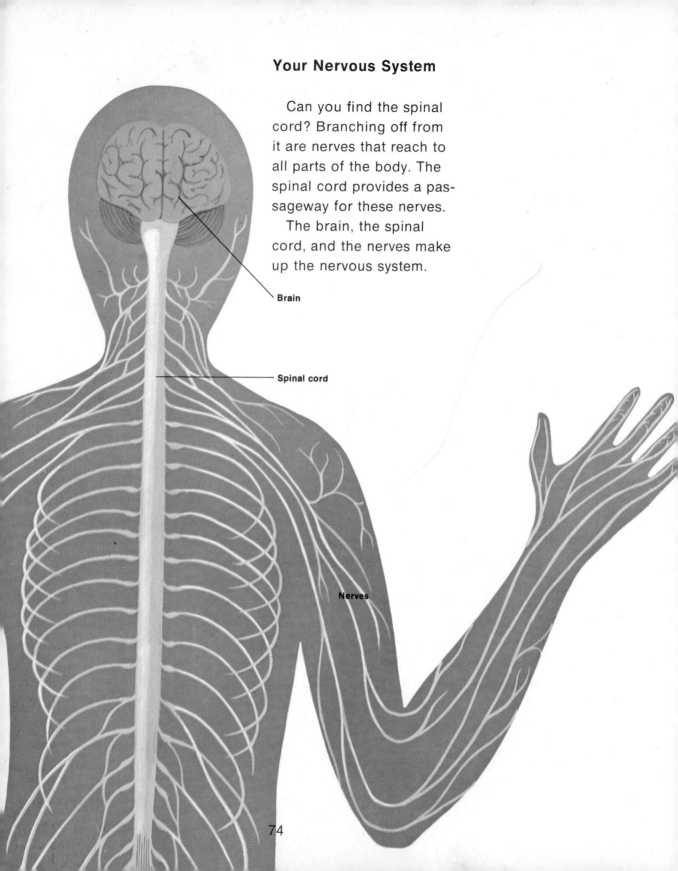

Your Nervous System

Can you find the spinal cord? Branching off from it are nerves that reach to all parts of the body. The spinal cord provides a passageway for these nerves.

The brain, the spinal cord, and the nerves make up the nervous system.

Brain

Spinal cord

Nerves

74

A Pioneer in Medical Science

One of the scientists who studied the brain was David Ferrier. He was a Scottish doctor who worked in England over a hundred years ago.

Dr. Ferrier did research with the brains of dogs. He temporarily made a dog enter into deep sleep to prevent pain. Then he opened the dog's skull to see the brain.

With a wire that carried an electric current, Ferrier would touch an area of the brain. When he touched one certain area, a certain part of the dog's body moved. If he touched the top of the motor area, the dog's toes would wiggle. If he touched the next section down, the foot would move. The next section made the legs move.

Suppose Ferrier touched the *right* side of a dog's brain. The movements took place on the dog's *left* side.

This scientist was one of the first to learn about control centers of the brain. He discovered that the brain is an "orderly place." There are special centers for seeing, hearing, touching, tasting, smelling, and moving. For example, nerves from the eyes go to the vision center only. Nerves from the ears go to the hearing center only.

Continuing research, Ferrier also noticed something else. Damage done to a control center, such as the hearing center, could result in deafness. Damage to the seeing center could result in blindness.

A lot more has been learned about the brain since then. Much valuable knowledge has come from brain surgeons who have had to operate on human brains. But Dr. David Ferrier was one of the pioneers in the study of the brain.

WRITE IT

There are many interesting things about the senses and the brain that you can find out for yourself. You can look in the encyclopedia and in library books. Then you can make reports to your group.

Maybe you will want to make your report into a chart. You might even make a puzzle.

Here you can see reports that some children made. Some good topics for your reports might be these. How many topics could you add to this list?

Cornea Transplants
Keeping Your Eyes Safe
The Amazing Brain

Odors

There are many kinds of smells, or odors. Maybe there are a million or so. But all these odors are a mixture of a few main kinds. Here are some of these kinds:

flower odors
spicy odors
fruit odors
putrid or goat odors

Connie

Some Signs of Eye Trouble

Here is a puzzle. Read these sentences with the words all run together. What are signs that you might need to have your eyes examined?

Dothingslookblurredwhenyouread?

Doyouoftenloseyourplacewhenyouread?

Doyoureyesoftenwater?

Doyouoftenhaveredeyesorsties?

Doyoushutoneeyewhenyouread?

Doyouholdyourbookverycloseorveryfarfromyoureyeswhenyouread?

Doyoukeeptippingyourheadtoonesideasyouread?

Doyouoftenhaveheadaches?

If you have some of these signs, tell your family. Or tell your teacher or the school nurse.

Erik

Color Blindness

People who cannot see some colors are said to be "color blind."

Most people who are color blind have trouble seeing reds, greens, and browns. These people can see blues and yellows.

A few people who are color blind cannot see blues and yellows.

Some people can see bright colors but have trouble seeing pale ones.

Today there are special contact lenses that people can wear. With these lenses the people can now see reds, greens, and browns. Once they were not able to.

José

Signs of Possible Ear Trouble

Having to ask people often what they have said.

A "running ear" — liquid coming out of the ear or a painful earache.

A turning of the head to one side to listen.

Sally

Things to Do

1. Do you know there are ways to talk without using your voice? Maybe you have seen someone on TV give the news or a tornado warning with *handtalk.* In handtalk, deaf people talk by finger spelling. They form words letter by letter with the fingers of one hand. On this page is a finger spelling alphabet. What is this word?

You may want to learn more about finger spelling. Or you might want to learn about another way in which deaf people talk. This is called *signing.* In signing, one or two hands make a word or idea. For example, this says *help.*

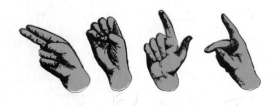

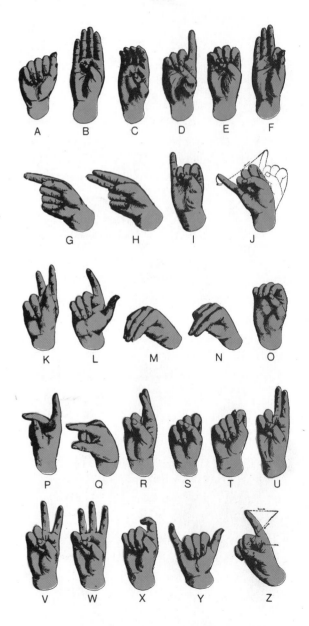

2. Here is a way to see how your sense of touch sends a message to your brain. Hold out the palm of your hand, close your eyes, and have a partner trace on your palm a letter or a number. Can you tell what the letter or number is?

3. Did you know that you have a "blind spot" in each eye? This is the spot at which the optic nerve leaves the eye to go to the brain. You cannot see an object if its image falls on this blind spot. Here is how you can test for your own blind spot.

On a piece of white tablet paper, draw a circle slightly smaller than a dime. Color the circle black.

About 4½ centimeters to the *left* of the circle draw a cross. Each part of the cross should be about 5 millimeters.

Close your right eye. Hold the piece of paper 30 centimeters in front of your left eye. Move the paper slowly toward you as you look steadily at the black circle. Does there come a time when you cannot see the cross out of the corner of your eye? When this happens, the image of the cross is falling on your blind spot.

This is part of a Braille page.

4. Find out about how blind people read books written in what is called *Braille*. One book that can help you is *Seeing Fingers: The Story of Louis Braille* by Etta Degering (McKay). Where else might you find information?

Special Research

Look for information about a reading machine for the blind. It is called the *Optacon*. You can find out about it in the book called *Let's Talk About the New World of Medicine* by M. W. Martin (Jonathan David).

Can You Show What You Know?[1]

Page numbers show you where to look back in the chapter for information, if you need it.

1. Tell why you need your five main senses. (41)

2. Mention three other senses that you have. (41)

3. Explain what happens that enables you to see an object such as a pen. (48)

4. Describe what happens to enable you to hear a bell ring. (53–54)

5. Describe what happens to enable you to taste some ice cream. (60–61)

6. Tell what happens that enables you to smell a flower. (63)

7. Explain what is meant by the "skin senses." (65)

8. Tell why your brain is needed to help you see, hear, touch, taste, and smell. (68)

9. Tell about the three parts of the brain and about what each part does. (68, 70, 72)

10. Explain how messages get to and from the brain. (68)

[1]Behavioral objectives in the cognitive area are stated here directly to students themselves.

Review It

Page numbers show you where to look back in the chapter for information, if you need it.

1. What kind of map could you make of your tongue? What main areas would you show on it? (60)

2. Why is it that when you have a cold you may not be able to taste your food? (59)

3. How might a hearing aid help a person hear better? (58)

4. What does it mean to be nearsighted? (49)

5. Why do you think a child might roll the tip of the tongue over a candy sucker? (60)

6. How do sounds get started? (51)

7. Why do you get a tickly feeling if you touch a tiny hair on your arm with a finger or a pencil? (65)

8. How do messages get to your brain from your fingertips? (68, 74)

9. How is the brain protected? (68)

Copy each numbered item from List A. After each item, write the letter and words from List B that best describe it. For example:

10. auditory nerve   h. hearing nerve

List A

10. auditory nerve
11. cerebral cortex
12. cerebrum
13. cochlea
14. cornea
15. iris
16. lens
17. optic nerve
18. pupil

List B

a. opening in center of iris
b. largest part of brain
c. seeing nerve
d. colored part of eye
e. colorless cover over pupil and iris
f. grayish-pink cover of cerebrum
g. snail-shaped part of inner ear
h. hearing nerve
i. part of eye that focuses light rays on retina

Health Test for Chapter Two

Copy each number on a piece of paper. After each number write the correct answer, *true* or *false*. Rewrite each false statement to make it true.

1. Tears help keep the cornea of the eye clean and moist.

2. When you go into a dark place, the pupils of your eyes become smaller.

3. The eyeball is filled with air.

4. An audiometer is used to check the eyes.

5. A person who is farsighted sees faraway things very clearly.

6. Sounds are caused by vibrations.

7. The sclera covers the eye.

8. Special centers for each of the senses are in the brain.

9. The cerebral cortex is very smooth.

10. Scientists know all there is to know about the human brain.

11. The cerebrum is divided into two halves.

12. Messages from the eyes go to the vision center of the brain.

Copy each sentence and fill in the missing word or words.

13. The part of the brain that helps your muscles work together is the _____.

14. The part of the ear that stretches across the auditory canal is the _____.

15. You taste sweet things strongly on the _____ of the tongue.

16. The "chemical senses" are those of _____ and _____.

17. Sensory nerves carry messages to the _____.

18. The olfactory nerve carries messages of _____.

19. Part of the eye that can bend light rays is the _____.

20. The semicircular canals in the ear help you keep your _____.

Number of Answers   20
Number Right   _____
Score (Number Right X 5)   _____

What Do You Think?

What is one thing this chapter told you that you wanted to know? Write about it on a piece of paper.

SCHOOL & HOME

Because your eyes are so important, you will want to take good care of them. One thing you can do is to develop good television watching habits. These habits are ones you can share with your family at home. If you have little brothers or sisters, you can help them learn these habits.

How to Watch Television

Sit a safe distance from the TV set. A good distance is about five times the width of the television screen.

Have some light in the room. A dark room and the bright light of the TV cause trouble. The muscles of the iris get tired. It is hard to try to adjust the pupils to light and dark at the same time.

Don't watch TV hour after hour. Prolonged watching tires your eyes. It causes general fatigue. Too much TV watching may also keep you from getting the exercise you need. It may keep you from doing other interesting things. Some of these things may be reading or working on a hobby or visiting with friends.

3 Your Skin, Hair, and Nails

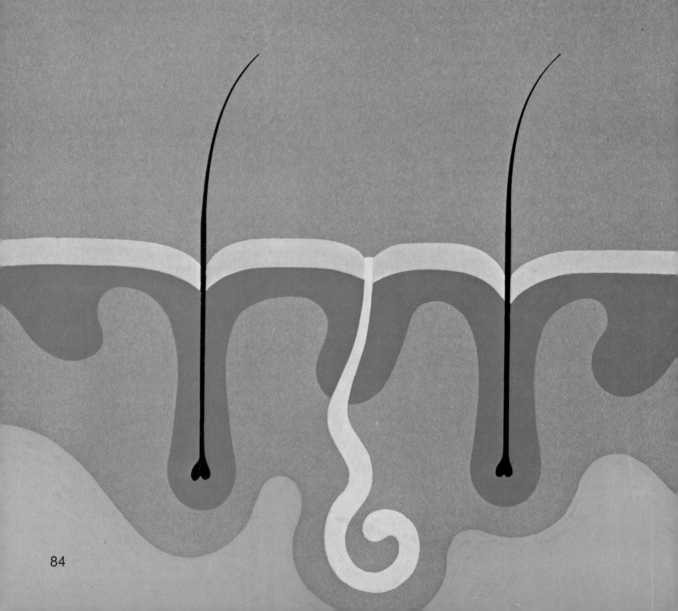

Why do you think the skin is called "one of the body's most complicated structures"?

What have you always wanted to know about your skin, hair, and nails?

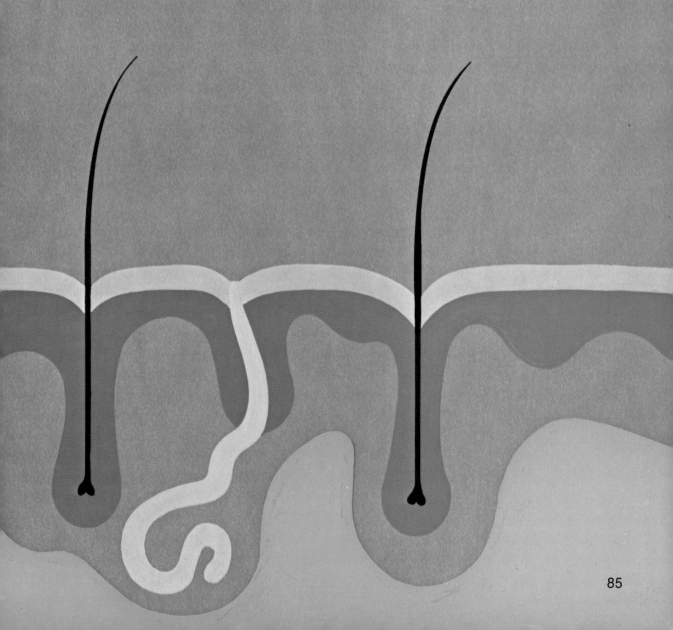

Preview It

Quickly look through this chapter. What questions do the six main titles ask? Look for the answers as you study. These answers will tell you some important things about skin. Think of your own questions as well. Are your questions about skin like any of these?

Is the skin you are wearing today the same as last year's?

Why is the color of skin different in people?

Why doesn't your skin crack?

What are goose pimples?

What are freckles?

When you wash your hands, why doesn't the water soak right through them?

Why doesn't it hurt when your hair and nails are cut?

What causes naturally curly hair?

Be alert for information to help you answer your own questions too.

What Is the Epidermis?

The *epidermis* is the outer part of your skin. It is made up of four or five layers of skin cells. The epidermis helps keep germs out of the body.

A Closer Look at the Epidermis

Suppose you could look at the skin on the back of your hand through a magnifying glass. You would see the little folds or creases in the skin better. You also might notice how the folds smooth out when you close your hand tightly.

These folds make it possible for your skin to stretch easily when you move. These same folds are catching places for dirt. That is one reason why you need to wash often.

While looking at your skin through the magnifying glass you might also see little hair pits. These pits have tiny hairs growing out of them. Oil comes up through these pits from the oil glands. The oil helps keep the skin soft and smooth. It prevents cracking and it waterproofs your skin. The oil helps keep water from soaking right through your skin. Look at the picture. Can you find some tiny hairs and oil glands?

There are some other things a magnifying glass can't show you. The live, growing skin cells in the lower part of the epidermis keep making new cells. Your skin makes millions of these cells daily. As the millions of old cells are pushed upward each day, they die. These dead skin cells have changed into a dry, flaky material. These dead cells are the topmost layer of skin you see and feel.

You rub off these dead cells when you wash. These dead skin cells are rubbed off on the clothes you wear. Your dead skin cells also rub off when you shake hands. When you get a sunburn, flakes of skin peel off. Then what happens?

The top layer is replaced by the next layer of cells. You are always shedding dead skin cells. The outer skin you are wearing today is not the same skin you wore last year.

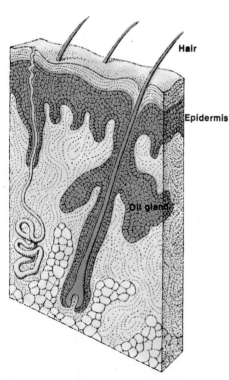

Hair

Epidermis

Oil gland

Cross section of the skin

Skin Color

Another interesting thing about the skin is its coloring. Normally, the color of your skin is a mixture of *pigments,* or coloring matter. The brown pigment called *melanin* is scattered through the epidermis. Another pigment found only in the red blood cells is known as *hemoglobin.* A pigment found in the fatty parts of the skin is *carotene.* It produces a yellowish tint.

Every person has the same set of pigments. And every person inherits skin color from parents. But, when a person does not inherit the pigment melanin, he or she is an *albino.* Albinos have pale skin, light hair, and pink eyes.

Long exposure of your skin to the sun may cause more pigment to be produced. The result is called suntan. The lighter the skin, the more noticeable the change.

Some people have melanin scattered unevenly through the epidermis. The brown pigment is found in little patches. You recognize these patches as *freckles.*

Other dark spots on the skin might be *moles.* Some are flat. Others are raised above the surface of the skin. Moles should be left alone. However, if a mole becomes sore, bleeds, or grows larger, you should see a doctor.

People's skin differs only in the amount of each pigment found in the epidermis. Otherwise, everyone's skin has the same structure and does the same jobs. What do some other parts of the skin do?

Sum It Up

What is meant by the term *epidermis?*
What are freckles? Moles?
Why do you have the color of skin that you have?

Books to Read

Elgin, Kathleen. *The Human Body: The Skin* (Watts).
Showers, Paul. *Your Skin and Mine* (Crowell).
Silverstein, Alvin and Virginia. *The Skin* (Prentice-Hall).

What Is the Dermis?

The layer of skin known as the *dermis* is often called the true skin. See the picture on page 93. The dermis contains important nerve endings for your sense of touch.

This layer also has live skin cells, fluid around those cells, blood vessels, and glands. Can you find these parts of the dermis in the picture on pages 94 and 95?

Blood Vessels in the Skin

Did you notice those many tiny blood vessels in the dermis? Your rosy colored nails and lips come from blood vessels showing through the thin layer of tissue. If you cut your finger, blood will flow from the opened blood vessels.

Some of the larger blood vessels are *arteries.* The blood flowing in the arteries carries oxygen. The blood also carries digested food in liquid form to the skin cells. The oxygen and liquid food are what keep your skin cells and all your other cells alive.

Other blood vessels in the dermis are called *veins.* Veins carry away waste substances and carbon dioxide from the cells. All the arteries and veins are connected by tiny tubes called *capillaries.*

Sweat Glands

The *pores* in the skin are openings for tiny tubes, or *ducts.* These ducts begin in sweat glands in the dermis. Can you find some sweat glands on pages 94 and 95?

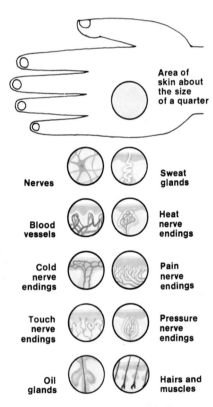

Area of skin about the size of a quarter

Nerves

Sweat glands

Blood vessels

Heat nerve endings

Cold nerve endings

Pain nerve endings

Touch nerve endings

Pressure nerve endings

Oil glands

Hairs and muscles

You can see why the skin is a complicated structure. In an area of skin about the size of a quarter, all the things listed above can be found.

Sweat glands take in liquid from the spaces around skin cells. The sweat glands send the liquid up through the ducts and pores to the skin surface. This salty liquid is perspiration.

You perspire all the time. Most of the time you do not see perspiration. It goes into the air, or *evaporates.* You see perspiration on your skin in hot weather or after exercise.

As perspiration evaporates, the body cools. This is one way the body keeps itself from getting too warm.

Perspiration does not just cool the body. It helps keep skin from getting too dry. And it also carries off small amounts of waste material.

Oil Glands

Also in the dermis are little pits, or *hair follicles.* Hairs grow out of these hair follicles. Near the roots of the hair are the oil glands. Oil flows from the oil glands along the hair shafts to the skin surface. Can you find some oil glands in the picture on pages 94 and 95?

The amount of oil made by the oil glands varies among people. If the oil glands make a lot of oil, a person's skin is oily. If the glands make a very small amount of oil, the skin is dry.

Tiny muscles are located at the root of each hair. When you are cold, these tiny muscles *contract,* or become shorter and thicker. The muscles do the same thing when you are frightened. The contracting muscles cause the tiny hairs to stand straight up. That is why you sometimes have little bumps around the raised hairs. These bumps are called goose pimples or goose bumps.

What Do You Think?

If you dipped a finger in water and then held it up in the air to dry, how would the finger feel? Do you know why?

A Fatty Layer

Below the dermis is a layer of connective tissue. It is sometimes classed as a part of the dermis. It is made up of threadlike parts with many spaces. The spaces are filled with fluid and fat. You can see this fatty layer in the picture on page 93. This fat helps cushion you from bumps. It also helps hold in body heat during cold weather. If a person is much overweight, a lot of fat may be found in this layer. This can be unhealthy.

Ridges in the Skin

In the same picture you can see connecting ridges. The artist has separated the dermis and epidermis so you can really see what these ridges look like. These ridges reach up from the dermis into the epidermis. If you look at the tips of your fingers, you can see a network of ridges. A magnifying glass helps you see them better.

Suppose you press your fingertip on an ink pad and then on clean paper. You can see the design on paper that these ridges make. This print of ridges in your fingertip is called a *fingerprint.* No other person's fingerprints are exactly like yours. So the fingerprint is a good means of identification.

Your fingerprints never really change. Suppose you should burn your finger. The same fingerprint will appear each time after a burn heals. If the burn is too deep, it may leave a scar.

Each of your ten fingers shows a different fingerprint. Usually all fingers are used when fingerprints are taken for identification.

Sum It Up

What parts are found in the layer of skin called the dermis?

Why are fingerprints and footprints a good way to identify people?

Do You Know?

When babies are born in hospitals, their footprints are sometimes taken instead of fingerprints. Can you figure out why? Was a footprint made when you were born? How do you know?

The Skin Is More Than a Cover

Your skin is a waterproof covering. But it has other functions too. It helps regulate temperature. It is a sense organ as well, because within it lie the many different kinds of nerve endings.

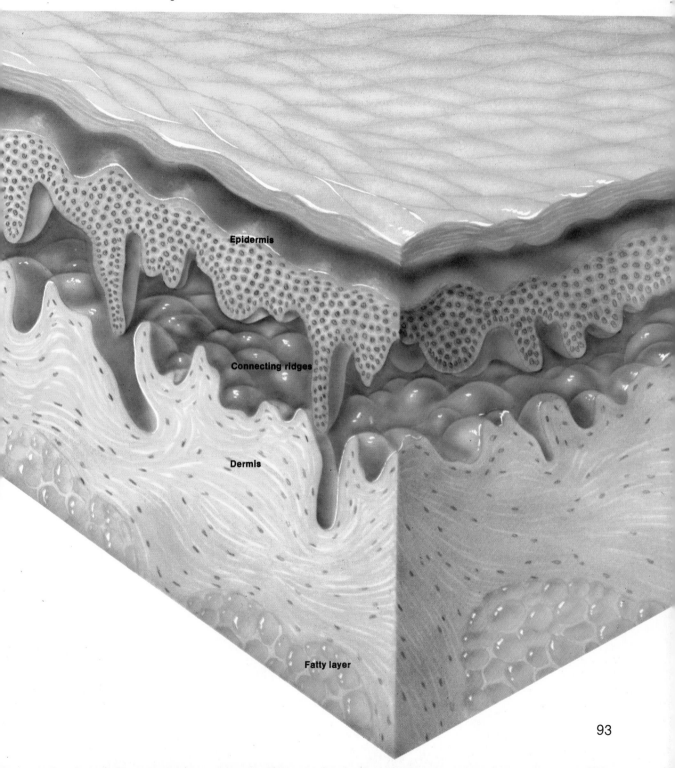

Epidermis

Connecting ridges

Dermis

Fatty layer

93

Here is a cross-section of the many interesting things found in the dermis.

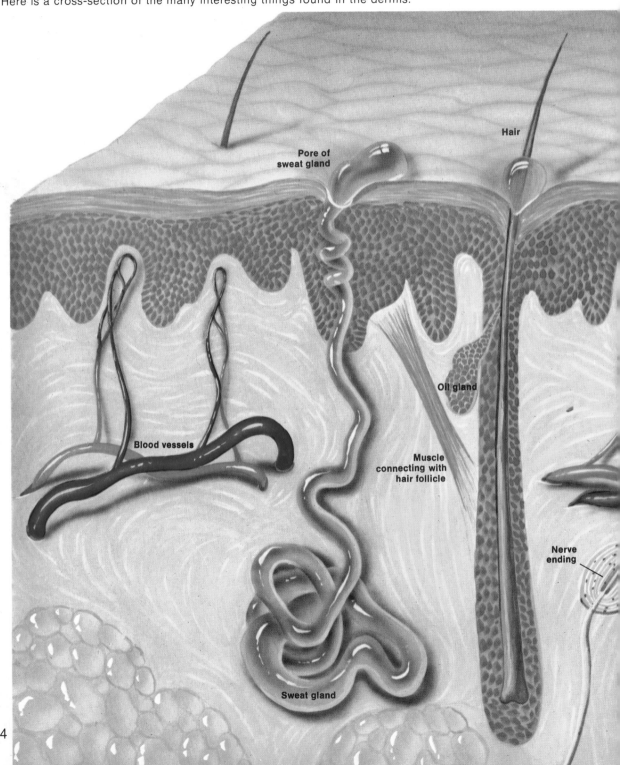

Pore of sweat gland

Hair

Oil gland

Blood vessels

Muscle connecting with hair follicle

Nerve ending

Sweat gland

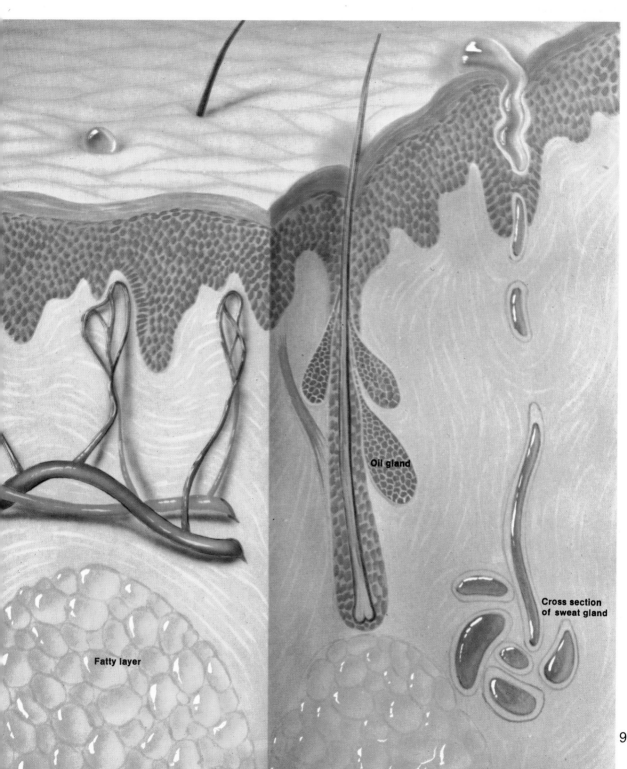

Oil gland

Cross section
of sweat gland

Fatty layer

Notice the many variations in skin tone. Notice, too, variations in appearance of the skin in people of different ages.

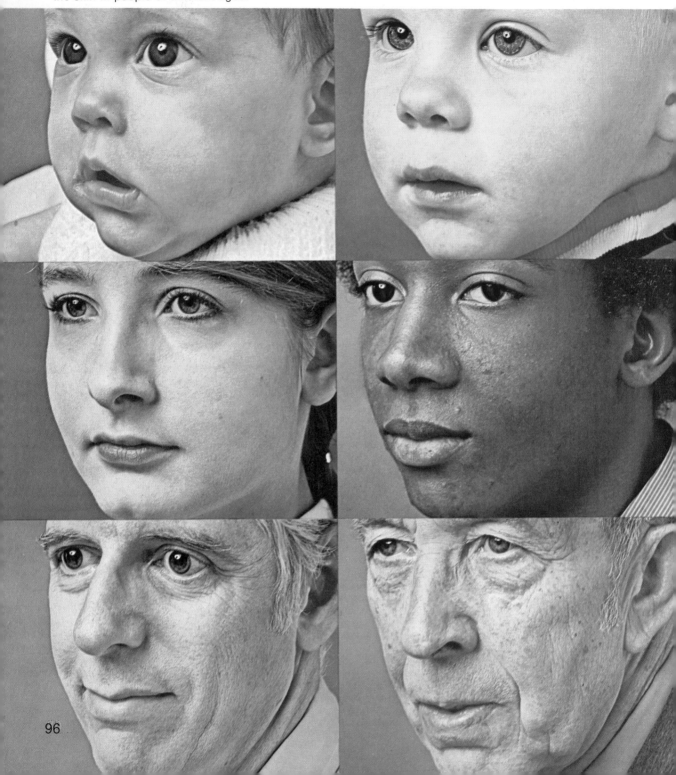

As people grow older, less oil may be in the skin and less fat under it. Then the skin may become somewhat wrinkled.

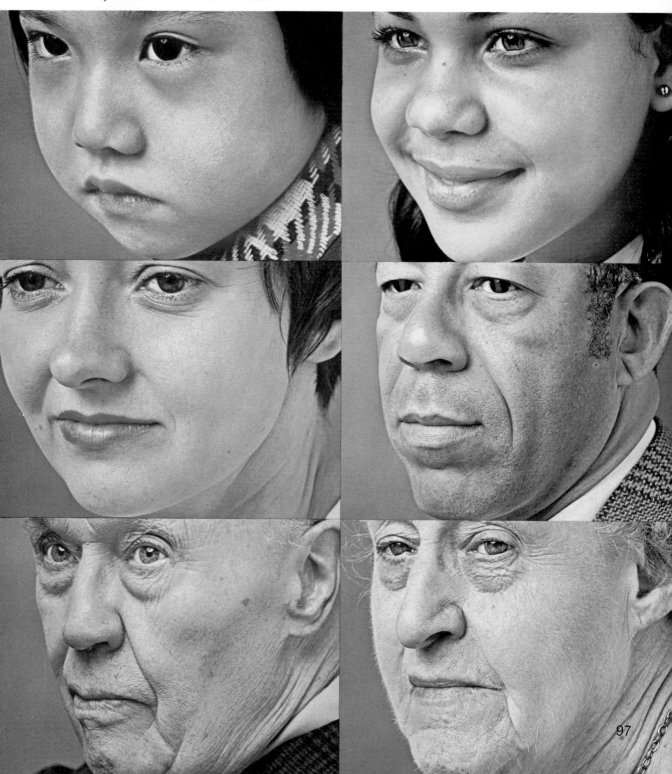

ENJOY IT

Thumbprint

In the heel of my thumb
are whorls, whirls, wheels
in a unique design:
mine alone.
What a treasure to own!
My own flesh, my own feelings.
No other, however grand or base,
can ever contain the same.
My signature,
thumbing the pages of my time.
My universe key,
my singularity.
Impress, implant,
I am myself,
of all my atom parts I am the sum.
And out of my blood and my brain
I make my own interior weather,
my own sun and rain.
Imprint my mark upon the world,
whatever I shall become.

Why can it be said that the heel of your thumb
has a "unique design"? How might it serve as your
"signature"?

Below are four main groups of fingerprints. What
are they? Which type of fingerprint do you have?

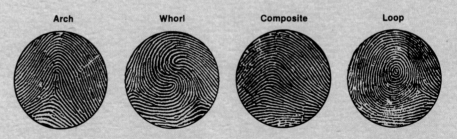

Arch   Whorl   Composite   Loop

How Does Your Skin Function?

What have you found out so far about how skin helps you? There are some other important things you may want to know.

The Skin and Body Temperature

Your body continually makes heat. The heat is brought to your skin by the warm blood in the blood vessels. Some of the heat goes from the blood into the air around the skin.

What happens when you go out into the cold? The blood vessels in your skin will contract or become smaller. Thus, less blood is able to enter the blood vessels of the skin. Less heat goes from the blood into the air. And more heat is kept inside the body.

When your body gets very warm, tiny blood vessels in the skin expand or get larger. More blood is able to flow into these blood vessels. And more heat from the blood passes from the blood into the air. As this heat leaves by way of the skin, the body is cooled. This is how the blood vessels in your skin help control body temperature.

What else helps cool the body besides the change in the size of blood vessels in the skin?

The Skin as a Storehouse

The fatty layer under the dermis is like a roomy storehouse. Water and fat are stored there. These stored materials are returned to the blood as needed from time to time. When do you think these materials carried by the blood might be needed?

Do You Know?

Tissue fluid surrounds all the body cells. Another function of the skin is to keep tissue fluid inside the body. You would dry up and die if you had no skin to prevent the escape of tissue fluids.

The Skin Helps Remove Wastes

Water that is not used or stored in your body each day is moved out in various ways. One way is as sweat through the pores of your skin. Another way a little water is removed is when you *exhale,* or breathe out. Most water, however, is removed through the kidneys as *urine.*

The Skin Helps Heal Small Cuts

When you cut your skin, blood flows out from the injured blood vessels. The flowing blood washes away some dirt and germs from the cut.

Next the blood vessels in the skin contract. This usually stops the flow of blood. Soon a thickened mass of blood, or *clot,* forms. This clot fastens itself to the sides of the cut. The blood clot starts to shrink. It eventually pulls the two sides of the cut closer together.

Later, threadlike connective-tissue cells move toward the cut. These cells begin to build new tissue. Skin cells growing from each side of the cut join at the center of the cut. Sometimes a scar remains where the skin cells join.

The Skin and Vitamin D

Invisible ultraviolet rays of the sun that shine on your skin change a substance in the skin into vitamin D. Thus, vitamin D is often called the "sunshine vitamin."

Vitamin D is needed to help build strong bones and teeth. Today vitamin D-fortified milk helps supply this vitamin all year round. Why is this necessary? How would heavy air pollution affect the amount of vitamin D you need?

Sum It Up

What are five things the skin does for you?

What does the skin have to do with production of vitamin D?

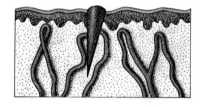
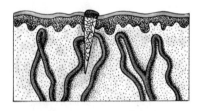
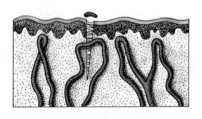

These drawings can help you tell the story of how a cut heals.

How Can You Take Care of Your Skin?

You have learned some important things about your skin. But what about its care? One good way you can help take care of your skin is to try to keep it clean.

Washing Your Hands and Face

Your face needs a thorough washing at least once a day. Use a clean washcloth to work the lather into your face and neck. Rinse with warm water. Follow with a second rinse of cold water. Then dry the skin with a soft towel. If you have dry skin, you may want to use a very small amount of soap.

Your hands should be washed before you eat and after you use the toilet. What are some other times when you should wash your hands?

Baths

Some people take a bath every day. Others take a bath several times a week. Just how often you bathe depends on how much dirt is on you. The temperature outdoors can make a difference too. In warm weather you may be hot and sweaty. You may need to bathe more often.

The best baths are the kind in which you use warm water and soap. The soap is needed to help remove oil that is mixed with dirt and bacteria on the skin. This can help prevent a skin infection.

If you rub yourself well with a towel after bathing, fresh oil will flow from the oil glands. This keeps your skin soft and smooth.

Something to Do

Find out how to save money when buying soap. Look in a grocery or drugstore at the price of soap bars the same size. How much do the prices vary?

If you want to save money, keep in mind that there is little difference among popular brands of soap. One is as good as another. When you pay top prices, you are usually paying for a pretty color, a fancy wrapping, or a special scent.

If your skin is very dry, you may not want to bathe every day. Too much oil from your skin may be removed. In this case, take a few baths a week instead of a daily bath. Putting bath oil in the bath water may help some people who have very dry or sensitive skin.

Baths do more than clean your skin. When you are tired, a warm bath can often make you feel relaxed and rested.

Try not to waste water when you take a bath. You can get clean with a small amount of water. So do not put too much water in the tub.

Showers

Many people prefer showers because they are quicker than tub baths. A shower is fine as long as soap, a washcloth, and warm water are used. Try not to waste water. You can get clean without letting the shower water run and run.

"Stand-up" Baths

An efficient "stand-up" bath can be taken if no tub or shower is available. Use a washcloth, soap, and warm water. The water can come from a washbowl or from a warm-water tap. Wash each part of the body and then dry it with a towel. Campers, people on safaris, and many others use "stand-up" baths.

Shampooing Your Hair

Your scalp and hair should be shampooed several times a week or more often if you wish. A lot of dirt gets in your hair. Not all of it can be brushed out.

To shampoo the hair, use a liquid or cream shampoo if you can. Such shampoos are easier to rinse out than bar soap. Rinse the hair thoroughly. Rub the hair well with a dry towel. When the hair is dry, brush it. Brushing helps make the hair shine.

Clothes to Suit the Weather

Wear clothes to suit the weather. This will help your skin regulate body heat.

Your body is always making and losing heat. In warm weather you want to make it easy for heat to leave the body. The heat leaves through the skin. Thin clothes made of cotton or other lightweight material let the heat pass easily into the air.

In cold weather, you want to keep as much heat as you can from leaving the body. Wear clothes made of materials, such as wool, that help keep heat from passing quickly to the outside air.

In wet weather, you do not want the body to use up too much of its heat trying to dry out damp clothes and damp shoes. Sudden cooling of the skin in this way may cause the body to become chilled. That is why you should keep your clothes and shoes dry in rainy weather. Wear boots or rubbers whenever possible. Wear a raincoat too. Or carry an umbrella.

Avoiding Sunburn

Another way to take care of your skin is to avoid sunburn. When you are going to be out in the sunshine for long periods of time, wear a hat or cap to protect your head. Wear clothes to cover your arms and legs. How can you protect your eyes?

If you want a suntan, it helps to use tanning lotions. But do not count on lotions to protect you for prolonged periods.

Sum It Up

What are three ways to take care of the skin?

How can you protect your skin from getting too much sun?

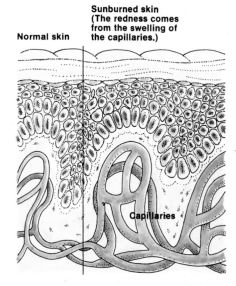

Normal skin

Sunburned skin (The redness comes from the swelling of the capillaries.)

Capillaries

How Do Your Hair and Nails Grow?

Remember the dermis? Your hair grows out of little pits in the dermis. The part of the hair that starts in each little pit is called the *root.* The hair root is alive and growing. It gets its food from blood that is brought into the skin by tiny blood vessels. If you pull a hair out by the root, you feel a twinge of pain.

The cells in the hair roots grow from the bottom up like skin cells. New cells push the old cells upward. The old or dead cells form the part of the hair you see on the skin. You can cut these dead cells without feeling any pain.

The hairs on your head grow for about two to six years. Then they rest. Resting hair tends to fall out easily. When you brush or comb your hair, you may notice that a few hairs come out. This is normal. A hair that falls out is replaced by a new one. And a hair is lost permanently only if the root of the hair is destroyed.

Your fingernails and toenails also grow from the bottom up. The nails grow out of live roots under the skin. As the cells in the nails grow out from their roots, they die. The dead cells change into the horny material you can see. What happens when you cut your fingernails or toenails?

Do You Know?

Your hair and nails may give a hint about your health. Suppose your nails are brittle and break easily. Or suppose they show little lines or ridges on them. These may be signs that you are not getting enough of the right kinds of food each day.

Lack of an adequate diet may cause your hair to become dry and dull-looking.

How Do You Take Care
of Fingernails and Toenails?

Your fingernails help protect the tips of your fingers. So you should keep these nails trimmed and rounded to the right length. If your nails are too short, they will not protect your fingertips. They will not help you pick up small objects. If the nails are too long, they will collect bacteria. They will also break easily.

Which picture at the right shows a hand with fingernails rounded to about the right length?

Besides keeping your fingernails the right length, try to keep them clean. How will you do that?

Do you know how to cut toenails? They should not be rounded. Instead they should be cut straight across. Then you won't get ingrown toenails. With an ingrown toenail, the flesh overlaps the toenail. Then the edges of the toenail cut into the flesh. Why should you try to prevent this from happening?

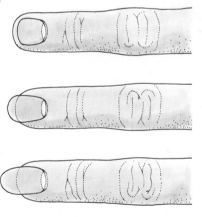

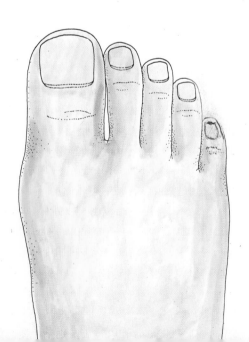

TELL IT

You may still want to know more about the skin. For instance, what are warts, calluses, and hangnails? Here are some oral reports by boys and girls your age. What information do they give you?

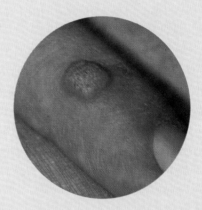

Warts

There are little ridges that grow up from the dermis to the epidermis. The ridges fasten these layers together.

Sometimes some of these little ridges keep on growing. They grow until they form a small, hard lump on the skin. This lump is called a *wart.*

If the wart grows on the bottom of the foot, it is called a *plantar wart.*

Most of the time these warts are hard and dry. Sometimes, though, tiny blood vessels grow in them.

It is believed that warts are caused by a virus.

If you want something done about a wart, you should see a doctor. Sometimes warts go away by themselves.

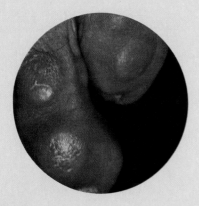

Calluses

If there is a lot of rubbing on the outside part of your skin, the skin gets tough and thick there. The thick spot on the skin is called a *callus*.

The callus helps keep the inside parts of the skin from being hurt by rubbing.

In time the callus will go away if the rubbing on the skin is stopped.

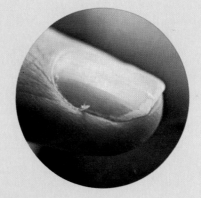

Hangnails

There is hard skin around the nails. This hard skin is called the *cuticle.* There is not much oil in the cuticle. So it cracks and gets rough edges sometimes.

If the rough edges aren't cut or softened, they get longer. Then they tear into the nearby skin. This causes *hangnails.* Hangnails can hurt.

Push back the cuticle when you wash your hands. Use a towel or washcloth. This is one way to prevent hangnails.

WRITE IT

Maybe you will want to write a report about the skin, hair, or nails. Below and on the next page you can see reports that other children have written. What information do these reports give you?

Some topics you might write on are the following:

What Is a Bunion?

Why Does Hair Change Color?

Why Does Skin Sometimes Get Wrinkled?

How Does Skin Get Chapped?

To help you find information, use books like the ones listed on page 89. You might also look up words like *skin, hair,* and *bunion* in an encyclopedia.

What Are Corns?

Corns are little, cone-shaped places that can form on the skin. They usually form on the toes.

Shoes or socks that do not fit right can cause corns. The outer layer of skin gets thick. The thick layer grows into skin layers underneath. Then you have a corn. It can hurt.

Sometimes a foot doctor has to remove the corn. It may go away if you stop wearing shoes or socks that don't fit.

Amy

What Makes Curly Hair?

Hair grows out of little pits in the skin. These pits have different shapes. Round pits send out hairs that have a round or oval shape. Hairs like these are straight.

Some hair pits are oval or sort of flat in shape. Hair that comes out of the flat oval pits is likely to be curly.

Jerry

Why Do Some People Bite Their Fingernails?

I talked to the school nurse about why some people bite their fingernails. The nurse says people do this sometimes when they are worried or unhappy. They may stop when they get over their upset feelings.

The school nurse says a good way to get over upset feelings is to talk things over with someone.

Some people have a habit of biting their nails and will do so even when they are not worried or upset. It is a good idea to ask a doctor for help when this happens.

John

HEALTH AROUND US

Do you know that skin can be *grafted?* That means it can be moved from one part of a person's body to another. This is done in case part of a person's skin is destroyed. Then the skin can't grow back. It must be replaced.

Suppose a person has a badly burned arm. A piece of skin from the person's thigh can be transplanted to the burned area on the arm. The transplanted skin will grow alongside the skin next to it. In time, the transplanted skin will cover the injured area completely.

Only the outer layers of the skin are taken from a healthy part of the body for the transplant. These very thin layers will grow back in two weeks or so.

A machine called the *dermatome* carefully removes healthy skin. The skin is then grafted over a badly injured area. Below is one kind of dermatome used to remove skin for grafts.

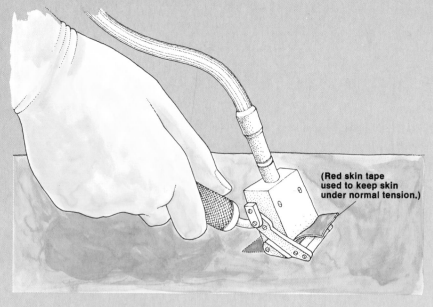

(Red skin tape used to keep skin under normal tension.)

The thickness of the skin removed for grafting could be as thin as this line _____.

1. Make a *Fingerprint Exhibit.* Display the fingerprints of everyone in your group. What will you need to make the fingerprints?

2. Suppose you read this advertisement in a newspaper or magazine.

To have shining hair...
use Perfect Hair Oil

Use what you have learned about the skin and hair to answer this question. *What can you do at home to make your hair shine without buying any special hair oil?*

3. Your skin helps control body temperature. Your body keeps at about the same temperature whether you are in a hot or a cold place. So you are said to be "warm-blooded." Now use a book or encyclopedia to find out what it means when certain animals are called "cold-blooded." You might use the book *The Skin* by Alvin and Virginia Silverstein.

Special Research

1. Look up information about these topics: *Pimples, Dandruff.*

2. Find out how doctors and dentists go about washing their hands to kill any germs that may be on them.

3. Make a report on how to treat such injuries to the skin as splinters and small cuts.

Can You Show What You Know?[1]

Page numbers show you where to look back in the chapter for information, if you need it.

1. Tell two important functions of your skin. (87, 99, 100)
2. Tell some things that are found on the surface of the epidermis. (87–88)
3. Explain why water doesn't soak through your skin. (88)
4. Discuss what gives a person's skin its color. (89)
5. Describe some things that are found in the dermis. (90)
6. Tell what is unusual about a person's fingerprint. (92)
7. Tell how blood vessels in the skin help control body temperature. (99)
8. Describe how the skin helps heal a small cut. (100)
9. Explain the connection between the skin and vitamin D, the "sunshine vitamin." (100)
10. List three things you can do to help take care of your skin. (101–103)
11. Explain how fingernails and toenails should be cut. (105)

[1]Behavioral objectives in the cognitive area are stated here directly to students themselves.

Review It

Page numbers show you where to look back in the chapter for information, if you need it.

1. Where does perspiration come from? (91)

2. What helps keep the skin from cracking? (88)

3. Why doesn't it hurt when you cut your hair or nails? (104)

4. How would you explain why some people have naturally curly hair? (109)

5. What helps keep the cells of the skin alive? (90)

6. What might be some effects of shoes that do not fit? (108)

7. How can you help prevent hangnails? (107)

8. What is a wart? (106)

9. What should you do if you want a wart removed? (106)

10. How can you help prevent a painful case of sunburn? (103)

11. Why do you need baths? (101–102)

12. How should you shampoo your hair? (102)

Copy each numbered item from List A. After each item, write the letter and words from List B that best describe it. For example:

13. albino   f. person who lacks a skin pigment

List A

13. albino
14. callus
15. corn
16. dermis
17. epidermis
18. fingerprint
19. perspiration
20. pigment
21. pore

List B

a. coloring matter in skin
b. tiny opening in epidermis
c. sweat
d. thick spot on skin
e. outer layers of skin
f. person who lacks a skin pigment
g. print of ridges in fingertip
h. cone-shaped thickening of skin that grows into layers underneath
i. true skin

Health Test for Chapter Three

Copy each number on a piece of paper. After each number write the correct answer, *true* or *false.* Rewrite each false statement to make it true.

1. Perspiration comes out of pores.
2. The epidermis is the true skin.
3. Pigment is found in the dermis.
4. Oil in the skin helps prevent it from cracking.
5. The skin helps keep bacteria out of the body.
6. Your fingerprint never changes.
7. Calluses result from a poor diet.
8. A freckle is another name for a wart.
9. As perspiration on the skin evaporates, the body becomes warmer.
10. There are many tiny blood vessels in the dermis.
11. The cells in the hair and nails you see are live cells.

Copy each sentence and fill in the missing word.

12. Perspiration helps _____ the body in hot weather.
13. The part of the hair that starts in each little hair pit is the _____.
14. Salty liquid that comes out through the pores is _____.
15. To get your hands really clean, you need warm water and _____.
16. Every day your epidermis sheds millions of skin _____.
17. A person's skin color is _____ from that of his or her parents.
18. Another name for vitamin D is the _____ vitamin.
19. Oil on the skin flows up from tiny oil _____ in the dermis.
20. The design made by the ridges on your fingertip is called your _____.

Number of Answers	20
Number Right	_____
Score (Number Right X 5)	_____

What Do You Think?

What did you learn in this chapter that you think is worth knowing? Write your answer on a piece of paper.

SCHOOL & HOME

Sometimes you injure your skin in various ways. These injuries may often happen at home. You will want to know how to treat the injuries safely.

One thing you can do is to make a first-aid booklet. Copy the first-aid treatments here. Take them home and talk them over with your family. Why is this a good thing to do?

First Aid for a Small Cut

Wash the cut with soap and water to help kill germs in and around it. Wash away from the cut to keep germs out.

Put a Band-Aid or a sterilized bandage over the cut. Press down on it to stop bleeding.

First Aid for a Splinter

Wash the skin around the splinter with soap and water.

Sterilize a needle by holding it over a flame.

Use the sterilized needle to remove the splinter. Then press above the wound to cause a little bleeding. This helps clean out the wound.

Put on a Band-Aid or bandage.

4 Your Bones and Muscles

All of us often take our bones and muscles for granted. What do you think is remarkable about them? What are some things you want to learn about your bones and muscles?

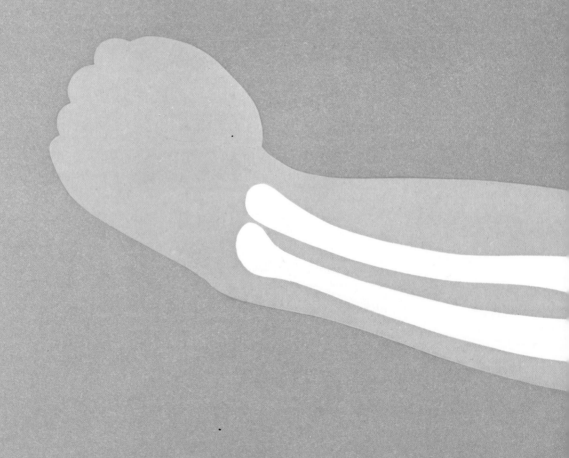

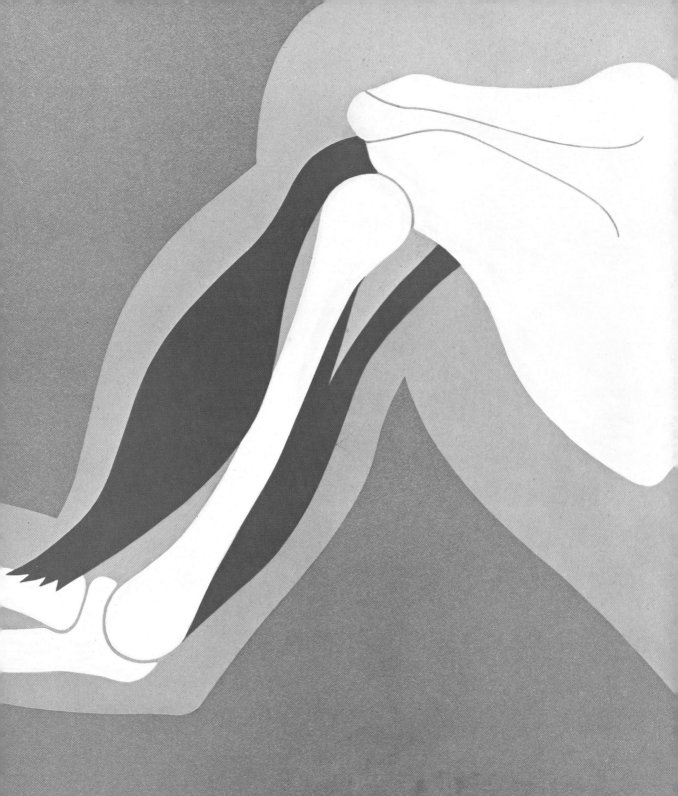

Preview It

Look through this chapter quickly. Find the seven main title questions. Which one interests you the most?

As you study this chapter, look for answers to those questions. You might also want answers to questions you have considered. How would you go about finding answers?

Along with the main ideas in this chapter, there is other information. You will be able to find answers to questions such as these.

About how many bones are in the skeleton?
Which bone in the skull can move?
What are floating ribs?
What are flat feet?
What part of the body is the trunk?
What are the body's shock absorbers?
Why has the skeleton been called "a masterpiece of design"?

What Is the Make-Up of the Skeleton?

You have a framework of bones from the top of your head down to your feet. This framework of bones is the *skeleton.* The skeleton gives the body its general shape. It also supports the body and protects many organs.

Your skeleton has more than 200 bones in it. There are little bones and big bones, flat bones and round ones, long bones and short ones. What may seem to be one bone, such as the skull, may really be many bones. See the picture.

Now look at the pictures on pages 120 and 121. This may give you an idea of how many different kinds of bones there are. Each bone is the right size and shape to do its work. For this reason, the skeleton is sometimes called "a masterpiece of design."

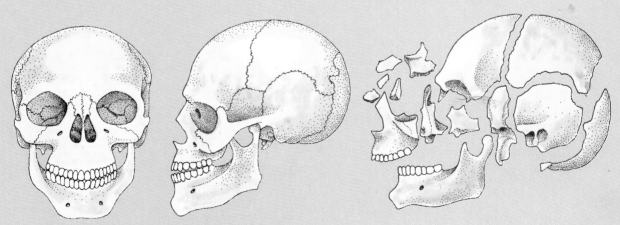

Skull bones are bones that enclose the brain.

The Wonderfully Designed Skeleton

Notice the many kinds of bones in the skeleton. Where are some of the different sizes and shapes you see pictured?

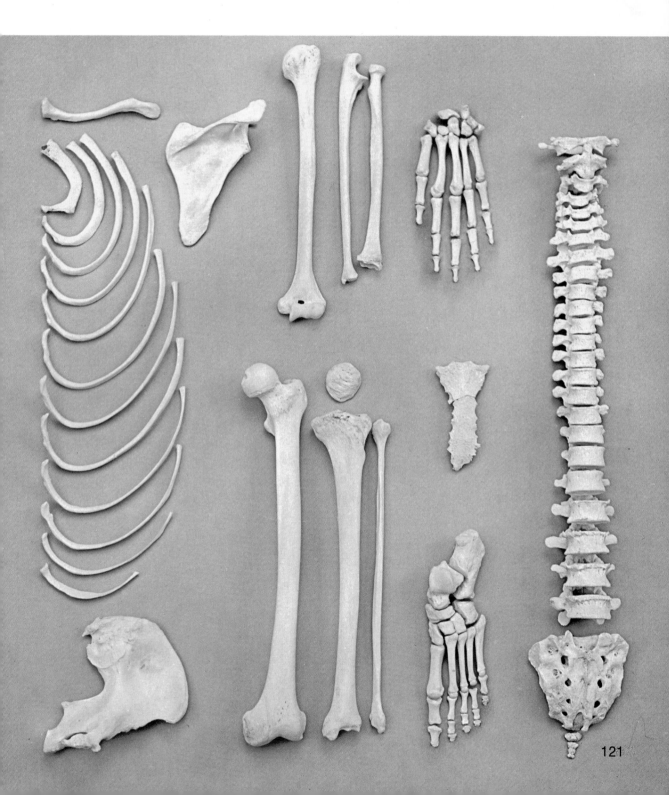

121

The Skull Bones

Skull bones include the *cranium,* or bones that enclose the brain. Cranium bones are flat bones that are firmly held together. The upper part of the cranium is hard and thick. It protects the brain from injury.

The skull also includes the bones of the face. In the skull are found eye sockets. These form a safe "pocket" for your eyes.

One of the bones in the skull is a moving bone. This is the jawbone. Your jawbone moves up and down and sideways when you chew, talk, or sing.

The Backbone

Now let us see how the backbone, or *spine,* is designed to do its special work.

The backbone is fastened to the skull at one end and to the hipbones at the other end. The backbone, together with the strong back muscles, helps hold you erect.

The backbone is made up of many little bones, or *vertebrae.* The spine lets you bend and twist. See the picture on page 123. There are pads of *cartilage,* an elasticlike material, between the 24 vertebrae. These little pads act as shock absorbers. When you walk, run, or jump, these pads cushion your bones. The pads keep the bones from bumping together.

There are two other bones at the end of the spine. These two bones are called the *sacrum* and the *coccyx.* Each one is made up of four or five vertebrae usually fused together.

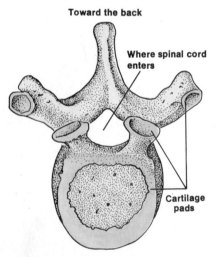

Toward the back

Where spinal cord enters

Cartilage pads

This is a single vertebra. Each vertebra in your backbone has a hole in it. The holes form a passageway for the main nerve cord—the spinal cord.

The backbone, or spine, is made up of many vertebrae. The vertebrae are lined up end to end and held together by muscles and strong bands of tissue. How do the cartilage pads between the vertebrae help the body?

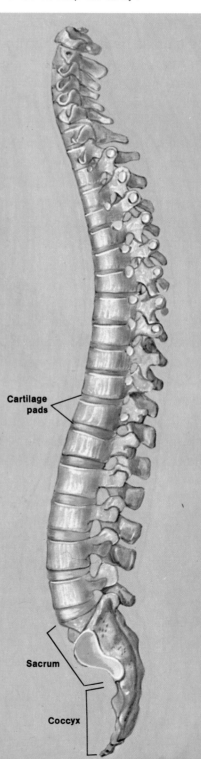

Cartilage pads

Sacrum

Coccyx

The Ribs

The *ribs*, along with the breastbone in the front and the spinal column in back, form a kind of cage. See the picture at the left.

The ribs are also joined together in such a way that they move up and down during breathing. This makes it possible for the chest cavity to get larger and smaller as you breathe.

You have 12 pair of ribs which are all connected to the spine in back. Ten of these pairs curve around the body. They are fastened to the breastbone in front with cartilage. The last two pairs are attached only to the backbone. These two pairs are called "floating ribs" because they are free in front. Try to find them in the picture here and on pages 128 and 129.

The Hipbones

The *hipbones*, with the sacrum and the coccyx of the spine, form a large bony bowl. See the picture on page 125. The bowl has a big opening at the bottom. This bowl-shaped cavity is the *pelvis*.

The pelvis helps support the upper part of the body. It also protects some of the organs in the lower abdomen. The lowest and strongest parts of the hipbones are what you sit on. Find the hipbones in the pictures on pages 128 and 129. Did you notice the bowl-shaped pelvis?

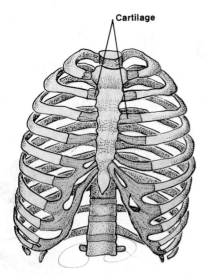

Cartilage

This rib cage protects such important organs as the heart and the lungs.

When you stand, your weight is supported by the bones of your legs down to your feet. But when you sit, the weight is supported by the arches of bones below the winglike parts of the hipbones. What is the pelvis? How does it help the body?

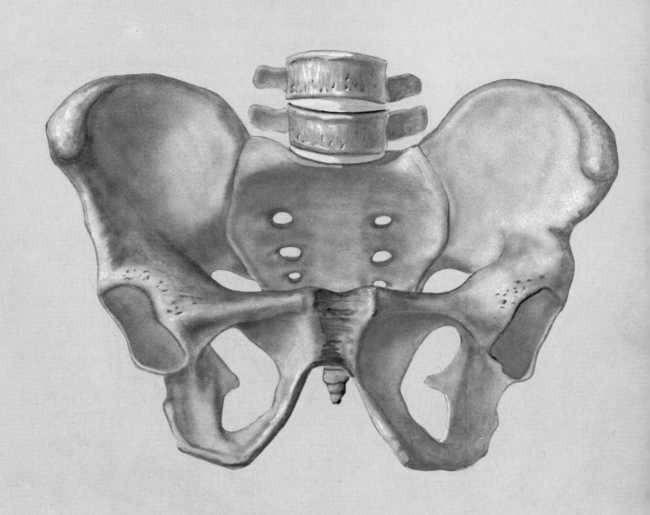

The Hand Bones

How do you make those short, fast movements with your hands? You have many short bones in your wrist, palm, and fingers which help. Do you notice anything about the finger bones in the picture on this page?

The Foot Bones

The bones in each foot are set in arches. These foot arches give a lot of support to the body. They look like arches that support a bridge.

Your foot arches bend and spring back each time you take a step. This keeps you from being jarred as you move about. Your toes help by moving and gripping as you walk.

What about people with flat feet? Someone with this difficulty has foot arches that are flat instead of curved. Notice the normal foot and flat foot on this page. Not all flat feet cause trouble. But those that are painful may need special care.

The Leg Bones

The long bones of the leg are designed for special jobs. One job is to help bear the body's weight. The leg bones can do this easily because the bones are almost hollow. They are *porous,* or full of many tiny holes. They are also stronger than if your long bones were solid. Columns of long solid leg bones would weigh too much. They would make it hard for you to move about.

The long bones of the legs also help the body make large motions. Where else in the body would you expect to find long bones? Use the pictures on pages 128 and 129 to find out.

What movements can you make with your hands? How does the thumb help?

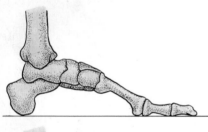

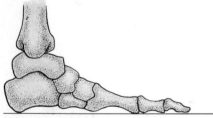

Which is the flat foot?

126

How Do Bones Fit Together?

Look again at the pictures on pages 128 and 129. Do you notice places in the skeleton where one bone ends and another begins? Places where two bones join and fit against one another are called *joints.*

Kinds of Joints

Some joints in your body are *fixed joints.* As you would guess from their name, such joints will "give." But they do not move very much. Most of the joints in your skull, for example, are fixed joints. Other joints, such as those between the bones in your spine, move just a little and give increased support.

The two kinds of *movable joints* are shown on this page. What are they?

Ball-and-socket joints, such as those in the shoulders and hips, allow back-and-forth and rotating motions. Look at the rounded end of one bone. See how it fits into the hollow socket of the other bone.

Hinge joints, such as those in your knees, fingers, and toes, allow movement in only one direction. What would happen if your knee had a ball-and-socket joint instead of a hinge joint?

Movable joints have a fluid around them which keeps them moist. They are able to move smoothly. The fluid also keeps the joints from getting stiff. How would you move about without this fluid?

**Hip joint
(ball-and-socket joint)**

**Knee joint
(hinge joint)**

Kneecap

Where else in the body are there joints like these?

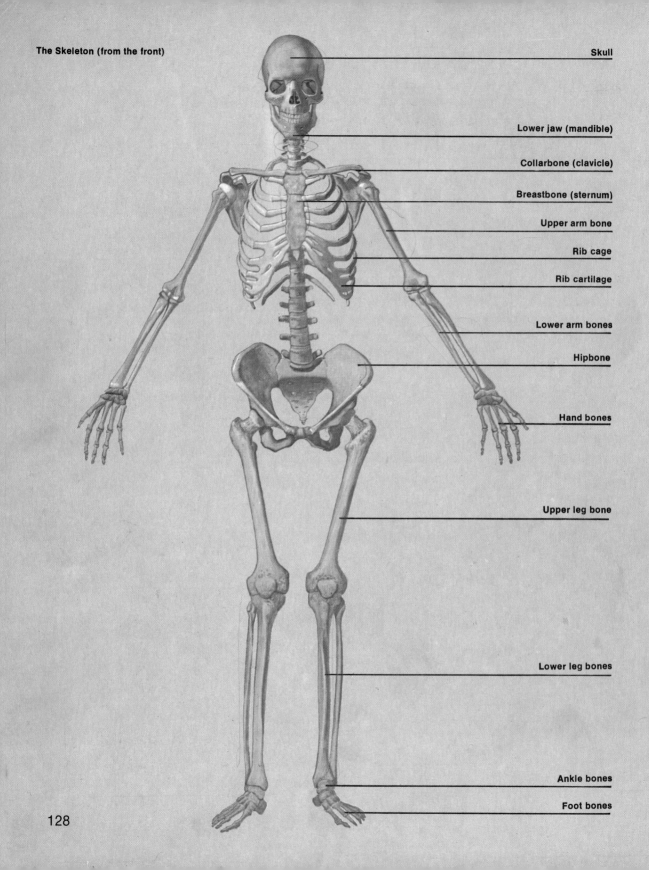

The Skeleton (from the front)

Skull

Lower jaw (mandible)

Collarbone (clavicle)

Breastbone (sternum)

Upper arm bone

Rib cage

Rib cartilage

Lower arm bones

Hipbone

Hand bones

Upper leg bone

Lower leg bones

Ankle bones

Foot bones

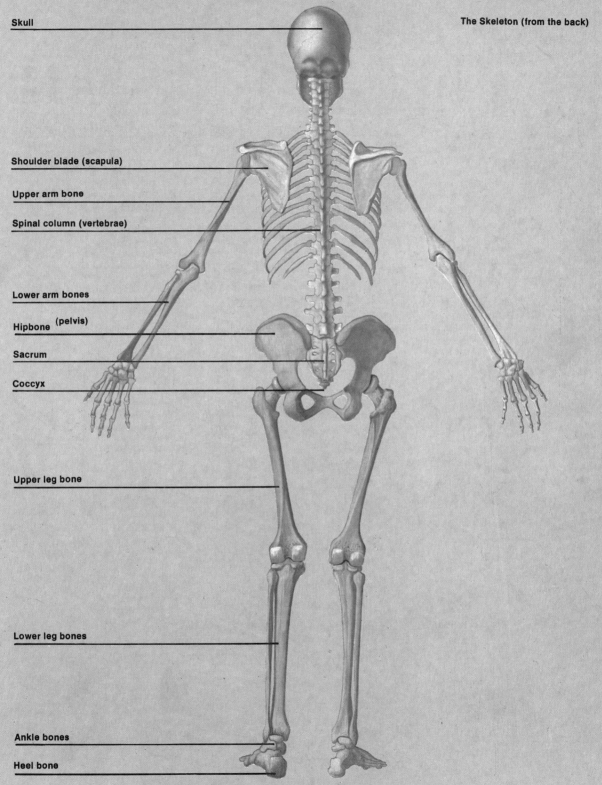

Skull

The Skeleton (from the back)

Shoulder blade (scapula)

Upper arm bone

Spinal column (vertebrae)

Lower arm bones

Hipbone (pelvis)

Sacrum

Coccyx

Upper leg bone

Lower leg bones

Ankle bones

Heel bone

129

How Do Your Bones Look— Outside and Inside?

Suppose you were asked to tell how bones look on the outside. You might describe bones as smooth, whitish, and hard. You might even mention the thin covering which contains nerves and blood vessels. Some nerves and blood vessels go into the bones.

All the outer layers of your bones are made of hard material called *compact bone.* If you looked inside the bones you would see a porous material. This kind of bone is called *spongy bone.* The little holes make it look like a sponge. But spongy bone is not soft. It is made up of a network of many criss-crossing bony tubes. This lightweight network gives strength to the bones. It helps give the body support it needs. Notice the spongy bone inside the long bone on page 131.

The Long Bones

The long bones in your body are the heavy-duty bones. Arm and leg bones are long bones. In the long bones, the spongy part is found at the rounded ends.

The Flat Bones

Flat bones in your body are put together somewhat like a sandwich. Rib bones are an example. They have two layers of compact bone outside. Spongy bone and a soft substance called *marrow* is found between them. Some flat bones are pictured on pages 128 and 129. Which ones are they?

Something to Do

Thousands of years ago, people found that the bones of animals they hunted and killed were very useful. Find out some of the uses that were found for bones in long-ago times. One book that will help you is *Bones* by Herbert S. Zim (Morrow).

This view of a piece of long bone shows the end of the long bone and the hollow shaft where yellow marrow is located.

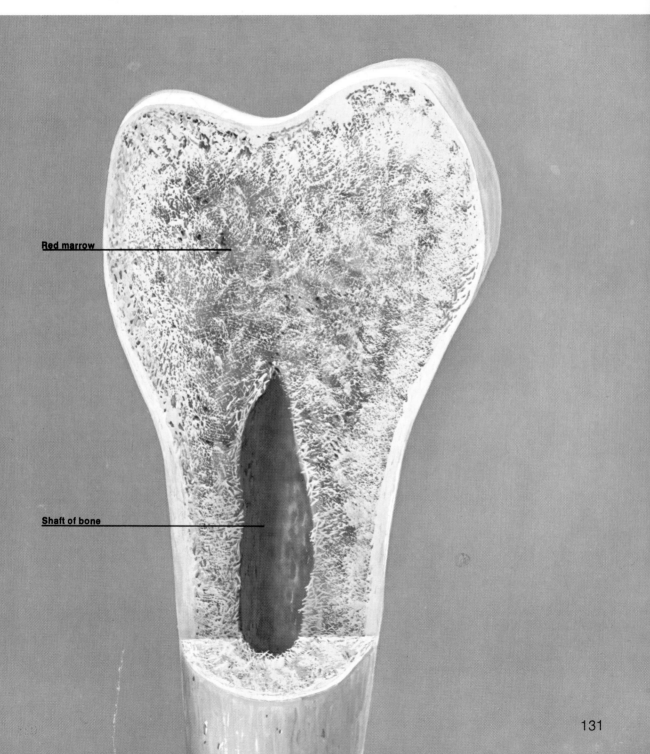

Red marrow

Shaft of bone

Marrow

Remember the hollow part in the long bones where it is filled with marrow? This marrow is yellow and mostly made of fat.

The marrow in the ends of the long bones is red. Red marrow is often called a "factory." Do you know why? It makes red blood cells which are sent into the bloodstream. They give blood its red color.

Red blood cells also pick up oxygen in the lungs and carry it to all parts of the body. And these cells carry waste carbon dioxide back to the lungs.

The red blood cells made in the marrow usually live for three or four months. As millions of your red blood cells die each minute, they are replaced by millions of these healthy new cells. These new cells pass through the very thin walls of the capillaries, or tiny blood vessels, which are in the marrow.

The marrow in your bones also makes some of the white blood cells. White blood cells fight germs that come into your body.

Sum It Up

What are some different kinds of bones found in the body?

How does the make-up of the backbone help you bend and twist?

What are some bones that help protect body organs?

What is the only bone in the skull that can move?

What are the "floating ribs"?

What are joints? Why are these useful?

What are two kinds of joints?

Why is red marrow important?

Books to Read

Look for books about the skeleton at the school or public library. Here are some you may find.

Balestrino, Philip. *The Skeleton Inside You* (Crowell).

Silverstein, Alvin and Virginia. *The Skeletal System, Frameworks for Life* (Prentice-Hall).

Weart, Edith. *The Story of Your Bones* (Coward).

Zim, Herbert S. *Bones* (Morrow).

How Do Your Bones Grow?

When you were a baby, your bones were mostly elasticlike cartilage. There was little calcium or other mineral matter in your bones.

As you grew older, your bones began to grow larger and stronger. Important minerals like calcium and phosphorus were needed. The bones took these minerals from digested food carried by the blood. Some of the needed minerals are found in fruits and vegetables. Most are found in milk.

While your bones are growing, you especially need a balanced diet. This includes not only milk but foods from the four food groups. It takes food from all these groups, in the right amounts, to keep you healthy and strong.

To build strong bones, the bone cells must have plenty of vitamins C and D. Vitamin C is found in citrus fruits, berries, tomatoes, and leafy vegetables. Vitamin D comes from cod-liver oil, some fish, and egg yolks. Vitamin D is also made from a fatlike substance in the skin. This happens when the skin is exposed to ultraviolet rays of the sun.

Growth in Thickness and Length

As you grow older, your bones grow thicker. The outside cover of the bones forms new hard bone cells.

Your bones are also growing in length. The picture will help you understand how this happens. Find the part called the *growth plate.* This growth plate is made of soft cartilage. The growth plate is separated from the end of the bone for a long time. As you continue to grow, changes take place in the growth plate.

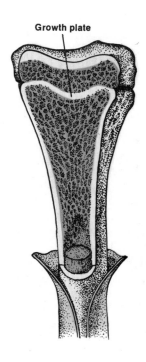

Growth plate

During your growth years, the ends of your long bones are fastened to the shafts by the growth plate. Gradually hard new bone cells grow out from the shaft.

When they grow out, they replace the soft cartilage. The cartilage is pushed toward the ends of the long bones. As the cartilage pushes outward, the long bones grow. By the time you are eighteen to twenty years old, hard bone cells have replaced the cartilage in the growth plate. Then the bones cannot grow longer. And you can grow no taller.

Ligaments and Tendons

As you think about the different bones in the skeleton, you may wonder why they do not slip out of place.

Your bones are kept in place by tough, stringy bands called *ligaments.* The ligaments reach from one bone to another and hold them together. You can see ligaments in the picture on this page.

There are other tough, stringy bands that fasten the nearby muscles to bones. These bands are called the *tendons.* See those pictured. How would you explain the difference between a ligament and a tendon?

Sum It Up

Why is an adequate diet important for building strong bones?

How do bones grow thicker?

How do bones grow longer?

Why don't bones slip out of place as you move?

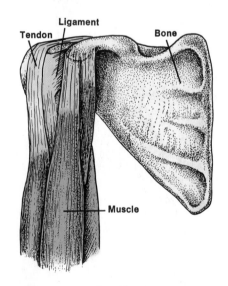

Bones, muscles, ligaments, and tendons work together to move the body. Here you see these parts in the arm and shoulder.

Ligament

Tendon

Bone

Muscle

HEALTH AROUND US

Do you know that there are artificial joints? These joints are made of plastic or metal. Artificial joints can be used to replace real ones that are worn out.

Cartilage covers the ends of bones where they meet in the joint. The cartilage protects the ends of the bones. It also helps hold them together.

With some diseases, though, the cartilage becomes worn and thin. At times the cartilage is all worn out. Then the ends of the bones in the joints rub on each other. The joints become painful and stiff. Sometimes they twist into various shapes.

One disease that affects joints is *arthritis.* Older people are more likely to have arthritis. But young people may have it. There are many kinds of arthritis. When arthritis attacks the cartilage in joints, it is called *osteoarthritis.*

Today artificial joints of plastic or metal can be inserted during an operation. The new joints may work as well as the real ones did.

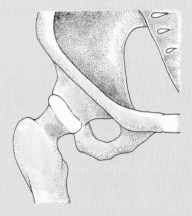

This is a normal ball-and-socket joint in the hip.

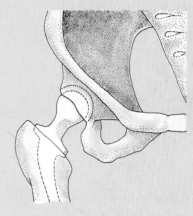

The joint in this hip has been replaced with an artificial ball-and-socket joint.

135

What Do Skeletal Muscles Do?

Muscles that cover the skeleton are called *skeletal muscles.* The flesh in your body is really more than 600 skeletal muscles along with some fat. The skeletal muscles round out the body and give it shape. See the pictures on pages 140–145.

Skeletal muscles allow your bones to move. They also help hold your bones in place. This is how the body is held straight.

Skeletal muscles do other things too. By squeezing the blood in the veins, they help return it to the heart. Skeletal muscles are in action much of the time. They help make a good part of the body's heat.

Skeletal muscles are of different sizes and shapes. The muscles of the face, for example, are small and thin. They are involved in chewing and in closing the eyes. These same muscles help you make facial expressions. Look at the facial muscles shown. Now put *your* facial muscles into action. Do these things: smile, frown, wink, laugh, yawn, close your eyes. Can you feel the facial muscles at work?

Muscles of the Trunk

The *trunk* is the part of the body from the shoulders to the top of the legs. The trunk of the body is another example of muscles that are well-designed.

No bony structure protects organs such as the stomach and liver. Only the front muscles of the trunk form a wall which protects these and other organs behind it. Meanwhile, the large muscles of the back help hold your backbone straight. Both front and back muscles make it possible for you to bend and twist.

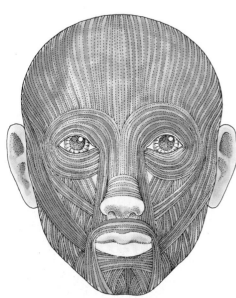

What muscles do you see here? You can learn more about these and other muscles in the book *The Human Body: The Muscles* by Kathleen Elgin (Watts).

Arm and Leg Muscles

Where you find long bones in your body, you will find long, strong muscles. Large actions are required. Let us see, for example, how the long muscles in your arms are designed for large action. This may be as simple as helping arms bend and straighten out.

The arm muscles are fastened at one end to the shoulder bone. At the other end they are fastened to the arm bones. The muscles pull to make your arm move. They do this by contracting. They become shorter and thicker. When muscles relax, they stretch out and become longer.

Feel the large muscles in your upper arm as you bend the arm. This gives you an idea of the shape of these muscles. They have a thick middle part. But they become smaller toward each end where they form a tendon.

To make a bone move, two muscles are needed. One muscle contracts and becomes shorter and thicker. At the same time the other muscle relaxes and stretches out. The shortened muscle pulls one bone toward the other. You can see these muscles pictured on this page. If the arm were straightened out, what would happen to the contracting muscle?

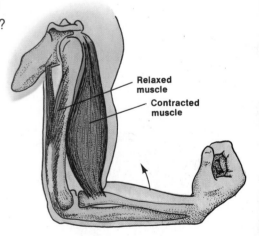

Relaxed muscle

Contracted muscle

Notice how the upper arm (biceps) muscle changes shape as it contracts to help move the bone.

137

What Are Voluntary and Involuntary Muscles?

Your skeletal muscles move on command when you want to walk or run. You can also chew, swallow, or talk. This is done when your brain sends messages over the motor nerves. The messages go to certain muscles in your body. Then these skeletal muscles contract or relax. Muscles that you can make work as you wish are *voluntary muscles.*

There are other muscles in the body that need no orders to start or stop. They are called *involuntary muscles.* These muscles are found in the blood vessels. Involuntary muscles are also found in such organs as the stomach, large and small intestines, and the bladder. The heart muscle also works without any orders.

Your involuntary muscles can be affected if you feel angry or fearful. They may not work properly. You may feel weak or sick or "tied in knots."

Your voluntary muscles may be affected by strong feelings too. When you are feeling upset, these voluntary muscles may tremble.

Striped Muscles

Suppose you could look through a microscope at the muscle fibers in your voluntary muscles. You would see tiny light and dark markings or stripes across the fibers. Because of their markings, voluntary muscles are sometimes called *striped muscles.*

Every muscle is made up of thousands of thread-like fibers fastened together. When we talk of muscles, we really mean bundles of these little fibers.

Voluntary (striped) muscle fibers

Smooth Muscles

Suppose you could look through a microscope at the fibers in most of your involuntary muscles. You would see how they differ from the striped voluntary muscles. The involuntary muscles are sometimes called *smooth muscles.*

Heart Muscle

How do the muscle fibers of the heart look under a microscope? They look a little like the striped voluntary muscles. But they work like involuntary muscles. Muscle fibers in the heart have some qualities of both striped and smooth muscles. However, heart muscle is quite different from either. The heart contains a special set of involuntary muscles that keeps your heart beating regularly all by itself. Heart muscle is also called *cardiac muscle.*

How You Can Build Strong Muscles

Muscles must be used regularly to keep them in their best working order. When they are not used for a long time, muscles do not work very well. They may become weak and even smaller.

Strong muscles are not built in a few weeks or months. They are built by following healthful practices year after year. One such practice is exercising regularly. Eating an adequate daily diet and getting enough sleep and rest most of the time are other healthful practices.

Remember that the more you use certain muscles, the more skillful you become in using them. What is your favorite exercise? What muscles do you think you are learning to use more skillfully?

Sum It Up

What are four things that skeletal muscles do?
What are voluntary muscles?
What are involuntary muscles?
How can emotions affect the muscles?

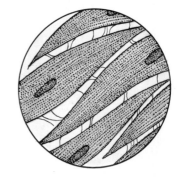

Involuntary (smooth) muscle fibers

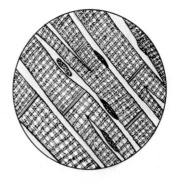

Heart (cardiac) muscle fibers

Muscles—The Body's Movers

Your framework of bones gives you a shape. Your muscles fill out that shape.
Muscles are the movers of your body. Every movable bone has muscles to move it.

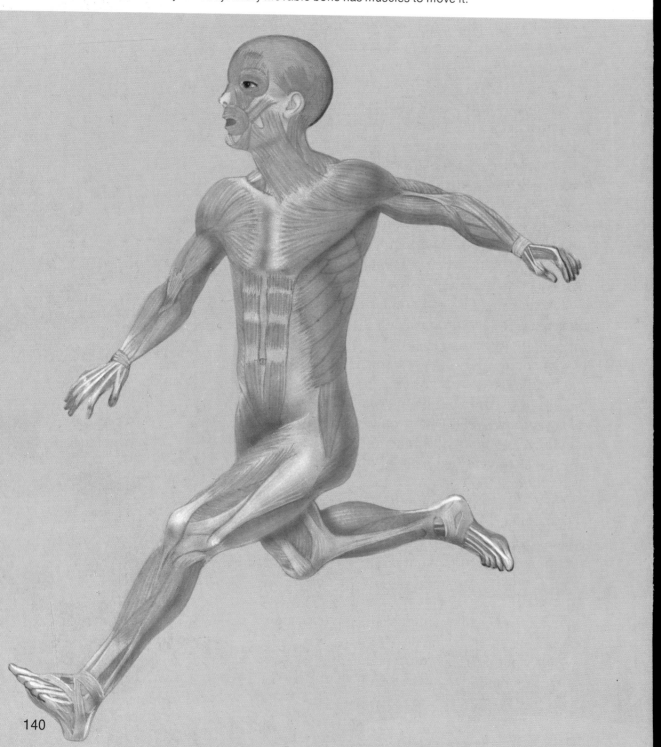

What muscles are in action here? How can a person become more skillful in using these muscles?

Notice the long, strong muscles in the trunk of the body. These muscles give this part of your body great power. What else do they do?

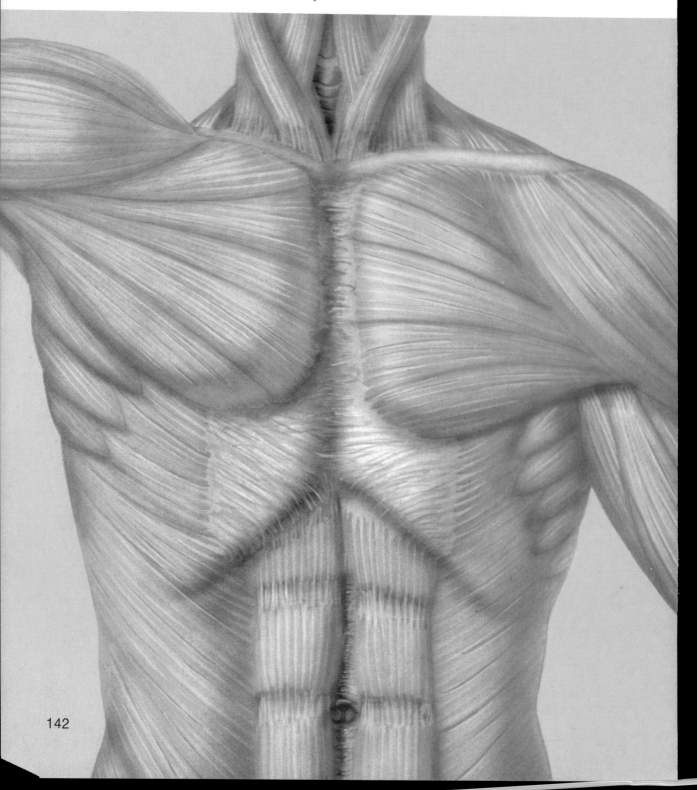

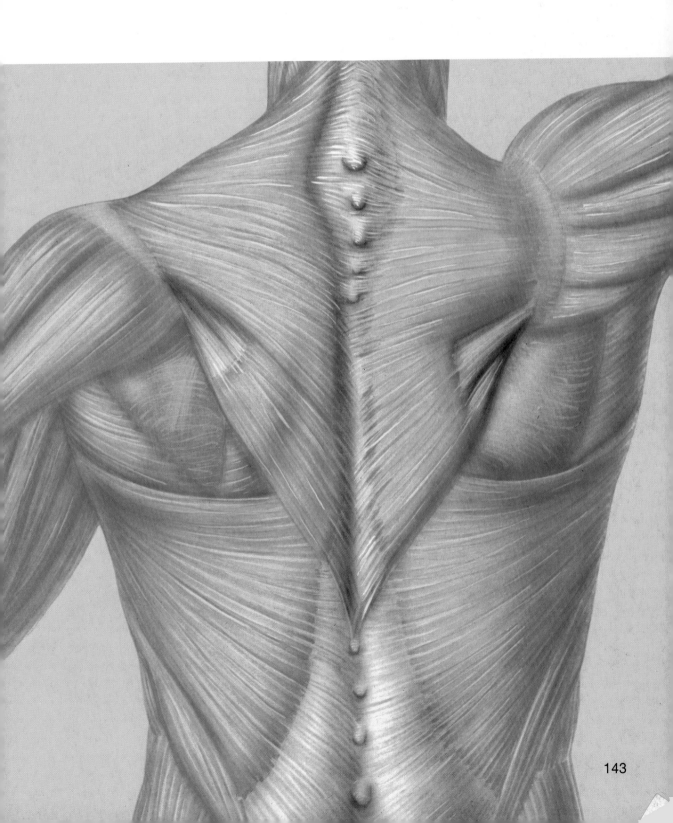

The muscles of the body are of many shapes. Some muscles overlap each other. Some are twined in or around each other. Others are squeezed in between other muscles and bones. All work together to produce action.

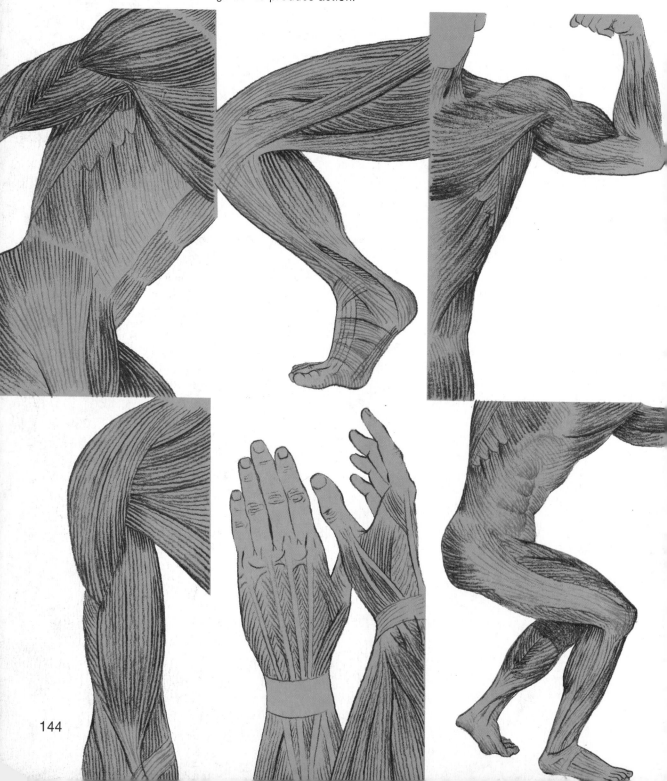

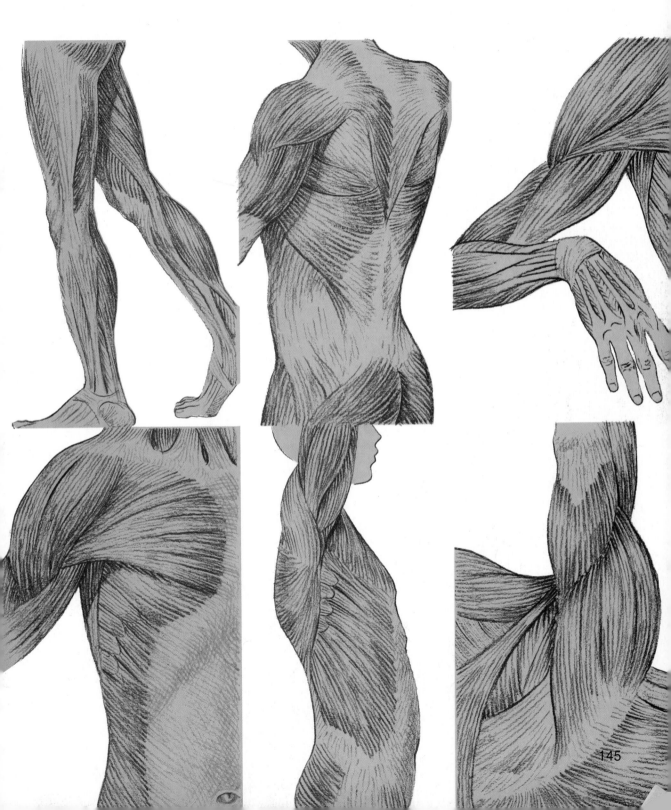

145

WRITE IT

There are many interesting things about the bones and muscles you can find out about for yourself. Begin with an encyclopedia and library books. From these you can make reports to your group.

Here is a report one person made on "What Happens When a Bone Breaks?" What *does* happen?

Other topics to consider for your reports might be these:

What Are the Sinuses?

What Is a Bunion?

What Is the Soft Spot on a Baby's Head?

What Is the "Funny Bone"?

What Is a Sprain?

What Happens When a Bone Breaks?

A bone breaks into two pieces and the broken ends do not push through the skin. This is called a <u>closed</u> <u>fracture</u>. This type of break is considered clean. An unclean break is when the bone splinters and there are bits of bone around the break.

If the ends of a broken bone push through the muscles and skin, the break is an <u>open</u> <u>fracture</u>.

The doctor puts the bone in a cast. The cast holds the broken pieces of bone together. After a while the broken bone heals. Such a break may take six weeks or longer to heal.

How does a broken bone heal? Threadlike connective tissue forms over the break. Then new bone cells keep forming. At last the break heals.

Ed

What Can You Do About Your Posture?

Just what is posture? Posture is the way you hold your body when you stand, sit, and move about.

Each person differs somewhat in his or her posture. That is because each person differs in the make-up of the joints. Each person differs, too, in the structure of the muscles. Such differences make it impossible for all people to stand alike, walk alike, or sit alike. Your posture depends a great deal on the structure and shape of your body.

There are things you can do, though, to avoid poor posture. For example, posture is poor when your body is being carried stiffly erect. You will look uncomfortable and unnatural. Poor posture hinders the normal workings of the body and can spoil your appearance. See the pictures on this page.

Good posture means your bones, muscles, and nervous system are all working together to keep you "in balance." Your bones can easily do the work they are designed to do. Your weight is spread properly over the body parts designed to support weight. You can stand or sit or move about without quickly getting tired. Good posture helps you feel comfortable. It also makes you look more attractive.

Just how can you maintain good posture or improve it? Try keeping your body in balance as you sit and stand and walk. *The most important thing you can do is to keep strong and well. Follow the guides for healthful living.* Do you know what some of these guides are?

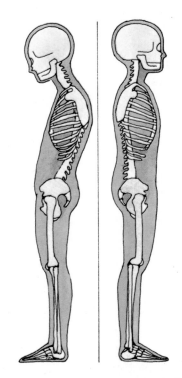

Which picture shows a body "in balance"?
Which picture shows posture that might spoil a person's appearance?

147

Perhaps getting enough of the right kind of food comes to mind. You know that good food builds strong bones and muscles. Strong muscles help hold bones in place. Bones can help you hold your body straight.

Getting enough sleep is also important. Can you show how people stand or sit or move about when they are tired?

Exercise is necessary for good posture too. Exercise helps build strong muscles that give good support to your body.

Shoes affect your posture. Can you explain or demonstrate how people might walk when their shoes don't fit?

Strong emotions can affect your posture. Which picture on pages 148 and 149 shows discouragement? Upset feelings?

Which picture has posture that suggests feelings of confidence or joy? Why do you think so?

ENJOY IT

People over the years have been fascinated by the wonders of the human body.

Here you can see some sketches of the body made by the famous artist, Leonardo da Vinci. These drawings were made about five hundred years ago. Yet they are so accurate that some are still used in medical books.

What parts of the body do these sketches show?

Anatomical drawings by Leonardo da Vinci, courtesy of The Royal Library, Windsor Castle, Copyright reserved.

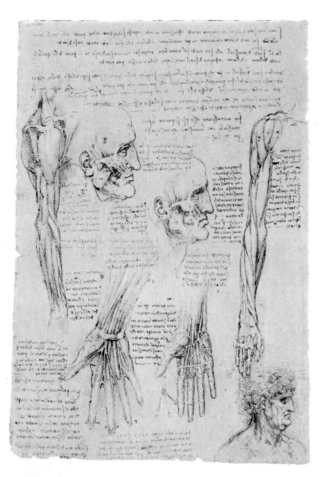

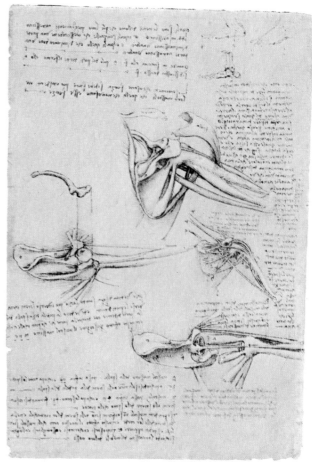

Things to Do

1. Ask a butcher for some bones. Make an exhibit of your collection. Label and identify those which are good examples of the following: spongy bone, marrow, flat bones, long bones, and joints.

2. Tell in which of these activities you direct the voluntary muscles.

      chewing   swimming   running
      writing   breathing   digesting

3. Can you unscramble these words to find the names of some bones? What are the bones? Write their names.

      cyxocc   rumsac   abckbneo   llusk

4. Look at the puzzle. Find five words that have to do with bones or muscles. Write the words. After each word, write a simple explanation of it.

```
L C D G J K M J O I N T S
C A R T I L A G E O X Z Q
E R A Q W E F M P O I U Y
V B N M A R R O W I U Y T
O W T E N D O N S Y Y R R
P I O Y T E W Q X B V D X
I Y R X L I G A M E N T S
```

5. Here is an active game that can help you build strong and skillful muscles. Read the directions. Be ready to explain to others how to play the game.

Run-Up-and-Kick-Back Relay
Equipment: 6 soccer balls or play-
               ground balls
Players: Even number, divided into
               5 or 6 teams, line formation
Place: Playground, playroom, or
               gym

The first player on each line runs with the ball to a goal. The goal is about 9 meters in front of the teams. Each runner then turns, puts the ball on the goal line, and from that point kicks the ball back to the team.

The next player on each team receives the kicked ball and runs with it to the goal line. There the player stands in front of the first player and kicks the ball to the third player on the team.

The first team to be lined up behind the goal line wins.

6. Look at the exercises shown below. How do you do them? Tell what muscles are being used as you do each exercise. What are some other exercises you can do?

Can You Show What You Know?[1]

Page numbers show you where to look back in the chapter for information, if you need it.

1. Explain what is meant by the term *skeleton.* (119)
2. Give some examples of the wonderful design of the skeleton. (122, 124, 126)
3. Tell what joints are. (127)
4. Describe how bones look on the outside and inside. (130–132)
5. Explain the importance of the red marrow. (132)
6. Describe how a long bone grows in thickness and in length. (133–134)
7. Explain what skeletal muscles are and how they help you. (136–137)
8. Tell how muscles make a bone move. (137)
9. Explain the difference between voluntary and involuntary muscles. (138–139)
10. Explain what is meant by posture. (149)
11. Tell two or more things a person can do to maintain good posture. (147–148)

[1]Behavioral objectives in the cognitive area are stated here directly to students themselves.

Review It

Page numbers show you where to look back in the chapter for information, if you need it.

1. Look back at the questions asked on page 118. How would you answer them now? (119, 122, 124, 126, 136)

2. What are the skull bones that help protect the brain? (122)

3. How does it help that the bones of the feet are set in arches? (126)

4. How do the bones of the skeleton fit together and how do they remain in place? (127, 134)

5. What bones protect the spinal cord? (122)

6. What bones help protect the heart and lungs? (124)

7. If your long bones were solid, how would this affect all of your movements? (126)

8. What parts of the body can be replaced by artificial ones? (135)

9. Which muscles in the body are the smooth muscles? (139)

10. Which muscles in the body can you tell what to do? (138)

Copy each numbered item from List A. After each item, write the letter and words from List B that best describe it. For example:

11. compact bone   d. hard outer bone

List A

11. compact bone
12. coccyx
13. cranium
14. fixed joint
15. hinge joint
16. pelvis
17. spine
18. tendons
19. trunk

List B

a. end-of-spine bone
b. joint that allows movement in one direction
c. joint that allows little movement
d. hard outer bone
e. bands that fasten bones to muscles
f. backbone
g. bones that enclose the brain
h. bowl-shaped cavity formed by hip-bones
i. part of body from shoulders to top of legs

Copy each number on a piece of paper. After the number write the name of the thing that best answers the description.

1. Movable bone in the skull.

2. Protective cage of bones.

3. Tough, stringy bands that hold the bones together.

4. Tough, stringy bands that fasten muscles to bones.

5. Hard, outer layer of bone.

6. Soft yellow or red substance inside some bones.

7. Places where the ends of two bones fit together.

8. Muscles that work according to orders from the brain.

9. Muscles that work without orders from the brain.

10. Many little irregular-shaped bones of the spine.

11. Muscles that, with some fat, cover the skeleton.

12. All the bones of the head.

13. Bowl-shaped cavity formed by hipbones and end of the backbone.

14. Body joints that do not move.

15. Joints that allow movement back and forth in only one direction.

16. Joints that allow movement in all directions.

Copy each number on a piece of paper. After the number write the letter that goes with the *best* answer choice.

17. In the skeleton there are (a) some 1000 bones, (b) some 200 or so bones, (c) some 40 bones.

18. Ribs are connected in back to the (a) kidneys, (b) hipbones, (c) backbone.

19. Movable joints are protected by a special fluid that (a) keeps them moist and moving smoothly, (b) glues them together, (c) manufactures red blood cells.

20. Involuntary muscles are found (a) on the skeleton, (b) in the sacrum, (c) in the body organs.

Number of Answers	20
Number Right	___
Score (Number Right X 5)	___

What Do You Think?

What did you think about this chapter? Write your ideas about it on a sheet of paper.

SCHOOL & HOME

Do you know what to do if someone should fall and possibly break a bone?

Study these first-aid steps that everyone should know. Copy them and take them home. Talk over the steps with your family. If you are keeping a First-Aid Scrapbook, put this material in it.

First Aid for a Broken Bone

If you should be around when someone falls and possibly has a broken bone, follow these steps:

1. Use a nearby telephone to call a doctor or have someone else make the call.

2. Do not move the injured person. Leave that for the doctor or a trained adult. If the bone is broken, moving the injured person could cause even more damage.

3. Keep the injured person warm and comfortable until a doctor comes. Put a coat, sweater, or blanket over him or her if the weather is cool or if he or she seems chilled.

5 How Your Body Uses Food

Amazing things happen to the food you eat. For instance, do you know what your body does with food? Do you know how all parts of your body get the food you eat?

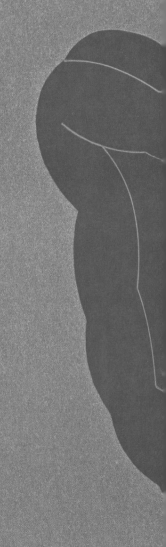

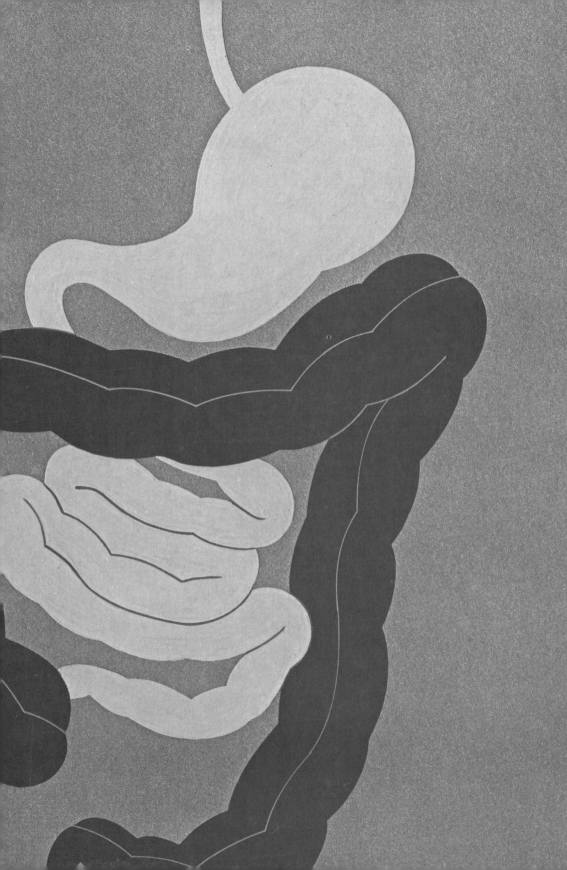

Preview It

Look quickly through this chapter. What questions do the four main titles ask? As you study the chapter, look for the answers.

You will also find out other things as you read, such as answers to questions that boys and girls your age have asked.

Could you swallow food if you were standing on your head?
How long does it take for food you swallow to reach the stomach?
What do emotions have to do with the way the stomach works?
What should you eat to keep strong and healthy?
Why do you need teeth of different shapes?

Be on the lookout for information to help you answer these questions too.

How Do Your Teeth Help You Eat?

Your teeth work by cutting, tearing, crushing, and grinding food. To do this, you need teeth of different shapes.

The front teeth, which cut food, are the *incisors.* There are four in each jaw. Incisors in the upper jaw come together with those in the lower jaw to cut the food you eat.

Then you move the food to the sides of your mouth. Here you use teeth called cuspids to tear up food into smaller bits. These teeth have a point, or *cusp,* on the chewing surface. Can you find your four cuspids? There is one on each side of the upper jaw. And there is one on each side of the lower jaw.

Next to the cuspids are primary molars. Between the ages of nine and eleven, you shed these teeth. *Bicuspids* replace them. The bicuspids have two points, or cusps. The bicuspids come together to crush your food into even smaller pieces. Adults have eight bicuspids in their permanent set of teeth. There are two located on each side of the upper and lower jaws.

The real work of chewing is done with the *molars.* They are in the back of your mouth. Molars have broad tops with four or five cusps on them. You use them to grind food into tiny bits. You will have twelve molars when all permanent teeth come in.

Look at the picture of a permanent set of teeth on page 162. Which of these teeth are in your mouth now? Which ones are not?

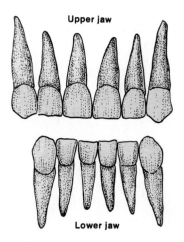

Upper jaw

Lower jaw

Do you see eight incisors and four cuspids?

Every tooth has its work to do in the cutting, tearing, and grinding of food. If even a few teeth are missing, food will not be broken up properly. How do teeth help you in speaking?

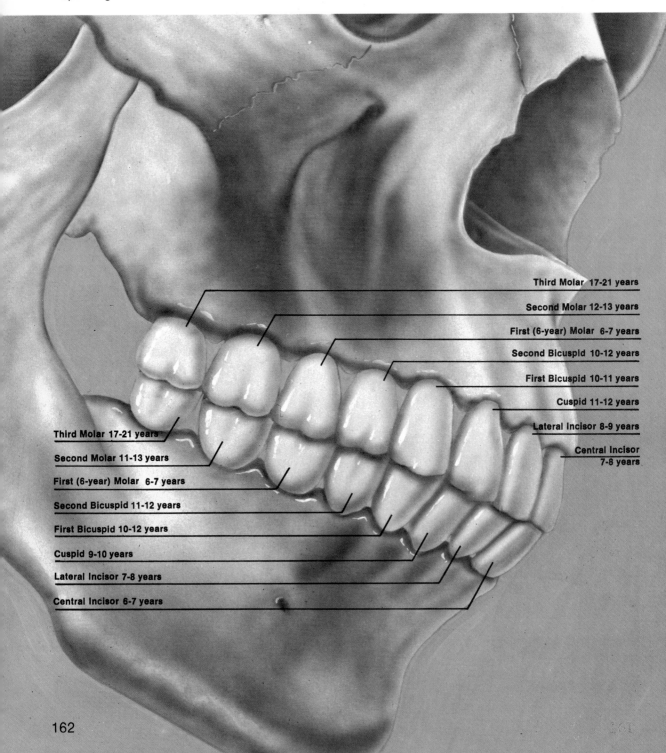

Third Molar 17-21 years

Second Molar 12-13 years

First (6-year) Molar 6-7 years

Second Bicuspid 10-12 years

First Bicuspid 10-11 years

Cuspid 11-12 years

Lateral Incisor 8-9 years

Central Incisor 7-8 years

Third Molar 17-21 years

Second Molar 11-13 years

First (6-year) Molar 6-7 years

Second Bicuspid 11-12 years

First Bicuspid 10-12 years

Cuspid 9-10 years

Lateral Incisor 7-8 years

Central Incisor 6-7 years

How Do You Take Care of Your Teeth?

You need all your teeth to break down your food so your body can use it. Teeth are important enough to take care of them. No other teeth will replace your permanent teeth. When teeth have to be *extracted,* or pulled out, false teeth are usually worn. False teeth are not as satisfactory as your natural ones.

The most common health problem among school-age children is *tooth decay,* or *dental caries.* Researchers have come up with one way to reduce decay: *Use a toothpaste that contains an approved fluoride.* Check the package for the seal of approval from the American Dental Association.

Another way to prevent decay is to cut down on sweet foods. Candy, cake, and soft drinks full of sugar encourage decay. If sweets are left on the teeth for even short periods, decay could result. To understand why this happens, you need to know about *plaque.*

Plaque is a sticky, colorless film of harmful bacteria that is always forming on the teeth. These germs are found even in a healthy mouth. In the presence of sweets, bacteria in plaque form acids. These acids cause cavities. Therefore, plaque should be removed daily. If you can, floss and brush after eating. Otherwise, do both thoroughly once a day. How will having regular dental checkups help?

Sum It Up
Why are teeth of different shapes needed?
What is plaque? How can it be removed?
How can you help prevent tooth decay?

FOR BEST RESULTS, SQUEEZE TUBE FROM THE BOTTOM AND FLATTEN IT AS YOU GO UP.

Accepted
COUNCIL ON DENTAL THERAPEUTICS
AMERICAN DENTAL ASSOCIATION

has been shown to be an effective decay-preventive dentifrice that can be of significant value when used in a conscientiously applied program of oral hygiene and regular professional care.

Council on Dental Therapeutics—American Dental Association

NET WT. 5 OZ.

Care of Your Teeth

Floss your teeth before you brush them. Flossing helps remove plaque from between the teeth. What is plaque?

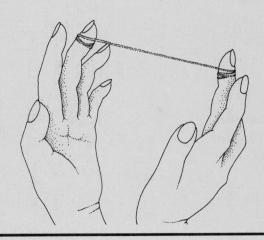

To floss the teeth, break off about one-half meter of floss. Wind most of it around one of your middle fingers. Wind the rest around your other middle finger.

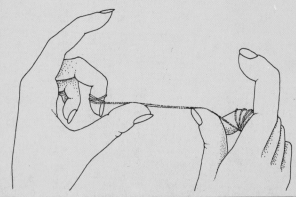

Now hold the floss between each thumb and forefinger. Allow about three centimeters between them, to guide the floss between the teeth.

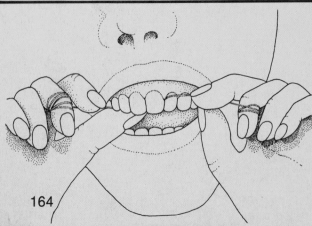

Hold the floss tightly. Move it back and forth to ease it between the teeth. Bend the floss toward the tooth as you do this. Gently slide it into the space between gum and tooth.

Now scrape the floss up and down against the side of the tooth. Do the same thing for each pair of teeth. Use a clean part of the floss each time.

Brushing

What can you learn from these pictures about a recommended way to brush your teeth? Be sure to use a flat, soft-bristled toothbrush.

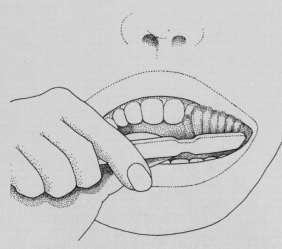

Place the ends of the bristles against the outside of your teeth. Angle the brush against the gums.

Move the brush back and forth. Use short, gentle strokes. Do this to the outside of all your teeth and gums.

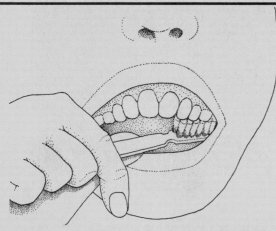

Brush the insides of your teeth and gums the same way you brushed the outsides, moving the brush back and forth. Brush the tops of your teeth too.

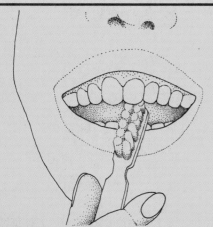

Brush the insides of your front teeth and gums up and down with the front end of your brush.

Another Way to Fight Plaque

There is a way to see if you are getting all the plaque off your teeth. Buy some disclosing wafers at a drugstore. The wafers are made of a harmless dye. The dye stains the plaque on your teeth. Chew a wafer, then brush your teeth. If there are still places colored with dye, you need to brush more. Brush until all the red-stained plaque is removed.

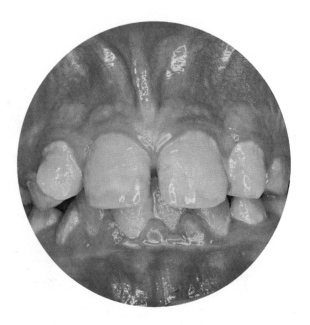

Teeth should be checked occasionally for plaque.

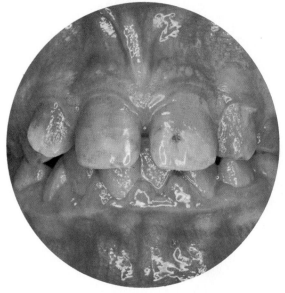

The color you see on these teeth is the plaque. Plaque is easier to see with a disclosing wafer.

How Does the Food You Eat Get Digested?

Many things must happen to food before your body can use it. The process of changing or breaking down food into a form the body can use is called *digestion.*

Your Mouth Helps

Digestion begins as soon as you put food into your mouth. As you chew, your teeth cut, tear, crush, and grind the food into small bits. At the same time, a liquid, *saliva,* is mixed with food in your mouth. Saliva comes from three pairs of *salivary glands.* These glands empty the saliva into your mouth. Just thinking of food can start the saliva to flow. The smell, sight, or taste of food can also start it to flow.

Saliva does several jobs. It moistens food, making it easier to swallow. Also, your body can digest and use food materials only in liquid form.

Saliva changes foods which do not dissolve in water. Bread and potatoes, for instance, are starches. Starches do not dissolve in water. Sugar does. Your saliva chemically changes starch to sugar so the food can be digested.

One other thing saliva does is help you taste your food. This is because food can be tasted only when it starts to dissolve.

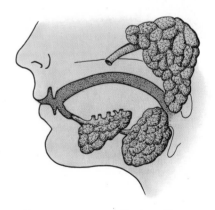

Here you can see three salivary glands on one side of the face. How does saliva get from them into the mouth?

Your body can digest food more easily if food is chewed well. Chewing helps break down and mix food with saliva. As you chew and moisten the food, your tongue is at work too. Your tongue forms the food into soft balls. Then it pushes these balls to the back of your mouth, or throat.

At the back of the mouth is the food tube, or *esophagus.* It leads from the throat to the stomach. Find the esophagus in the picture below.

What happens as food starts to move down this tube? A thin layer of cartilage, the *epiglottis,* covers the windpipe during swallowing. The windpipe is where the air you breathe is channeled to the lungs. This is how food is prevented from "going down the wrong way."

Food that goes down the food tube is pushed along by rings of muscles. The pushing and squeezing action of the muscles in the walls of the tube is called *peristalsis.* This action enables you to swallow food even if you are standing on your head. Food you swallow reaches your *stomach* in about five seconds. A glass of water can make the trip even faster.

Your Stomach Helps

What happens when food enters the stomach? Peristalsis continues to move the food along. Saliva mixed with food continues to break down starches into sugars.

The stomach is rather small when it is empty. It is a bag of muscle. As food enters, it stretches greatly. See the pictures on pages 169 and 170.

Gastric juices pour out of many small glands in the stomach walls. The gastric juices contain chemicals that break down proteins and a few fats. Muscles in the stomach walls twist and bend the stomach. These movements churn the food and mix it with the gastric juices.

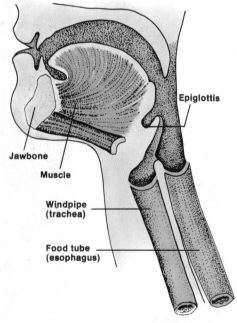

Epiglottis

Jawbone

Muscle

Windpipe (trachea)

Food tube (esophagus)

Which part shown here keeps food from going into the windpipe?

Here you see the twisting, bending movements of the stomach. How do these movements help digest food?

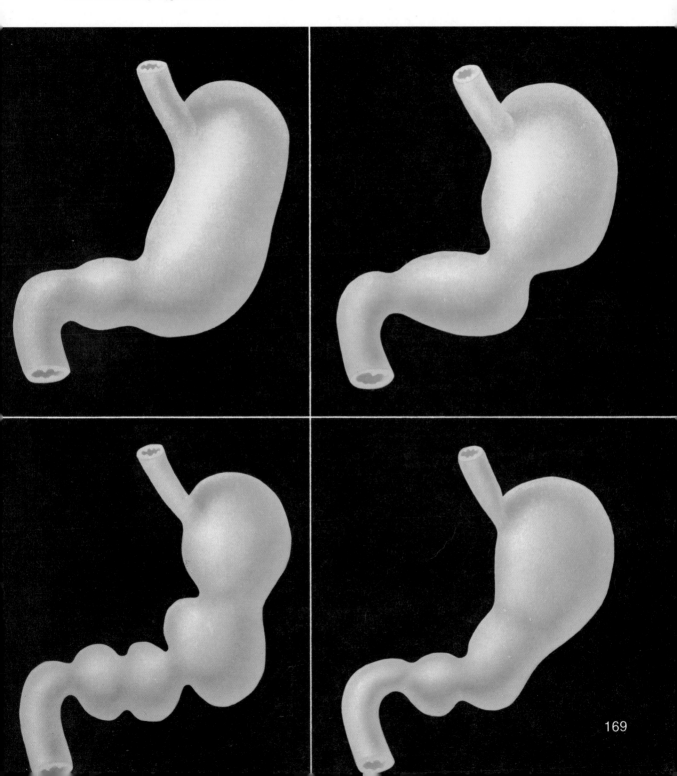

This model of a stomach—made in a health museum in Cologne, Germany—
shows how the stomach is supplied with blood by many blood vessels.

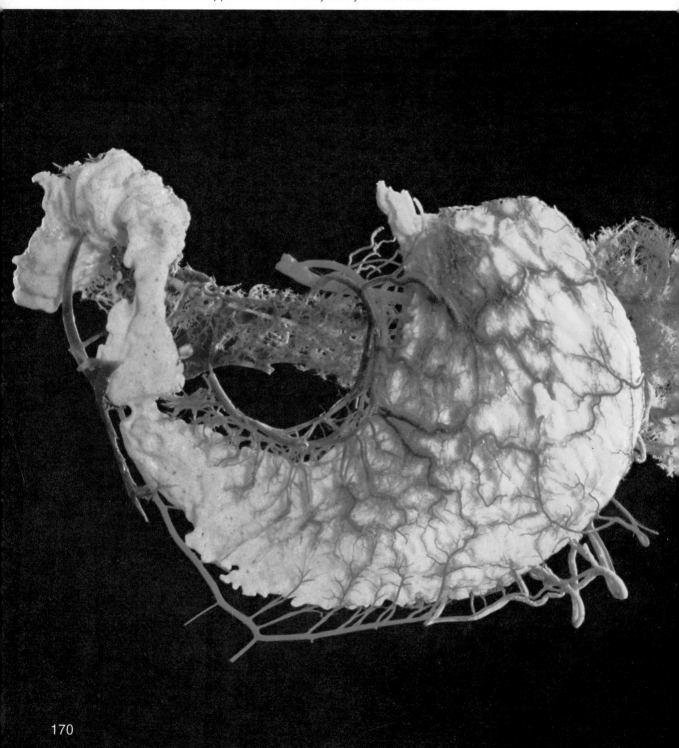

Why don't the strong gastric juices digest, or break down, the walls of the stomach? They would do just that if it weren't for mucus. *Mucus* is a slippery substance that protects the inside of the stomach walls. The mucus also helps food slide easily into the *small intestine.*

Some food is ready to leave the stomach shortly after a meal. It usually takes from two to four hours for all the food from a meal to move out of the stomach into the small intestine. Food material high in fat remains the longest in the stomach.

Food is partly digested in the stomach. Then the food material moves into the small intestine. It is in the form of a thick liquid called *chyme.* This thick liquid is squeezed out of the stomach by special muscles. It is sent into the small intestine a little at a time.

Your Small Intestine Helps

Your small intestine, or *small bowel,* is a coiled tube. If it were straightened out and measured, it would be about four times your height.

The small intestine is not very big around. It is called small because there is another kind of intestine in the body. This type is much larger around. You will learn more about this larger intestine later.

What happens as the partly digested food moves into the small intestine? Digestive juices come from the small intestine's walls. This juice is mixed with food by the movements of the small intestine.

Books to Read

Look in the library for books like these about the human body.
Elgin, Kathleen. *The Human Body: The Digestive System* (Watts).
Riedman, Sarah. *How Man Discovered His Body* (Abelard).

Other digestive juices are made by the *pancreas* and the *liver.* Juice made by the liver, called *bile* or *gall,* is stored in the gall bladder. See the picture on page 174. Bile helps digest fats. These juices are poured into the small intestine through little tubes, or ducts.

Digestion of food is completed in the small intestine. Most of the food by this time has changed into a thin, watery form that can be used by the body.

This liquid food material passes out of the small intestine and goes into the bloodstream. To do this, it does not pass through any opening. You may wonder how this can happen.

In the walls of the small intestine are many tiny, fingerlike parts called *villi.* Each of the villi is about the size of a comma on this page. The villi are in constant motion, waving back and forth. They contain blood vessels. The liquid food passes through the thin walls of these blood vessels and enters the bloodstream.

Then the blood carries the food material to all the cells of the body. The cells use the nutrients from the digested food to produce energy for the body's processes.

Not all digested food material is needed at once by the body. So it is changed into forms that can be stored until it is needed. Some is stored in the muscles. And some is stored under the skin as fat.

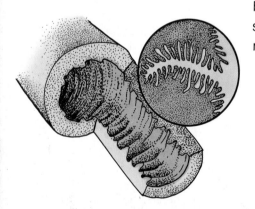

This is an inside view of the small intestine, showing villi. What have you learned about the villi?

Doctors can study X-ray pictures to see how well the body's organs are working. This X-ray picture shows the stomach and small intestine of a ten-year-old patient. The doctor gave her a special and safe chemical to drink that made these organs show up on the X-ray film.

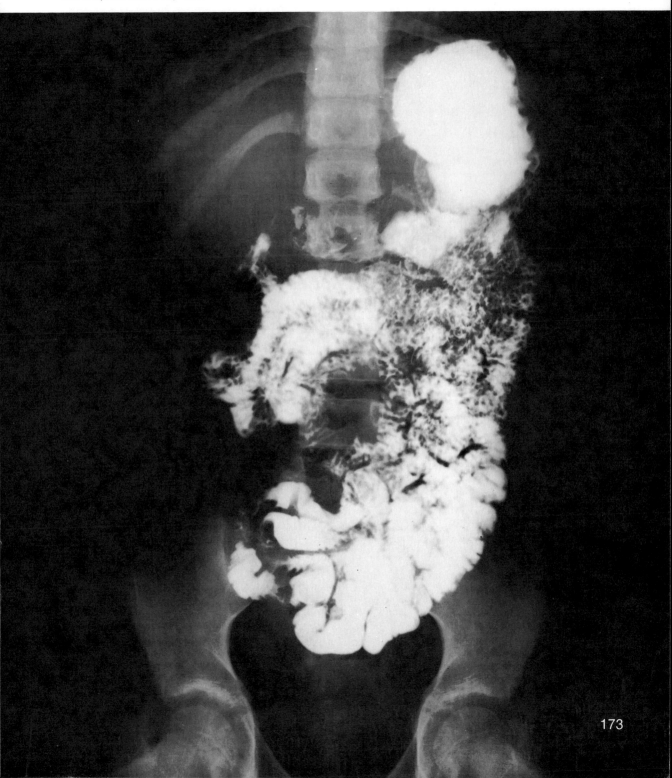

The Liver and Gall Bladder

This model shows a back view of the liver and gall bladder. Bile is made in the liver and stored in the gall bladder. Bile is sent into the small intestine. What foods does bile help digest?

Your Large Intestine

Some food cannot be digested, or broken down, in the small intestine. It does not pass through these walls. What happens to this undigested food? It is pushed by muscles of the small intestine into the *large intestine,* or *large bowel.*

The large intestine is a wide tube about two and one-half centimeters across. It is wider than the small intestine, but is not as long. If it were straightened out, it would be about as long as you are tall.

Undigested food is partly a liquid mass when it first enters the large intestine. Gradually most of the water is removed. This water goes through the walls of the large intestine into blood vessels. What is left is made up of such things as fruit skins, outer parts of grain, seeds, and the stringlike parts of some vegetables. Other materials in the large intestine are bacteria. There are some digestive juices too.

When your large intestine begins to fill up, the solid waste material pushes against the walls. The muscles in these walls then begin working. These muscles squeeze the material along to an opening at the end of the large intestine. Then the waste material is ready to be pushed out of the body as a *bowel movement.* The time from when food is eaten until the undigested food is passed from the body may be from 10 to 20 hours.

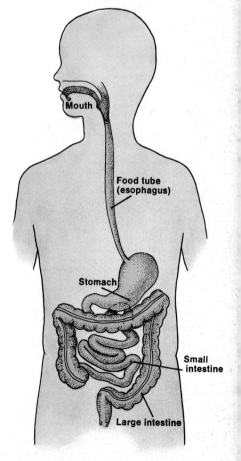

Mouth

Food tube (esophagus)

Stomach

Small intestine

Large intestine

What organs make up the digestive system?

175

Your Kidneys and Urinary Bladder

The large intestine gets rid of the solid wastes. But your body produces liquid wastes too. The *kidneys* and the *urinary bladder* help get rid of liquid wastes.

You have two kidneys. They are bean-shaped organs located in your back under your lowest ribs. You have one kidney on the left side and one on the right. Although you have two kidneys, you could live without one if necessary.

Thousands of little tubes in the kidneys work as filters. As blood passes through the kidneys, any excess water, cell wastes, and other materials the body cannot use are filtered out. These waste substances pass from the blood in the blood vessels into the tubes.

The liquid waste material is called *urine.* Urine flows through a tube from each kidney into the *urinary bladder.* The bladder is a muscular bag in the lower abdomen.

The bladder stores the urine until it is ready to leave the body. When the bladder is full, you are able to relax a special muscle at the lower end of the bladder. The muscle stays relaxed just long enough to allow you to urinate.

Sum It Up

Where does digestion begin?

How does saliva help digest food?

What happens to food in the stomach?

What happens to food in the small intestine?

How does digested food get into the blood?

What does the blood do with digested food?

Can you name the main parts of the digestive system?

How does the body get rid of liquid waste materials? Solid waste materials?

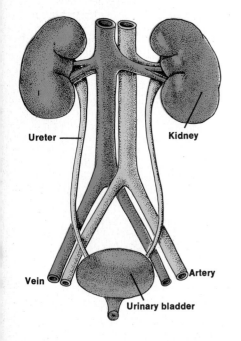

Ureter — Kidney

Vein — Artery

Urinary bladder

What can these organs do?

The Kidney

This model shows a single kidney and part of the tube that carries urine to the bladder. What wastes do the kidneys help get rid of?

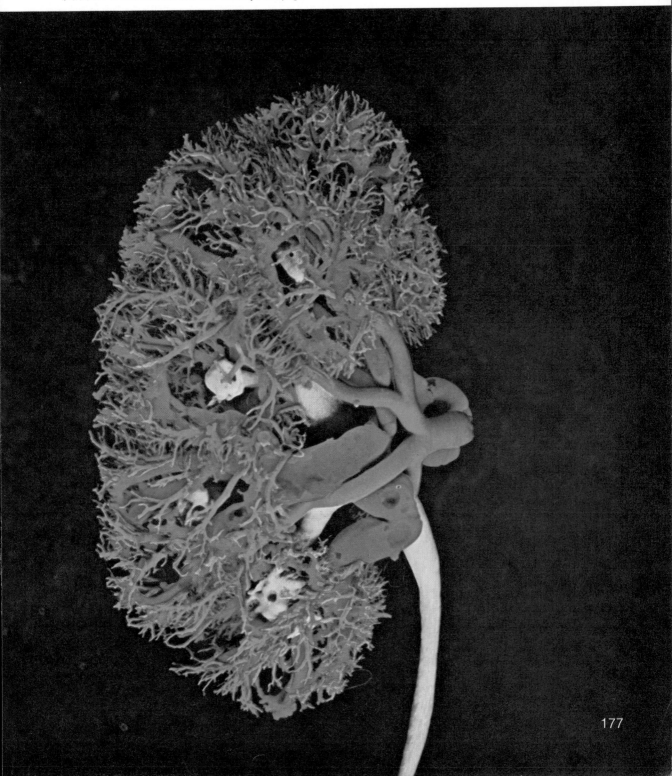

How Food Is Digested:
A Diagram

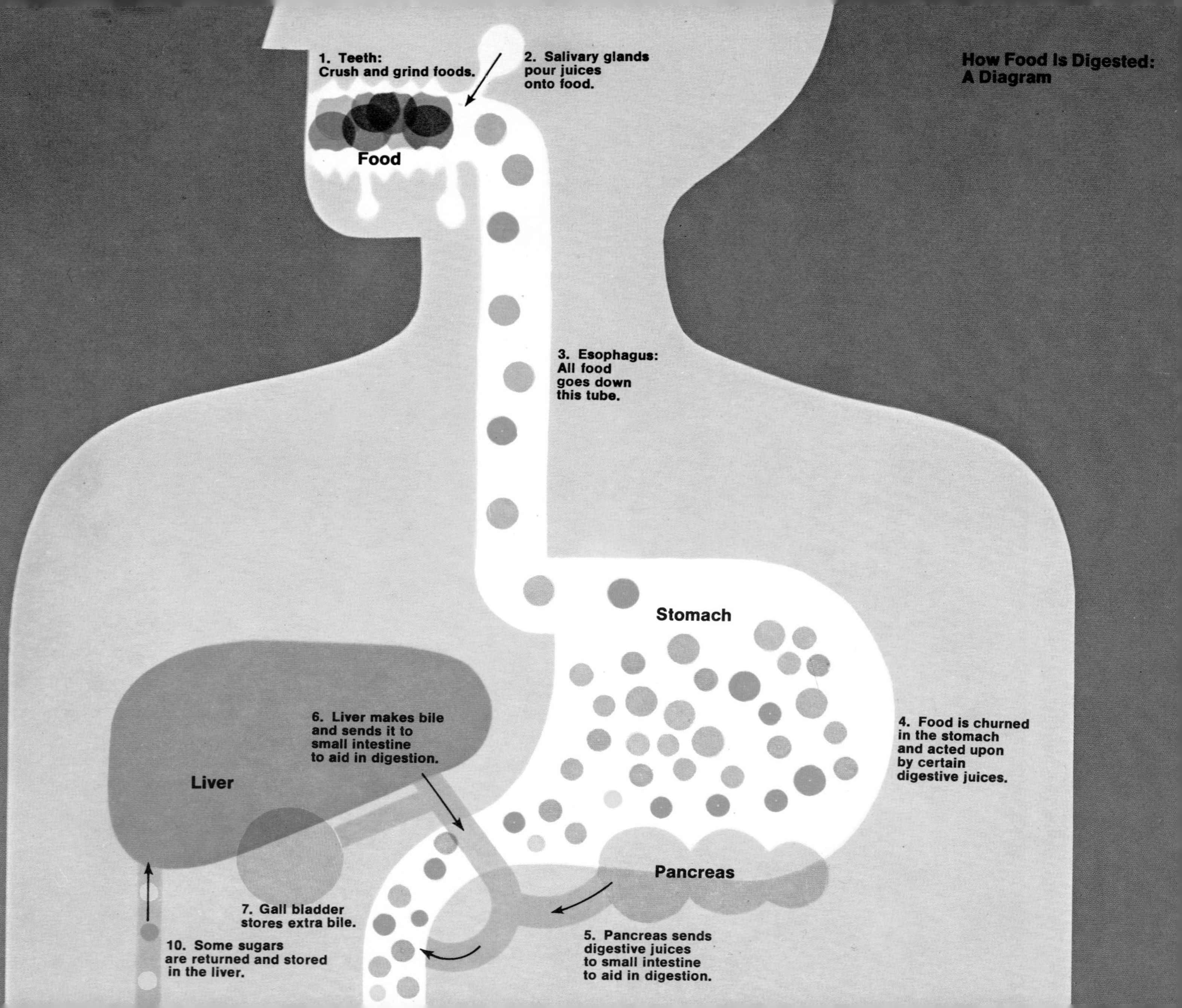

1. Teeth: Crush and grind foods.

Food

2. Salivary glands pour juices onto food.

3. Esophagus: All food goes down this tube.

Stomach

4. Food is churned in the stomach and acted upon by certain digestive juices.

Pancreas

5. Pancreas sends digestive juices to small intestine to aid in digestion.

Liver

6. Liver makes bile and sends it to small intestine to aid in digestion.

7. Gall bladder stores extra bile.

10. Some sugars are returned and stored in the liver.

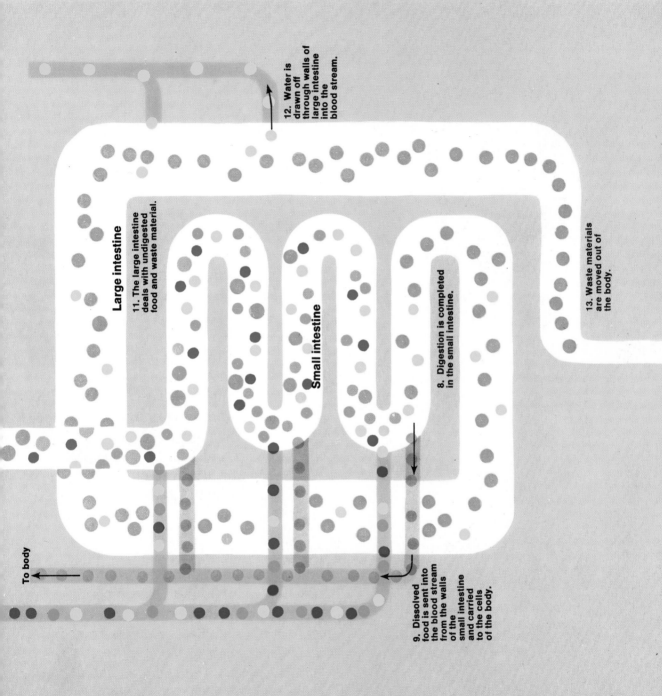

Large intestine

11. The large intestine deals with undigested food and waste material.

12. Water is drawn off through walls of large intestine into the blood stream.

Small intestine

8. Digestion is completed in the small intestine.

13. Waste materials are moved out of the body.

To body

9. Dissolved food is sent into the blood stream from the walls of the small intestine and carried to the cells of the body.

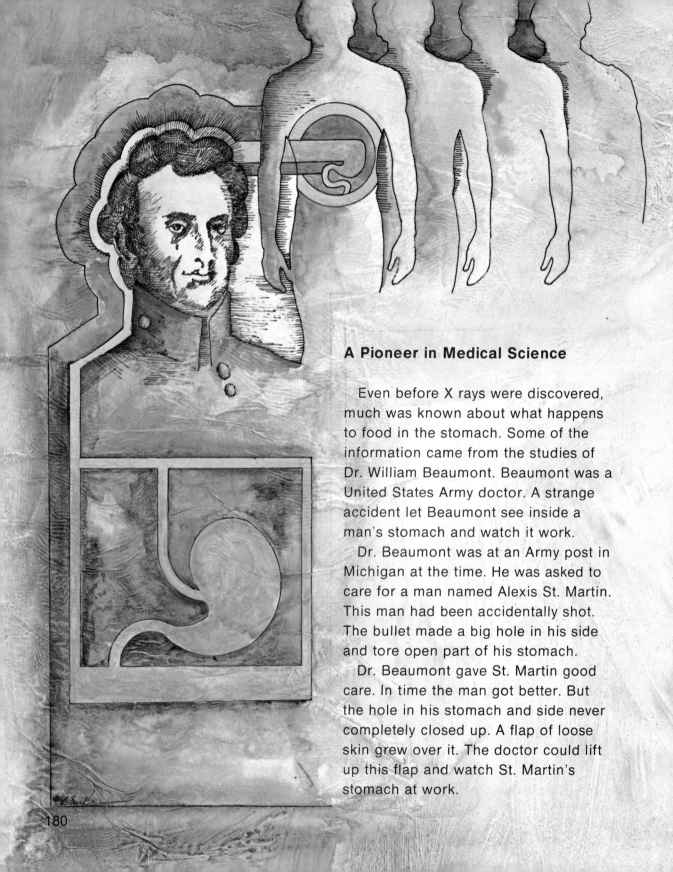

A Pioneer in Medical Science

Even before X rays were discovered, much was known about what happens to food in the stomach. Some of the information came from the studies of Dr. William Beaumont. Beaumont was a United States Army doctor. A strange accident let Beaumont see inside a man's stomach and watch it work.

Dr. Beaumont was at an Army post in Michigan at the time. He was asked to care for a man named Alexis St. Martin. This man had been accidentally shot. The bullet made a big hole in his side and tore open part of his stomach.

Dr. Beaumont gave St. Martin good care. In time the man got better. But the hole in his stomach and side never completely closed up. A flap of loose skin grew over it. The doctor could lift up this flap and watch St. Martin's stomach at work.

The doctor asked St. Martin's permission to try some experiments. St. Martin cooperated and later traveled with the doctor to other Army posts. There the experiments continued. In the next ten years, Dr. Beaumont did more than a hundred experiments. He kept a careful record of everything he learned.

Beaumont learned that the stomach finished its work more quickly with some foods than with other foods. Foods like bread and potatoes were ready to leave the stomach within an hour or so. But protein foods like meat and eggs stayed in the stomach for three hours or longer.

Emotions affected how St. Martin's stomach worked. When he was worried, angry, or unhappy, the gastric juices flowed less freely. With less gastric juices, the stomach could not do its work as well. However, when St. Martin was happy and calm, the gastric juices poured out freely. Then the stomach did a good job of churning food and mixing it with gastric juices.

St. Martin's stomach worked better when he was fairly quiet than when he was exercising. Sometimes he sat quietly for a while after a meal. Then his stomach worked better than when he was cutting wood.

Dr. Beaumont also noticed that alcoholic drinks made the lining of the stomach red and sore looking. Again the stomach did not work as well.

By watching the churning of food in the stomach, Beaumont discovered that the stomach has two kinds of movements: crosswise and lengthwise.

All this happened over one hundred fifty years ago.

HEALTH AROUND US

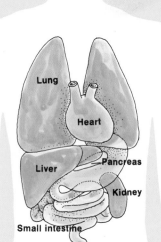

Lung

Heart

Liver

Pancreas

Kidney

Small intestine

In recent years many human organs have been transplanted. In a transplant, doctors take an organ from one person's body and place it in another person's body.

A transplant may be done when a person has a diseased organ. The person may die unless the diseased organ is taken out and replaced with a healthy one.

Transplanting an organ is often difficult. It requires an operation by specially trained doctors.

A problem with all transplants is *rejection.* The body does not want an organ from another person. So it fights off, or rejects, the transplant.

There are several ways to prevent rejection. One way is to match the donor of the new organ with the person who is to receive it. People who are similar in the chemical make-up of their blood and other tissues turn out to be good matches. There are drugs, too, that doctors use. These drugs help keep the body from rejecting a transplant.

The best results in transplants have been with *kidneys.* Thus, doctors take one healthy kidney from a volunteer giver. They transplant the kidney to the body of a person with diseased kidneys. Many people who receive kidney transplants live normal lives afterward.

How Does What You Eat Affect You?

You have just learned how digested food material is carried by the blood to all parts of the body. But how does your body use this food?

The digested food has nourishing materials in it called *nutrients.* The body needs these nutrients. The body uses them for growth, energy, and repair of body tissues.

The blood carries the digested food throughout the body. The different cells take out of the blood the materials they need for their work.

Some of the digested food nutrients are used to make you bigger and stronger. Some of the nutrients give the body energy for work and play. Other food materials help keep the body working well and in good health.

You Are What You Eat

In order to stay healthy, you need enough of the right kinds of food. You may eat "like a horse" three times a day or more. But if your meals do not contain the proper amounts of various nutrients, your body will not get what it needs. Nutrients are substances that keep you alive and well.

There are many different nutrients found in foods. But they can all be grouped under six main kinds. They are *proteins, minerals, vitamins, carbohydrates, fats*, and *water.*

To be well-nourished each day, you need to eat foods that contain these nutrients in the right amounts. Most foods contain more than one nutrient. But no single food contains all the nutrients in the amounts you need.

Something to Do

As you think about nourishing foods, you may want to look for cookbooks for young people your age. You may get ideas for foods you can prepare for your family. Look in the school or public library for such cookbooks as these:

Cadwallader, Sharon. *Cooking Adventures for Kids* (Houghton).

Cavin, Ruth. *1 Pinch of Sunshine, 1/2 Cup of Rain: Cooking What Comes Naturally* (Atheneum).

Van der Linde, Polly and Tasha. *Around the World in 80 Dishes* (Scroll Press).

A Daily Food Guide

There are four main groups of foods you should try to eat every day—or at least most days! You need all these foods to keep you healthy.

Compare the foods you eat every day with the ones that supply the nutrients you need. Vegetables, fruits, nuts, beans, peas, milk and milk products, eggs, meat, fish, poultry, cereals, and bread supply the important nutrients most people need.

Using a Daily Food Guide

There are some fifty nutrients you need in your daily diet. How can you be sure to get these nutrients? To make it easy for you, nutrition scientists have made daily food guides. An easy-to-use guide is shown on pages 184–187.[1]

Vegetable-Fruit Group

Four or more servings include:

A citrus fruit or other fruit or vegetable important for vitamin C

A dark-green, leafy or deep-yellow vegetable for vitamin A, at least every other day

Other vegetables and fruits, including potatoes

[1]Adapted from Leaflet No. 424, U.S. Department of Agriculture.

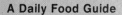

If you eat enough servings from the foods in the four food groups shown in the guide, you will get the nutrients you need. You can then add other foods as you wish.

How many servings from each food group are recommended? A "serving" would vary in size from small for a young child to large (or seconds) for active teen-agers and adults.

Meat Group
Two or more servings include:
    Beef, veal, pork, lamb, poultry, fish, eggs
    As alternates: dry beans, dry peas, nuts, peanut butter

You can follow this guide and still have a wide variety of meals. Different families can have very different menus. Yet by following the guide, all the menus can be nutritious ones. You don't need foods from *each* group at every meal. But try to include the suggested servings from each group sometime during the day. This can be in meals and in snacks.

Keep a food diary for the next few days. Write down what you have at each meal and in snacks. List the foods you eat each day under these headings: *Breakfast, Lunch, Supper, Snacks*. Count the number of servings you had each day from each group. How can a food diary of this kind help you?

Milk Group
Some milk for everyone
- Children under 9: 2 or 3 cups
- Children 9–12: 3 or more cups
- Teen-agers: 4 or more cups
- Adults: 2 or more cups
- As alternates: cheddar-type cheese, cottage cheese, cream cheese, and ice cream

Sum It Up

How does what you eat affect you?

Can you eat lots of food and still not be well-nourished? Explain.

What would be harmful about an all-milk-diet day after day?

What are four main food groups in a daily food guide? How many servings should you have from each group every day?

Bread-Cereal Group

Four or more servings include:

Whole-grain, enriched, or restored breads and cereals (such as rice, rolled oats, noodles, crackers, and cornmeal)

187

ENJOY IT

A Round

Spaghetti,
spaghetti,
heaped in a mound;

spaghetti,
spaghetti
winds and winds around;

spaghetti,
spaghetti,
twists and turns and bends;

spaghetti,
spaghetti
hasn't any ends;

spaghetti,
spaghetti
slips and dips and trips;

spaghetti,
spaghetti
sloops and droops;

spaghetti,
spaghetti
comes in groups;

spaghetti,
spaghetti,
no exit can be found. . . . . . .

What do you like about spaghetti?
What kinds of spaghetti sauce do you like?

TELL IT

Many people believe things about foods that are not true. Mistaken ideas about foods are *food fallacies.*

Here are oral reports some children gave about food fallacies. What are the fallacies? What are the facts? Can you think of any food fallacies after reading these?

One food fallacy is that white eggs are better than brown eggs. There is the *same* amount of nutrients in brown eggs as in white eggs.

When you buy eggs, the important thing is not the color. You should open the box and be sure you are not buying eggs that are cracked or broken. Harmful germs may have gotten into cracked or broken eggs.

Some people think fish is a brain food. They think you can get smart by eating a lot of fish. That isn't true. Fish doesn't make your brain work better. Eating enough of the right kinds of food can help your entire body work well.

Some people think that it is not safe to cook food in Teflon-coated pans. The fact is that such pans are perfectly safe to use.

Anita

Harry

Sharon

189

Things to Do

Look at the recipes here. Which one would you like to try? Copy your favorites and take the recipes home. Try them out if you can. What food groups are in each recipe?

Fruit Milk Shake
1 cup milk
$1/2$ cup sliced fresh fruit of any kind
   (bananas, berries, peaches, and
   melon are good to use)
1 raw egg
1 scoop of ice cream (if you wish)

   Wash the fruit. Peel it if necessary. Remove pits and seeds. Put everything in a bowl. Beat with an eggbeater.
   Serves one.

Apple Crisp
3 medium-sized apples
$1/2$ cup flour
$1/2$ cup butter or margarine
$3/4$ cup brown sugar
$3/4$ cup quick-cooking rolled oats

   Cut apples in quarters. Peel apples and remove cores. Slice apples in thin slices and put in lightly greased round pie pan.
   Mix oats, sugar, and flour. Add butter or margarine and stir until you have a crumbly mixture.
   Put mixture on apples. Bake for about 35 minutes in a 350° oven.
   Serves six.

Tuna Casserole
2 small cans of tuna fish
2 medium-sized cans of macaroni
   and cheese
$1/8$ teaspoon of pepper
$1/2$ cup of grated cheese

Open the cans of tuna fish and drain them. Put the tuna into a casserole dish. Break up tuna with a fork. Open the cans of macaroni and mix them with the tuna. Add the pepper and mix again. Sprinkle the grated cheese on top. Bake for 30 minutes in a 300° oven.
   Serves four.

Celery Sticks
1 bunch celery
1 package soft yellow cheese or
   cream cheese

Clean celery and stuff each stalk with cheese. Or stuff each stalk with peanut butter or liver sausage.

1. Find the names of four digestive organs in the puzzle below. Write their names on another paper. After each, write how the organ helps digest food.

```
T Y U Y T S A L M Z R O P I
C S T O M A C H R N M Q P T
W N K R Q W E R Z L I V E R
K K D P A N C R E A S F G D
S M A L L I N T E S T I N E
```

2. Help prepare an exhibit of tooth-paste containers. Use only those containers that have the seal of approval from the American Dental Association.

3. Here is a day's diet from one girl's food diary. Check to see if she had enough of the right kinds of foods. Use the food guide on pages 184–187 to help you.

Breakfast
    1 dish corn flakes
    1 cup milk
    1 orange

Lunch
    1 serving short ribs
    1 serving cabbage slaw
    1 slice cornbread
    1 serving cooked spinach
    1 cup buttermilk

Supper
    2 pancakes, syrup, and margarine
    1 cup milk
    1 peach

Snack
    1 peanut-butter sandwich

4. List several new foods that you tried and liked. Also draw a picture of the foods, or find magazine pictures of them. Be ready to tell why you liked each food you tasted.

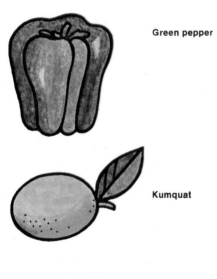

Green pepper

Kumquat

Bean sprouts

Special Research

Because many people are hungry in the world today, scientists are working on food problems. They are working to improve methods of farming, to seek new sources of food, and to develop new kinds of foods.

See what you can find out about one of the following topics. Be ready to report on one.

New Types of Seeds

Seaweed As a Food

Fish Farms on the Bottom of Oceans

Imitation Foods Made from Soybeans

How Project HOPE Fights Poor Nutrition

What UNICEF Does to Feed Hungry Children

Project CARE and Its Work

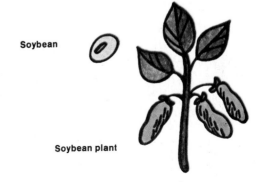

Soybean

Soybean plant

Can You Show What You Know?[1]

Page numbers show you where to look back in the chapter for information, if you need it.

1. Tell how teeth aid in digestion. (161–163)
2. Explain why you should floss your teeth. (163–164)
3. Demonstrate one way that is recommended to brush your teeth. (165)
4. Tell what is meant by digestion. (167)
5. Explain how the mouth helps digest food. (167–168)
6. Describe what happens to food in the stomach. (168–171)
7. Explain how the gall bladder and pancreas help in digesting food. (172)
8. Tell two things that happen to food materials in the small intestine. (171–174)
9. Explain what happens to nutrients in food once they get into the bloodstream. (172, 183)
10. Tell what happens to undigested material in the large intestine. (175)
11. Name some body parts that help get rid of liquid wastes; tell what they do. (176)
12. List three ways the body uses food materials. (183)
13. List the six main kinds of nutrients. (183)
14. List four food groups and the suggested number of daily servings from each group. (184–187)

[1]Behavioral objectives in the cognitive area are stated here directly to students themselves.

Review It

Page numbers show you where to look back in the chapter for information, if you need it.

1. What did Dr. Beaumont find out about the effects of emotions on the work of the stomach? (180–181)

2. How do the villi help your body use digested food material? (172)

3. What is one organ that can be transplanted with some success? (182)

4. Why doesn't food get stuck in your throat when you swallow it? (168)

5. Why should you take good care of your teeth? (163)

6. What is meant by plaque? (163)

7. How might you check to see if you are brushing all the plaque off your teeth? (166)

8. What kind of toothbrush should you use? (165)

9. How can a daily food guide help you? (184)

10. What are nutrients? (183)

Copy each numbered item from List A. After each item, write the letter and words from List B that best describe it. For example:

11. chyme   b. thick liquid into which food is changed by the stomach

List A

11. chyme
12. esophagus
13. gastric juice
14. peristalsis
15. plaque
16. urinary bladder
17. urine

List B

a. muscular bag that stores urine
b. thick liquid into which food is changed by the stomach
c. food tube
d. digestive juice made by the stomach
e. colorless film of bacteria on teeth
f. pushing and squeezing movement of muscles in walls of a digestive organ
g. waste liquid from the body

Copy each number on a piece of paper. After the number write the correct answer, *true* or *false.* Rewrite each false statement to make it true.

1. Your body gets energy from the food you eat.

2. The only function of saliva is to moisten food.

3. Another name for the food tube is the epiglottis.

4. Most of the time the food you eat goes down the windpipe.

5. Your small intestine is about as long as you are tall.

6. The pancreas and gall bladder send digestive juices into the small intestine to help digest food.

7. Digestion is completed in the large intestine.

8. Once digested food material gets into the bloodstream, it is carried to cells in all parts of the body.

9. The cells of the body need and use the food material carried to them by the blood.

10. The walls of the small intestine are lined with tiny parts called villi.

11. Food that is not needed at once can be stored in the body.

12. Emotions can affect the way your stomach works.

13. Digestion of food starts in the stomach.

14. The urinary bladder is a storage place for food.

15. A kidney can be transplanted to another person's body.

16. The front teeth are the molars.

17. Well-chewed food is easier to digest than food that is not chewed properly.

18. Sweet foods clinging to the teeth can help cause tooth decay.

19. Milk contains all the nutrients you need each day.

20. Proteins, minerals, and vitamins are important nutrients found in some foods.

Number of Answers ___20___
Number Right _____
Score (Number Right X 5) _____

What Do You Think?

What did you learn in this chapter that you plan to use? Write about it on a separate sheet of paper.

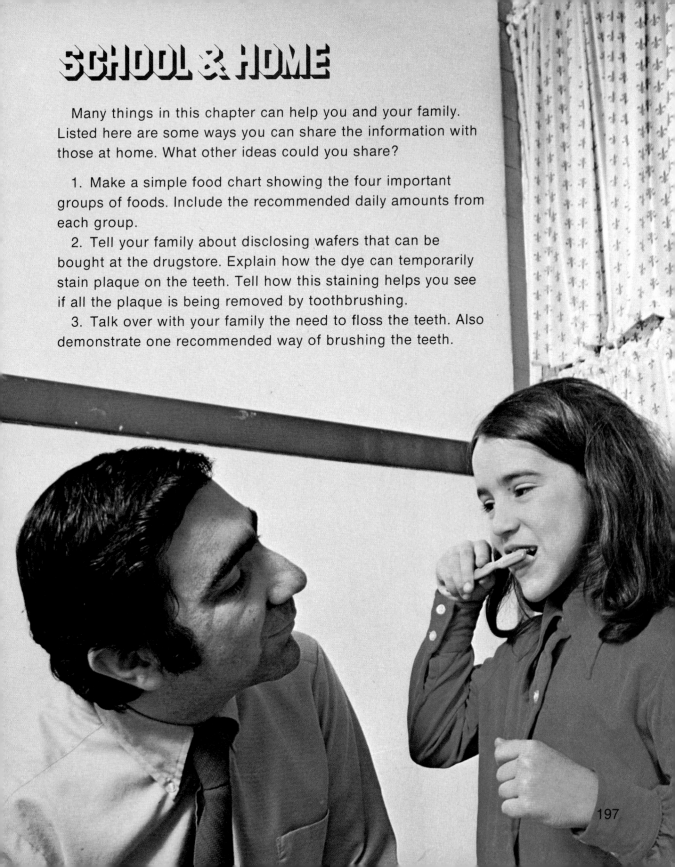

SCHOOL & HOME

Many things in this chapter can help you and your family. Listed here are some ways you can share the information with those at home. What other ideas could you share?

1. Make a simple food chart showing the four important groups of foods. Include the recommended daily amounts from each group.

2. Tell your family about disclosing wafers that can be bought at the drugstore. Explain how the dye can temporarily stain plaque on the teeth. Tell how this staining helps you see if all the plaque is being removed by toothbrushing.

3. Talk over with your family the need to floss the teeth. Also demonstrate one recommended way of brushing the teeth.

6 Your Heart and Lungs

What would you like to know about your heart and lungs?

Have you ever wondered why the heart is sometimes called "a mighty organ"?

Have you ever thought about what happens in the lungs? What exchange do you think takes place?

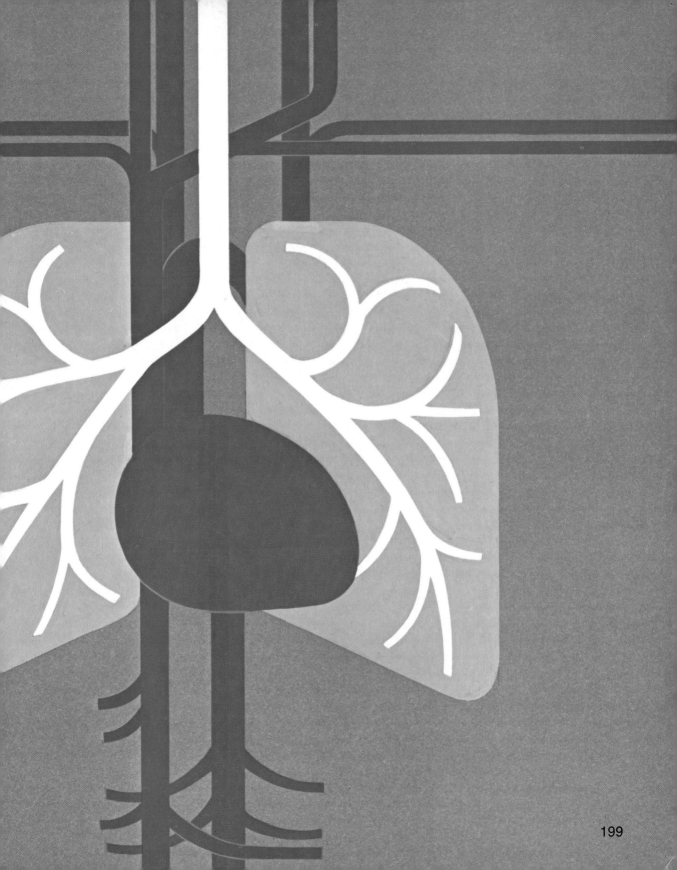

Preview It

Quickly look through this chapter. What two important questions are asked? As you study this chapter, look for detailed answers to these questions.

You will also find answers to other things you may have wondered about. For example:

How fast does the heart beat?
Is everyone's heartbeat the same?
What is blood made of?
What are blood types?
How do you breathe?
Could you stop breathing if you wanted to?

How Does Your Circulatory System Work?

The circulatory system is made
up of the heart, the blood vessels,
and the blood. This system has a
special job to do. It moves blood
around and around throughout
your body. This circulating blood
carries food materials and oxygen
to all your cells. The cells use
these substances to produce heat
and energy. Meanwhile,
wastes from the cells are
also being carried away
by the blood.

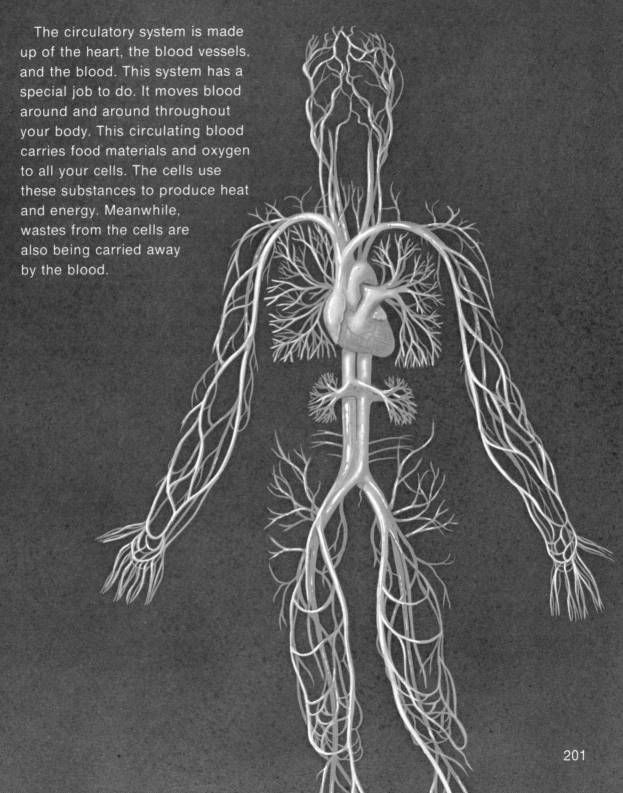

The Heart

The heart is behind the ribs in your chest. It is about the size of your closed fist.

If you put your hand over the left side of your chest, you should be able to feel your heart beating. It constantly beats and rests. Each beat pumps, or forces, the blood through your blood vessels. Your heart keeps blood moving.

Inside the Heart

A wall of muscle goes down the middle of the heart. It separates the heart into two parts called *chambers.* Both chambers act like two pumps side by side. Both work at the same time. Each chamber has an upper part called the *auricle.* The lower part is called the *ventricle.*

Each pump has a special job. The right pump sends oxygen-poor and carbon dioxide–rich blood to the lungs. In the lungs, the blood gets rid of the carbon dioxide and takes on a fresh supply of oxygen. Blood with wastes, such as carbon dioxide, is dark-bluish in color. Blood rich in oxygen and free of wastes is bright red.

The left pump receives the bright red, oxygen-rich blood from the lungs. It then sends the blood to all parts of the body through the main blood artery. This blood vessel is the *aorta.*

Use the diagrams and captions on page 203. They will help you trace the flow of blood in and out of the heart.

The heart is made of a special kind of muscle. One certain part of the heart, the *pacemaker,* has the job of timing. It sees that the two upper heart chambers beat together. They pump at the same time. They relax at the same time. Then the pacemaker sees that the two lower chambers beat together, pumping and relaxing. Therefore, you feel only *one* heartbeat instead of two.

Do You Know?

The heart beats about 90 times each minute in people your age. A baby's heart beats about 140 times. An adult's heart beats about 70 to 80 times. Everyone's heartbeat is not quite the same. The heart beats faster when you exercise. It also beats faster if you are angry, excited, fearful, or worried.

202

This shows the beginning of the pumping cycle. The auricles relax. Blood from the body enters the right auricle. Blood from the lungs enters the left auricle.

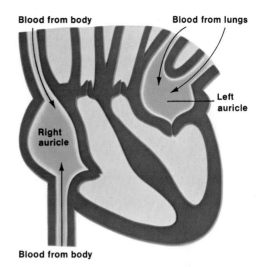

This diagram shows the blood being pumped into both ventricles. Blood from the auricles can enter them through valves. The valves work like one-way doors. The valves open to let some blood pass through. Then they snap shut. And the valves make sure the blood flows in one direction only.

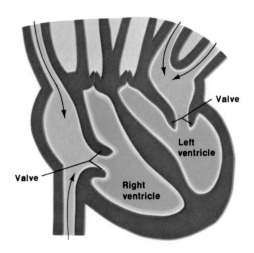

Here the ventricles are in a state of contraction or beating. Blood is forced out of the right ventricle and into a blood vessel leading to the lungs. Oxygen-rich blood from the left ventricle is forced into the aorta to be pumped throughout the body. This completes the pumping cycle. The cycle is continuously repeated.

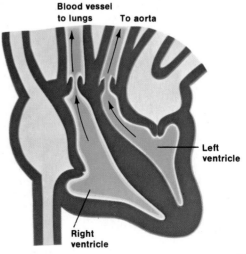

The Blood Vessels

Look again at the picture on page 201. Notice the many blood vessels. The picture cannot show all these vessels. However, it suggests how many are needed. Organs such as the lungs and kidneys require quite a network of blood vessels.

These blood vessels called *arteries* carry blood from the heart through the body. Blood vessels called *veins* carry blood back to the heart. Tiny blood vessels called *capillaries* connect the arteries and veins.

Capillaries are fifty times thinner than the thinnest hair. When blood from the arteries enters the capillaries, an important thing happens. Oxygen and digested food materials in the blood are drawn through the thin capillary walls into nearby cells. At the same time, carbon dioxide and other wastes from cells enter the blood through capillary walls.

The waste-filled blood flows from the capillaries into tiny veins. These veins branch into larger veins. Finally two large veins carry the blood back to the right side of the heart.

The large upper vein brings used blood from the head and arms to the heart. The large lower vein brings used blood from the trunk and legs.

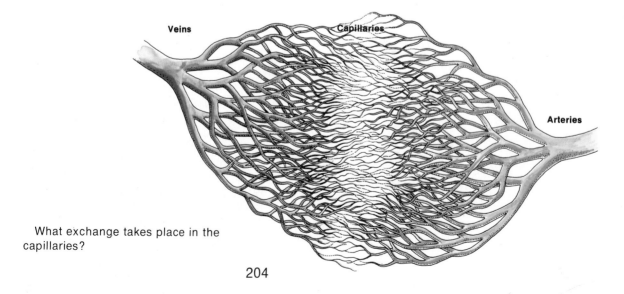

Veins   **Capillaries**   **Arteries**

What exchange takes place in the capillaries?

204

Look closely at your wrist. Do you see some tiny blue lines? These are some of the veins that carry used blood back to your heart. The arteries are deeper in your body. They carry the fresh or bright red blood from the heart through your body.

As blood is forced from the heart into the arteries, some room must be made for each spurt of blood. So the elastic walls of the arteries stretch. Then the heart rests. And the arteries spring back to their original size. Blood is pushed farther along when the arteries spring back. This way the blood is kept moving. The stretching of the arteries after each heartbeat is the *pulse.* You can feel your pulse at your wrist. Where else in the body do you think you can feel your pulse?

The Blood

Suppose you looked at a drop of blood under a powerful microscope. You would see many tiny *red blood cells* floating in a liquid. These red blood cells are shaped something like saucers.

You would also see other tiny, odd-shaped cells. Some of them are *white blood cells.* Others are *platelets.*

Red blood cells are made in the marrow of your long bones. Red cells give the blood its color. These cells are so small that 50,000 of them could fit on a pinhead.

Inside each red blood cell is a substance called *hemoglobin.* Hemoglobin carries the much-needed oxygen to all cells in the body.

The white blood cells are larger than red blood cells. Red cells, however, outnumber the white cells. Some white cells are made in bone marrow.

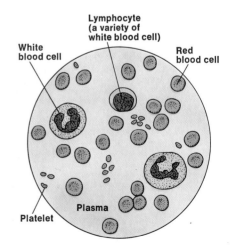

Make-up of the blood (greatly enlarged).

White blood cells are often called the body's "soldiers." Their number increases when the body is fighting disease germs. Certain white blood cells quickly move out of the blood vessels to where the germs are. These white blood cells kill the germs by surrounding them and "eating" them up. Some white cells form a wall around the germs. This keeps many germs from spreading through the body. White cells are found in pus around a sore or a boil.

Platelets in your blood serve as protectors too. They help control bleeding when you have a cut. If you accidentally cut a blood vessel, your platelets will come to the surface of the cut. Then they will begin to crumble.

Start **20 seconds** **50 seconds** **70 seconds**

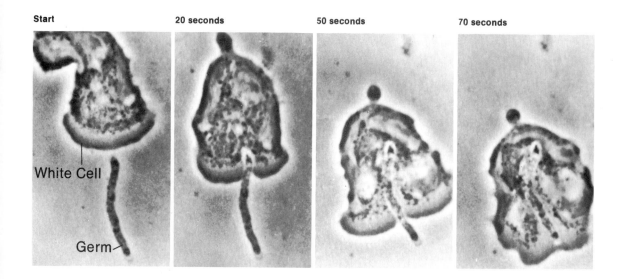

White Cell

Germ

A special chemical is produced by the platelets as they crumble. This chemical causes the blood to thicken, or *clot.* As the blood clots, the opening in the cut blood vessel is stopped up. The blood cannot flow to the skin's surface.

Red cells, white cells, and platelets all float in the liquid part of the blood. This liquid is called *plasma.* Plasma is made up mostly of water, but it contains other things too. For example, plasma contains food materials that the blood takes to body cells. Plasma also contains *antibodies.* The body makes these antibodies to protect it against certain germs.

Both whole blood and plasma are used in medicine. Medical workers take whole blood from the veins of a healthy adult who volunteers to donate. This is usually done at a hospital or blood bank.

Whole blood can be stored for a short time if it is refrigerated or frozen. The blood can be given by one person to another in a *transfusion* when needed. But there is one precaution. If someone needs blood during an operation, blood types must be matched.

Blood plasma is also used for transfusions. To get plasma, blood is put into a machine. The machine separates plasma from other parts of the blood. Plasma is then stored as a liquid at room temperature. Or it is made into a powder. The powder can easily be stored for long periods.

Powdered plasma is made liquid again by adding *sterile* water. Sterile water has no living germs in it. Plasma is good for transfusions in emergency situations. It is often given to a person who is suffering from shock.

Sum It Up

What are the parts of the circulatory system?
What is the special job of this system?
How do wastes get from body cells into blood?

Books to Read

Kalina, Sigmund. *Your Blood and Its Cargo* (Lothrop).

Showers, Paul. *A Drop of Blood* (Crowell).

Weart, Edith. *The Story of Your Blood* (Coward).

Zim, Herbert S. *Your Heart and How It Works* (Morrow).

Pioneers in Medical Science

Before the 1600s, no one knew how blood circulated in the body. Many doctors thought the liver changed the food into blood. They thought that blood went from the liver to the heart to be warmed. And then somehow blood disappeared into body tissues. It was believed the new blood was made in the body every day or so.

In the early 1600s, Dr. William Harvey began to question these ideas. The English doctor studied forty different kinds of animals. He noted what happened to the blood in their bodies. He also observed the human heart and blood vessels as he operated.

In 1628, Dr. Harvey made known his findings. He had discovered that *the same blood was being pumped around and around in the body.* He had noticed the valves in blood vessels kept the blood flowing in only one direction.

Harvey reported that the heart pumped blood into the arteries. From there the blood went into the veins. Then the veins brought blood back to the heart.

Dr. Harvey did not know *how* blood got from the arteries into the veins. But he knew that somehow it did.

In 1661, an Italian scientist discovered how the blood gets from arteries into veins. This scientist was Dr. Marcello Malpighi.

By this time the microscope had been discovered. Dr. Malpighi put a drop of water in the artery of a frog's lung. Then he looked at it under his microscope and waited. Soon he saw the watery spot in a vein. How do you think it got there? With his microscope, Dr. Malpighi was able to see the tiny, tiny blood vessels now called capillaries. The mystery was solved. Blood gets from arteries to veins through these tiny, tiny capillaries.

The Mighty Heart

The heart beats about 70 to 80 times a minute for an adult, 90 times a minute for a person your age. The heart beats all the minutes of all the years of a person's life. A healthy heart is a strong organ. Hard work or hard play usually won't hurt it.

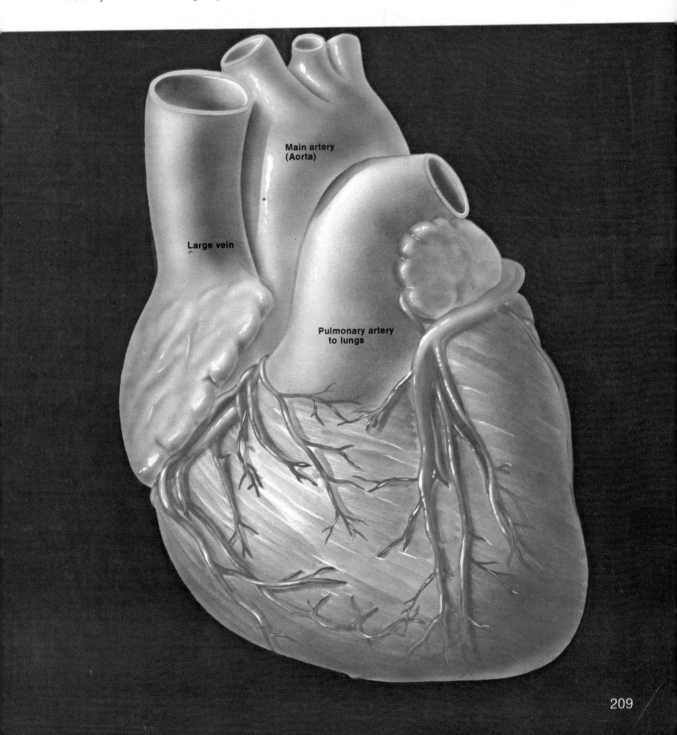

Main artery
(Aorta)

Large vein

Pulmonary artery
to lungs

The pictures on 210 and 211 are photographs of models. The picture on this page shows the heart's network of blood vessels.

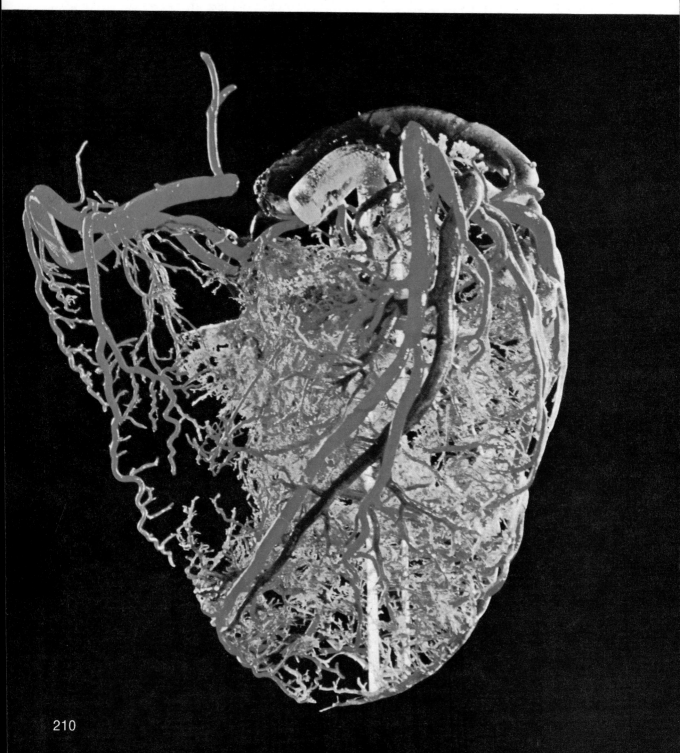

The outside of the heart has a covering over it. This covering keeps the heart from rubbing against the lungs and the walls of the chest. How does that help?

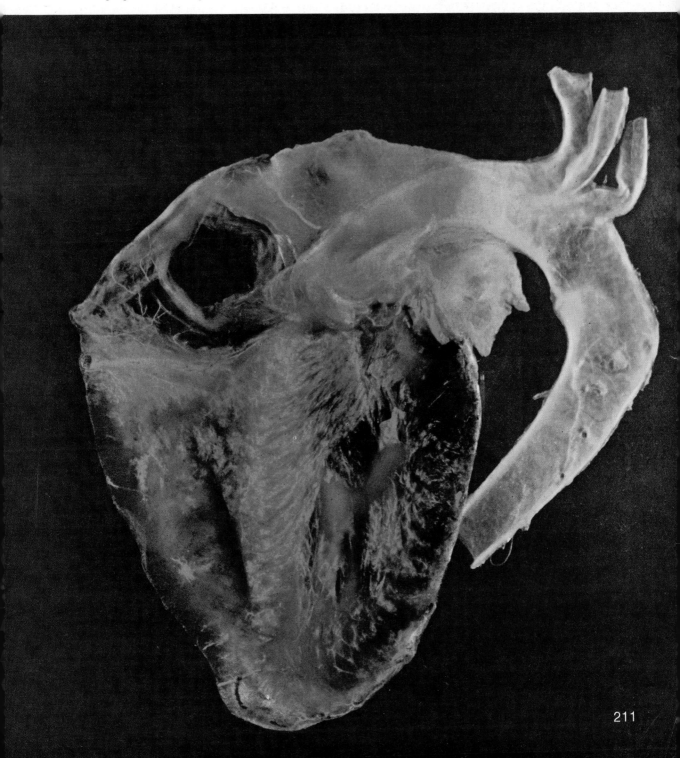

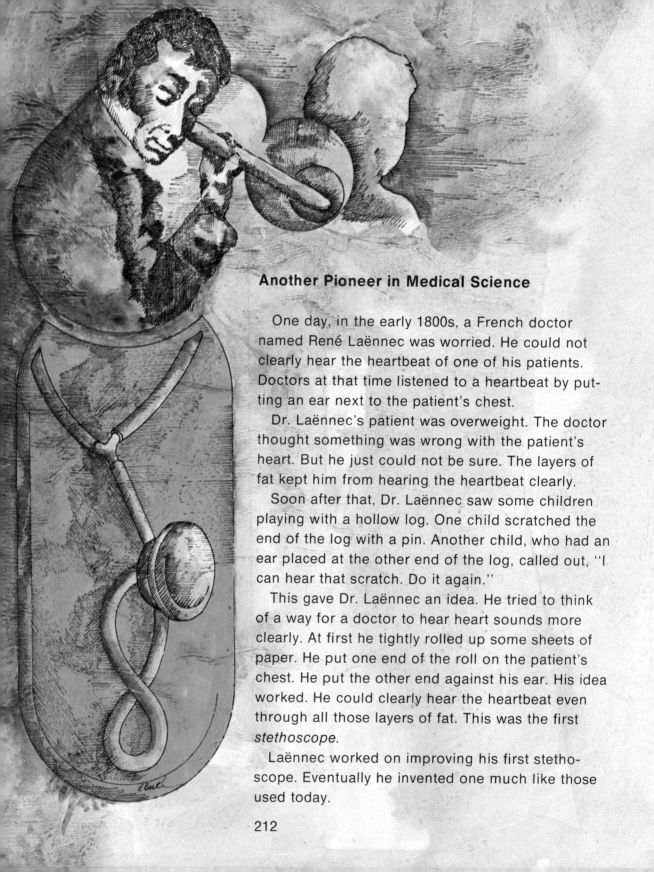

Another Pioneer in Medical Science

One day, in the early 1800s, a French doctor named René Laënnec was worried. He could not clearly hear the heartbeat of one of his patients. Doctors at that time listened to a heartbeat by putting an ear next to the patient's chest.

Dr. Laënnec's patient was overweight. The doctor thought something was wrong with the patient's heart. But he just could not be sure. The layers of fat kept him from hearing the heartbeat clearly.

Soon after that, Dr. Laënnec saw some children playing with a hollow log. One child scratched the end of the log with a pin. Another child, who had an ear placed at the other end of the log, called out, "I can hear that scratch. Do it again."

This gave Dr. Laënnec an idea. He tried to think of a way for a doctor to hear heart sounds more clearly. At first he tightly rolled up some sheets of paper. He put one end of the roll on the patient's chest. He put the other end against his ear. His idea worked. He could clearly hear the heartbeat even through all those layers of fat. This was the first *stethoscope.*

Laënnec worked on improving his first stethoscope. Eventually he invented one much like those used today.

212

HEALTH AROUND US

There is a machine that can make a record of the tiny electrical currents the heart makes. It is called an *electrocardiograph.*

First little wires are taped in place on a person's skin. The wires carry the electrical currents from the heart to the machine. Here they are *amplified,* or made larger. The wires are attached to a lever arm with a pen point on one end. The amplified but changing currents move the pen. The result is a pattern of waves on the paper.

The name of the record taken by the machine is an *electrocardiogram,* or *ECG.* Doctors study the ECG. They note the height and regularity of the waves. The stronger the electrical wave, the higher the line the pen draws. The pattern of the waves indicates to the doctors how well the heart is working. A heart that is not working properly shows patterns different from a normal heart.

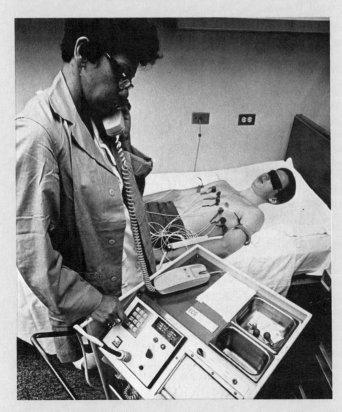

How Does Your Respiratory System Work?

You must have oxygen to stay alive. It is found in the air you breathe. Your breathing, or *respiratory system,* allows air to enter the body. It comes in through your nose or mouth and is drawn into the lungs. In the lungs, oxygen is picked up by the blood. The blood carries it to all the body cells. When you breathe out, a gas called *carbon dioxide* and some other wastes are sent out of your body.

Let's find out more about the different parts of the respiratory system. These parts are the *nose,* the *windpipe* or *trachea,* the *bronchial tubes,* and the *lungs.*

Your Nose Helps

Air goes into your body through your nose. Some can also go in through your mouth. It is best to breathe through your nose most of the time. Do you know why?

Air that comes in through the nose is prepared for the lungs. For one thing, the air is filtered by many tiny hairs in your nose. These hairs catch some of the germs and larger particles of dust you breathe in.

The sticky fluid called *mucus,* in the lining of your nose, also helps collect dust and germs. This mucus moistens the air passing through the nose.

Some of the dust and germs caught in the mucus is carried out when you blow your nose. Some is carried to the throat and can be swallowed. Or it is coughed up from your throat. In these ways many germs and particles of dirt are kept from reaching the lungs.

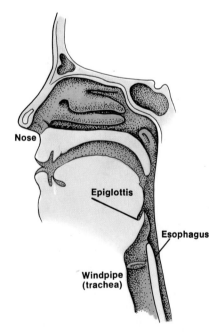

Nose

Epiglottis

Esophagus

Windpipe (trachea)

Which important parts of the respiratory system are shown here? What else do you see?

As the air comes in and passes over the folds of skin inside the nose, it is warmed somewhat. This helps keep the body from becoming chilled.

The nose is sometimes called the body's "air conditioner." That is because it moistens the air and filters out some impurities.

Suppose, however, that the air is very dirty. It contains harmful gases or other pollutants. Some pollutants may include those found in cigarette smoke. When you breathe, neither the hairs in the nose nor the mucus can prevent many of the pollutants from reaching your lungs. So you can see why air pollution is a serious health problem.

Your Lungs Get Air

The air that comes into the nose or mouth goes down a tube called the *windpipe,* or *trachea.* The voice box, or *larynx,* is at the upper end of the windpipe.

The windpipe extends down into your neck. Then it divides into two large branches called *bronchial tubes.* One bronchial tube goes to each of the lungs. See the picture below.

Look again at the nose, the windpipe, and the *epiglottis* on page 214. The epiglottis is a thin piece of cartilage. When you swallow food, the epiglottis covers the entrance to the windpipe automatically. Food is kept from going into the windpipe and choking you. Only rarely does food "go down the wrong way."

How You Breathe

The bronchial tube inside each lung branches into smaller and smaller tubes. The tiniest of these end in balloonlike air pockets, or *air sacs.* There are many air sacs in the lung tissue.

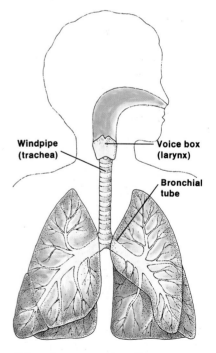

Windpipe (trachea)

Voice box (larynx)

Bronchial tube

What do you see here?

As the air sacs fill with air, they act like balloons. They get bigger. You can see a picture of some air sacs below.

How is air drawn into and sent out of the lungs? To understand this, you need to know about your chest. Study the pictures on the next page after you read.

Your chest is somewhat like a cage with walls attached to a floor that can move. The chest walls are made up of ribs with muscles between. The floor is made up of a big tentlike muscle called the *diaphragm.*

The lungs themselves cannot get larger and smaller to take in and force out air. They need help. The diaphragm and rib muscles furnish it. As the diaphragm contracts and flattens itself downward, the rib muscles pull the ribs upward and outward. The whole chest expands, or becomes larger. Air is sucked into the lungs. This is called breathing in, or *inhaling.*

In breathing out, or *exhaling,* the opposite actions take place. The diaphragm relaxes and moves upward. Rib muscles relax and move the ribs downward and inward. The chest becomes smaller. The ribs and diaphragm push on the lungs forcing air out. Then the lung tissue returns to its original size.

The act of breathing is largely automatic. You can hold your breath. But you can do it only for a minute or so. Your nervous system makes sure you breathe all the time. You do not have to control the movements of breathing or even think about them.

Do you know how many times you breathe in a minute? How could you find out?

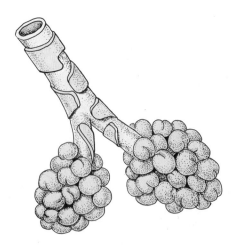

Air sacs in the lung (greatly enlarged). How does air get into the sacs?

These pictures show the movement of the diaphragm and the ribs during breathing. What is happening in each picture?

Breathing in

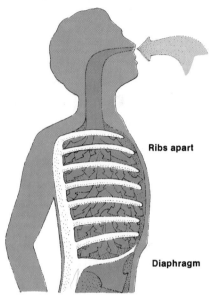

Ribs apart

Diaphragm

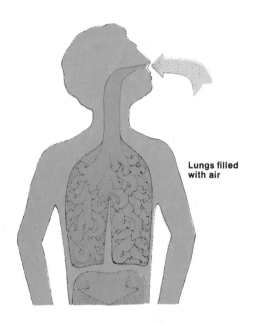

Lungs filled with air

Breathing out

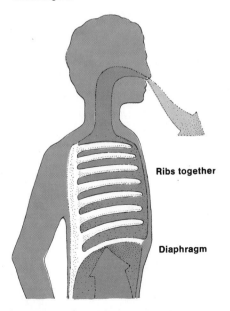

Ribs together

Diaphragm

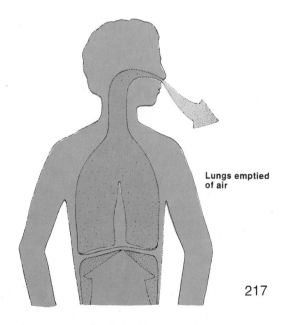

Lungs emptied of air

The Exchange in the Lungs

What happens when air enters the lungs? The oxygen from the air goes through the thin walls of the air sacs. Each air sac in the lungs is surrounded by a network of capillaries. Capillaries are the tiniest blood vessels. Blood in the capillaries absorb oxygen. At the same time, wastes, such as carbon dioxide, pass from the blood into the air sacs. Then these wastes are breathed out.

This is the important, lifegiving exchange that takes place in your lungs. The air breathed into your lungs loses its oxygen and takes on wastes to be breathed out. Blood pumped to your lungs gives up the wastes in exchange for the oxygen.

This is how the lungs keep the blood "fresh." And that is why the lungs are sometimes called the body's "cleaning plant."

When You Need More Air

Have you noticed that you breathe faster when you run, jump, or walk very fast? Strenuous exercise makes you breathe faster for a good reason. You need extra oxygen. Your blood takes this oxygen to your muscle cells. The cells then use it to create quickly needed energy.

Breathing faster also helps get rid of more carbon dioxide and other wastes. These wastes are produced by the contracting of the muscle cells.

Have you noticed that your feelings, too, sometimes cause you to breathe faster? What happened when you saw a scary TV program? What happened when you read an exciting book? Can you remember how your breathing changed after being frightened suddenly?

Do You Know?

There is something else that can make you breathe faster. It has been found that excessive noise around you can speed up your breathing.

At times like these you may have found yourself breathing faster than usual. Maybe you had to gasp quickly to take in more air.

You also need more air when you talk or sing. Actually you cannot make a sound at all if you do not take in air. This is also true if your voice box does not work properly.

Your Voice Box

At the top of the windpipe is a hollow organ. This organ is the *voice box,* or *larynx.* It is made of bone and cartilage fastened together by ligaments and muscles.

The *vocal cords* in your voice box are two straight, elasticlike bands. When you are not speaking or singing, these cords are relaxed against the sides of the voice box. Are they relaxed in the picture?

This is what happens when you start to talk or sing. Tiny muscles bring the vocal cords closer together. Air coming up the windpipe from the lungs makes the vocal cords move back and forth very fast, or *vibrate.* When vocal cords vibrate, sounds are produced. Your vocal cords work much like the strings on a guitar. When the strings vibrate, they make sounds.

Lots of air is needed to make the sounds for talking and singing. Try sitting quietly without making a sound. Then say your name out loud. What do you notice about air you need in each case?

Sum It Up

What are the main parts of the respiratory system?

What important exchange takes place in lungs?

What is needed for your vocal cords to produce some sound?

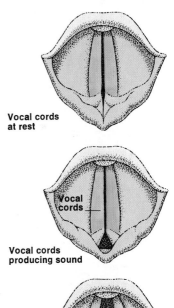

Vocal cords
at rest

Vocal cords
producing sound

Vocal cords
during breathing

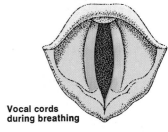

The voice box, when seen from above, shows how the vocal cords look when you are at rest (top), when you are making sound (middle), and when you are breathing (bottom).

Your Lungs

The lungs reach from the lower part of the neck down almost to the middle of your trunk. Here you see the branches of the bronchial tubes. What is at the end of the smallest branches?

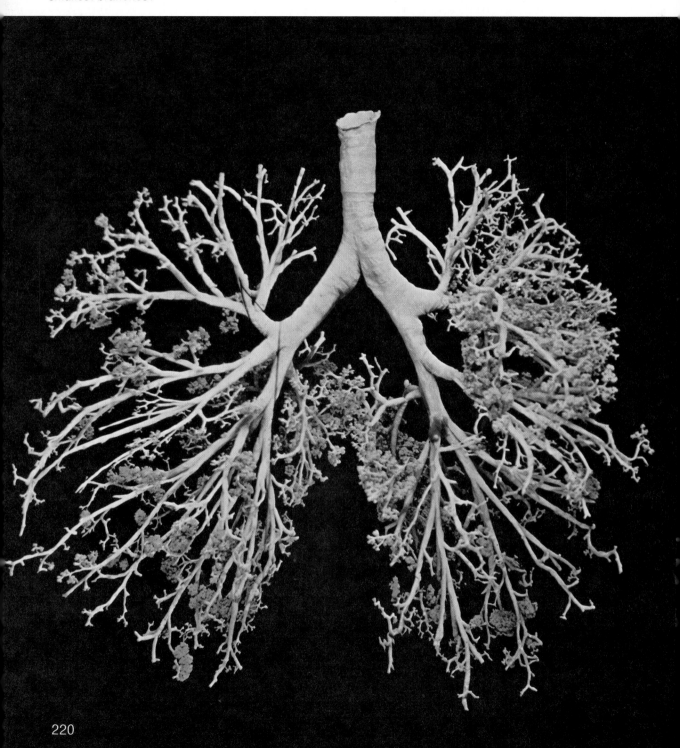

An important exchange takes place in the balloonlike air sacs of the lungs. What is that exchange? You can see here the network of blood vessels in the lungs. How does oxygen in the lungs get into the blood?

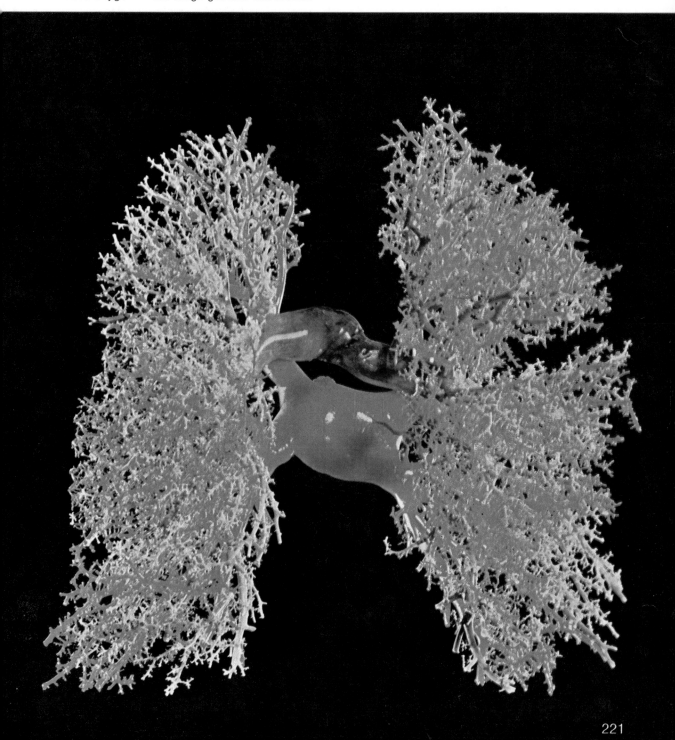

This model shows the position of the heart in relation to the lungs. Can you locate the heart? Some bronchial tubes? Some blood vessels?

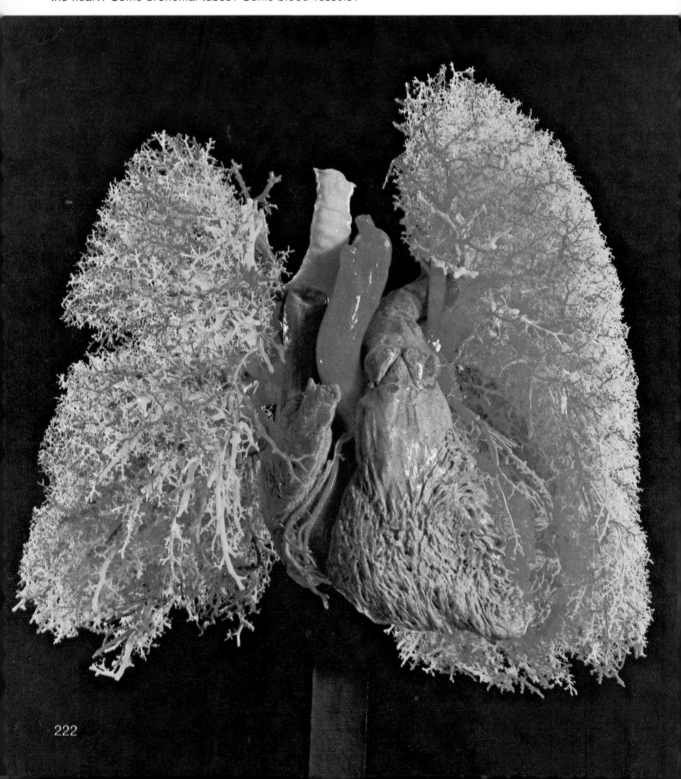

HEALTH AROUND US

Years ago doctors thought the heart could not be operated on. This was because the heart would have to be stopped during surgery. Today, many operations are done on faulty hearts. The operation can make the heart healthy again.

Why can the heart now be operated on? It is because of wonderful machines that are available today. One such machine is the heart-lung machine. This machine enables surgeons to operate on "resting" hearts that are temporarily emptied of blood.

The heart-lung machine acts as substitute heart and lungs during an operation. From two tubes put in the large veins, blood from the patient is pumped into the heart-lung machine.

You can see a picture of a heart-lung machine below.

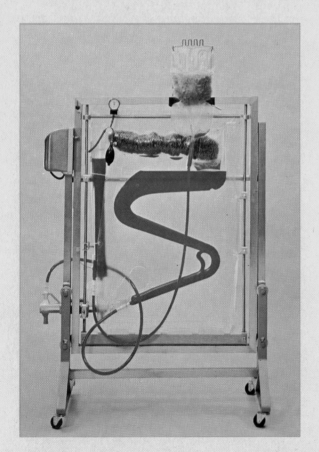

TELL IT

There are many other interesting facts about the heart and lungs. Look in an encyclopedia or library books for more information. Then share the information with your group.

Here is what some other boys and girls found.

Exercise helps your lungs. When you exercise, you breathe more deeply. Your lungs take in more air then. If you exercise day after day, your lungs get used to taking in more air. They do it more easily. They become able to hold more air too. You become able to exercise harder and longer without getting out of breath too soon.

If you want to help take good care of your heart, you should try not to be very much overweight. If you get too fat, the heart has extra work. It has to pump blood over more of your body.

Eric

Bill

I found out what doctors hear when they use a stethoscope. They put the stethoscope on your chest. Then they listen. They hear two sounds each time your heart beats. The first sound goes "lub." This is when blood enters the ventricles and the valves close behind it.

The second sound is high and short. It goes "dup." This is made when blood is squeezed out of the heart and the second set of valves snap shut. The heart goes "lub-dup." Those are the heart sounds.

If you get plenty of exercise each day, your heart grows stronger.

One way to take care of the heart is to get enough sleep. When you sleep, the heart makes fewer beats each minute. It gets a longer rest between beats too.

Amy

Sue

Marie

WRITE IT

Here are some topics related to the heart and lungs. You might want to write about one of them.

Which Side of the Heart Is Stronger?
How Does Cigarette Smoking Affect the Heart?
What Are Blood Banks?
What Happens When There Is a Hole Between the Two Sides of the Heart?
How Does Too Much Noise Affect the Blood Vessels?
Can You Live with Just One Lung?

Below is a report about blood types. What information does it give you?

Blood Types

There are four main blood types. Sometimes they are called blood groups. Scientists call these types Group O, Group A, Group B, and Group AB. Blood types are grouped according to substances in the blood. These four main blood groups are found among all people everywhere.

Suppose a transfusion of whole blood is to be given. Then blood types must be matched. The blood donor's type must match the blood of the person who gets the transfusion. If it is not matched, the person who gets the blood may be in trouble. The person could even die.

Frank

Here is another report. It is about cigarette smoking and health. What do you think about smoking after reading this?

Cigarette Smoking and Health

Cigarette smoking can damage the respiratory system. For one thing, it can cause bronchitis. This disease may lead to trouble with breathing. It can even cause someone to cough a lot.

Smoking cigarettes can also play a part in causing emphysema. With this disease, the lungs do not work well. A person may not get all the air that is needed in the lungs.

Cigarette smoking is a cause of lung cancer. A cancer spreads through healthy tissues and destroys them. People can die from lung cancer.

Colleen

Things to Do

1. Learn first-aid treatment for a bruise, a nosebleed, and bleeding from a cut. The procedures are given below.

How to Treat a Bruise

A bruise is caused by blood leaking from capillaries under the skin.

Put cold cloths on the bruise at once to reduce swelling and to relieve any pain. The body will gradually reabsorb the blood from the bruised area.

How to Stop a Nosebleed

If you have a nosebleed, *sit with your head straight.* Blood goes into the throat if you tilt your head back. *Use the thumb and forefinger to pinch the ends of the nostrils together.* This squeezes the blood vessels and helps them seal themselves with clots. If the bleeding does not stop, gently pack the lower ends of the nostrils with wet gauze. Then try pinching again. It may help to apply cold, wet towels to the face. This makes the blood vessels contract and less blood can flow through them.

How to Stop Bleeding

To stop bleeding of a cut, place a pad of sterile cloth over the cut and *press down.* If sterile cloth is not available, use a pad of any clean material. If necessary, use your bare hands.

This pressure squeezes the blood vessels against tissue, muscle, or bone. Then less blood can flow through the cut blood vessels. If a cut is large or deep, a doctor should care for it.

2. Make a report to the group about the work of Charles Drew. Charles Drew was a pioneer in medical science. He discovered how to keep blood and plasma from spoiling. He also helped plan blood banks where thousands of bottles of blood and plasma could be stored.

One book that you might look for at the library is *Charles Drew* by Roland Bertol (T. Y. Crowell).

3. Find out how fast your heart beats. To do this, you will need a friend who can time you. Use a watch with a second hand. Place your fingertips on your wrist to take your pulse. Count the beats. Have your friend tell you when the watch's second hand shows one minute is up. Write down how many times your heart beat for that minute.

Hop up and down on one foot fifteen times. Now sit down and take your pulse again for one minute. Did your heart beat faster? Check your friend's heartbeat while you call the time.

4. You know that cigarette smoking can be harmful to the lungs. How harmful is air pollution to the lungs? Try to find out the ways it can damage the lungs. Also find out what lung diseases air pollution may cause.

Here are some books that contain information you could use in your report.

Bloome, Enid. *The Air We Breathe* (Doubleday).

Elliott, Sarah M. *Our Dirty Air* (Messner).

Tannenbaum, Beulah, and Myra Stillman. *Clean Air* (McGraw-Hill).

Special Research

1. Find out if air pollution is a problem in your community. What is your community doing about it? What might *you* and your family do?

2. See what interesting things you can find out about how these animals breathe: *fish, frogs, grasshoppers, earthworms.* One helpful book is *What's Inside of Animals?* by Herbert S. Zim (Morrow).

Can You Show What You Know?[1]

Page numbers show you where to look back in the chapter for information, if you need it.

1. Tell about the special job of the circulatory system. (201)

2. Explain where blood goes as it circulates throughout the body. (202)

3. Tell what the right and left pump of the heart do. (202)

4. List three kinds of blood vessels and tell what each one does. (204)

5. Describe what can be seen in a drop of blood under a powerful microscope. (205)

6. List the four main parts of the respiratory system and explain what they do. (214)

7. Describe what causes air to be inhaled and exhaled. (215–217)

8. Explain the life-giving exchange that takes place in the lungs. (218)

9. Tell what you know about these pioneers in medical science: Harvey, Malpighi, and Laënnec. (208, 212)

10. Mention several ways to care for your heart and lungs. (224–225)

11. Name the four main blood types. (226)

[1]Behavioral objectives in the cognitive area are stated here directly to students themselves.

Review It

Page numbers show you where to look back in the chapter for information, if you need it.

1. What part of the heart does the timing? (202)

2. What helps keep blood moving onward through the blood vessels? (205)

3. What prevents blood from flowing the wrong way in the heart? (203)

4. What is the pulse? (205)

5. Which blood vessels carry dark-bluish red blood back to the heart? (204)

6. How does blood get from arteries into veins? (204, 208)

7. What are known as the body's "soldiers"? (206)

8. How do red blood cells carry oxygen? (205)

9. What could happen if you did not have platelets in your blood? (206)

10. How is food kept out of the windpipe? (215)

11. How is it you are able to talk? (219)

12. When do you need more air than usual? (218–219)

Copy each numbered item from List A. After each item, write the letter and words from List B that best describe it. For example:

13. aorta   e. the main artery

List A

13. aorta
14. arteries
15. auricles
16. capillaries
17. plasma
18. trachea
19. veins
20. ventricles

List B

a. liquid part of the blood
b. tiny blood vessels connecting arteries and veins
c. windpipe
d. lower chambers of the heart
e. the main artery
f. blood vessels that carry the blood from the heart throughout the body
g. blood vessels that carry blood to the heart from all parts of the body
h. upper chambers of the heart

Health Test for Chapter Six

Copy each sentence and fill in the missing word or words.

1. Parts called _____ prevent blood from flowing the wrong way in the heart.

2. Capillaries are tiny blood vessels that connect the _____ and _____.

3. The _____ side of the heart pumps blood to the lungs.

4. At the tiny ends of the lung's bronchial tubes are air _____.

5. Another name for the trachea is _____.

Copy each number on a piece of paper. After each number write the correct answer, *true* or *false.* Rewrite each false statement to make it true.

6. Your heartbeat slows down when you exercise strenuously.

7. You can stop your breathing for hours at a time.

8. Capillaries are large blood vessels.

9. The stretching of arteries after a heartbeat is the pulse.

10. There are four main blood types, or blood groups.

11. The vocal cords are located in the lungs.

12. Both sides of the heart pump together.

13. The blood in the veins of your hand is a bright red color.

14. Epiglottis is another name for the windpipe.

15. Plasma is the liquid part of blood.

16. The normal heart is not damaged by hard work or hard play.

17. The air you breathe out is full of fresh oxygen.

18. Hemoglobin in red blood cells carries oxygen.

19. Platelets help stop the bleeding from a cut.

20. The hairs in your nose help filter out dirt and germs.

Number of Answers	20
Number Right	_____
Score (Number Right X 5)	_____

What Do You Think?

Do you think your study of this chapter was worthwhile? Why or why not? Write your answer on a separate paper.

SCHOOL & HOME

Be sure to share at home what you have learned about first aid. Explain how you would treat a bruise, a nosebleed, and bleeding from cuts. You can also learn and share what to do in case of *choking*.

Choking results when food or another object gets stuck in the throat. Oxygen cannot get to the choking person's lungs. A person could die if proper first aid is not given *at once*.

Stand behind the person who is choking. Quickly wrap both arms around the victim's waist. One of your hands should grip your other wrist. Press upward forcefully into the victim's diaphragm, just below the ribcage and above the navel. Repeat if necessary. The pressing forces the object out of the throat with a force of air from the lungs.

The procedure was developed by Dr. Henry Heimlich and is called the "Heimlich Maneuver."

7 Your Questions About Safety, Drugs, and Smoking

What do you think you should know to help keep yourself safe?

What does everyone need to know about safety in using drugs?

What are some of your questions about smoking?

Preview It

Quickly look at the questions on pages 238–248. What do they suggest about the kinds of accidents that occur among people your age?

When could a person's use of drugs be unsafe? What do you think is unsafe about smoking? What happens when alcohol is taken into the body? You will find some answers to these questions in this chapter.

Before you start this chapter, you might do some thinking about drugs. It is a good idea to think in a broad way. A drug can be thought of like this. A drug is any prepared substance that if taken into the body causes changes in it. For example, the changes may affect the way the brain works. The changes may affect the respiratory system or the circulatory system. The changes may affect a person's emotions. A drug may cause other changes.

Medicines are a kind of drug that help treat an illness, prevent an illness, or stop pain. Alcohol is a drug, and there is a drug in tobacco and in marijuana. Some people use these substances to change how they feel. Even things like model airplane glue or gasoline can be considered as drugs. Such things are not intended to be breathed into the body. But sometimes this is done unwisely. Then a person's health may be affected.

If you were asked, then, to explain drugs, what would you say?

Could You Pass a Bicycle-Safety Test?

Suppose your community or your school sets aside time for some bicycle-safety tests. What questions might you have to answer on this test? What might you have to *do* on your bicycle?

Talk over these questions. Then turn the page. Compare your ideas with the tests shown there and on pages 238–241.

BICYCLE-SAFETY TEST
BRING YOUR BICYCLE
to the
SCHOOL PLAYGROUND
ANY SATURDAY THIS MONTH
9 a.m. – 3 p.m.

Bicycle-Safety Knowledge Test

Some typical questions and answers are given here to help you prepare for a Bicycle-Safety Test.

1. Name at least four safety violations of bicycle drivers.

A violation occurs when a driver:

drives too fast,

drives against traffic instead of with it,

fails to use hand signals when turning or stopping,

hitches a ride on a moving vehicle,

zigzags in traffic,

drives in the middle of the street,

drives abreast with two or three people,

fails to stop at intersections.

What other answers can you add?

2. Suggest at least six rules for a Bicycle-Safety Code. Be ready to give a reason for each one.

Carry packages in a basket, carrier, or saddlebag.

Use both hands to steer, except when signaling.

Walk the bicycle across busy intersections.

Stop and look in all directions before driving into a street from a driveway, sidewalk, or alley.

Use a light at night. Also wear something light-colored.

Do not drive on icy pavements. And do not drive during snow or heavy rains.

Use a reflector on back and front fenders and spokes. Use red for rear. Use white or yellow for front spokes.

What other items can you add to this Code?

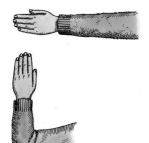

Hand signals

Left turn (top)
Right turn (middle)
Stop (bottom)

238

Performance Tests[1]

1. Drive slowly through a test lane about 18 meters long and about 91 centimeters wide. Tires should not touch the line on either side. This drive will test your ability to balance the bicycle.

2. Drive at an average riding speed toward a white STOP line about 30 meters ahead. Apply your brakes at the STOP line. Suppose your bike goes more than 3 meters beyond the STOP line. That means your brakes need to be fixed. (And you fail this part of the test!)

3. Drive through an obstacle lane. Start from a position back of the first obstacle so that you get your balance before you reach the first obstacle. Pass to the right of the first obstacle and weave in and out among the rest. When the last obstacle has been passed, return over the same route. (See the obstacle lane at the right.)

These are the standards for success on the obstacle test.

No foot touched the ground.

No tire touched an obstacle.

Bicycle went to the right and then to the left of the obstacles.

Brakes were not used excessively.

Rear wheel did not skid when you stopped.

An average amount of energy was used to control the bicycle.

4. Give the proper hand signals for turning and stopping. (Correct hand signals are shown on the opposite page.

Bicycle obstacle lane. Eight obstacle blocks made of wood or rubber are placed one and one-half meters apart on a straight line. What must the driver do in this line?

[1]Adapted from *Skill Tests for Pedal Pushers*, National Safety Council, 425 N. Michigan Avenue, Chicago, Illinois 60611.

Test of Bicycle Mechanical Condition
Use these checkpoints to find out
if your bicycle is in good condition.

Seat: Adjust height so leg bends only slightly with ball of foot at bottom of stroke. Tighten securely.

Coaster brake: Should take hold quickly and brake evenly. If bike has hand brakes, check them before your first ride. Must brake evenly every time, no slippage. Oil and adjust if necessary.

Safety flag

Reflector: Must be visible for 91 meters at dusk and at night.

Chain: Clean and oil often with light oil.

Light: Must be visible for 152 meters at dusk and night.

Warning device: Be sure it works properly, loud and clear. Must be heard at least 30 meters away.

Handlebars and grips: Set handlebars for proper height. Keep handlebar stem well down in the frame. Tighten securely. Fasten grips; replace if worn.

Fork bearings: Oil. Adjust for easy steering.

Wheels: Oil and tighten bearings and nuts. Be sure they rotate smoothly without wobbling from side to side.

Wheel reflectors: Be sure they are clean and fastened securely.

Crank hanger: Clean and oil. Adjust bearings if necessary.

Pedals: Oil and tighten bearings. Check pedal treads for wear.

Tires: Inspect for wear and leaks. Remove imbedded stones, nails, glass, etc. Keep inflated to the correct pressure that is stamped on the sidewall of the tire.

Spokes: Replace broken ones at once. Keep all of them tight.

241

SAFETY AROUND US

Bicycles are very popular with people of all ages. However, as more people use bicycles, there are more bicycle accidents. Many accidents are caused by drivers losing control. Can you think of other reasons why bicycle accidents might happen?

Below is a graph that gives you some information about bicycle accidents resulting in an injury or in damage to a bicycle.

Bicycle Accidents in a Recent Year

By Age of Boys and Girls[1]

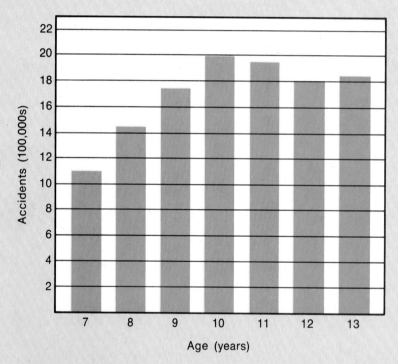

[1]Derived from information in *Bicycle Accidents and Usage Among Elementary Children in the United States*. Chlapecka, T. W., Schupack, S. H., et. al. March, 1975, National Safety Council.

What Should You Do in Case of Fire?

Suppose you discover a fire at home. What should you do?

Talk over this question with your group. Then turn the page and read on. Compare your ideas with the ones given on pages 244 and 245.

A Fire in a House

Suppose you discover a fire in your house. Alert your family at once. Have everyone leave the house. Do this even if the fire seems small. Once a fire starts, it grows with frightening speed. The fire department can be called from a neighbor's house.

It is best to have an adult call the fire department. But if you ever have to do it, follow these steps. Dial the fire department or the operator. Give your name and address. Then briefly tell what happened. Do not hang up until you are sure the message has been understood.

Once you are out of a burning house, do not go back into it.

Maybe fire and smoke have spread through the house before you can leave by the stairs or the hall. Then you will need another means of escape. Keep the room door shut. If possible, leave by a window. If need be, wait for the fire department on an upper porch.

Or stuff the cracks under the door with cloth of some kind. These cloths help keep out the smoke. Then stay by an open window. Keep your nose and mouth covered with a cloth, towel, or handkerchief. The cloth helps keep smoke and gases out of your lungs.

Safety experts advise that families have frequent fire drills. Then family members can practice what to do if a fire occurs. They should plan for different exits in case some are blocked. They should also practice what to do if they cannot escape from the house. Why do you think home family drills are a good idea?

Some common causes of fires in homes are cigarettes, electric heaters, worn electric cords, cleaning fluids, and oily rags. How might each of these things cause a fire?

Something to Do

Someone from your class might write to the National Safety Council, 425 North Michigan Avenue, Chicago, Illinois 60611 to inquire about prices on Safety Data Sheets on topics such as these: *Bathroom Hazards, Bicycles, Cigarette Fire Hazards, Electrical Equipment, Flammability of Wearing Apparel,* and *Flammable Liquids in the Home.*

244

A Fire in an Apartment

Most people who are killed in fires are suffocated by deadly gases and smoke. This happens before any flames ever get to the people.

Gases given off by burning objects and smoke are lighter than air. These gases rise through stairways, elevator shafts, laundry chutes, and heating vents. The gases and smoke quickly fill the upper floors.

If you and your family live in an apartment and find the building is on fire, follow these steps. Report the fire to the fire department if you are the first to discover it. Then crawl to the exit door with a handkerchief, towel, or other cloth over your nose and mouth. Staying near the floor will help keep you out of dangerous gases. These gases rise upward in a room. The cloth helps keep smoke and gases from getting into your lungs.

When you reach the door, touch it with your hand. *If the door is warm, leave it closed.* If it is cool, carefully open it a crack. Brace yourself against it as you open it. A blast of hot air could rush in and *suffocate* you and others. If no smoke or hot air comes in, it is safe to open the door.

Suppose the hall outside the apartment door is not full of smoke or flames. Then crawl down the hall to the nearest fire-escape stairs. Close the door when you leave the apartment. But leave the door unlocked. Close the door of the stairwell or the fire-escape stairs as you go out. This will help prevent drafts that fan the flames.

Maybe there is no safe way to get out of the apartment. Then stuff towels or other cloths around the exit door or doors. Dampen the cloths if possible. Open a window and stay near it. Wait for firefighters to rescue you. Or stand on a balcony. Why is this a good idea?

Something to Do

Work with others to plan and give some safety skits. The skits should show what to do when a fire breaks out in a home and in an apartment.

SAFETY AROUND US

Sometimes people are trapped on the top floors of modern high-rise buildings during a fire. At times a helicopter is used to rescue these people from the roofs.

If necessary, a fire department in a large city may send a helicopter to a burning building. The helicopter lands on the roof to get people. Or the helicopter drops a net to people. The people are lifted off the building in the net. Then they are pulled up into the helicopter.

What Causes Bumps and Falls?

Many accidents occur when someone falls or is bumped. People often fall off their bicycles. They can even get hurt from bumping into people or things.

How do you think these bumping and falling accidents happen? Think of all the reasons you can. Discuss them with your group. Then turn the page. Compare your ideas with the ones on page 248.

Many bumps and falls result from people who do not look where they are going. They do not keep alert for possible hazards as they move.

Carrying things in an unsafe manner is one example. Don't try to carry so much that you can't see in front of you. Try to watch where you step. Look ahead to where you are going. Avoid turning around and talking to someone as you walk.

Dresser drawers, cupboard doors, or even locker doors that are not closed are hazardous too. They often cause painful bumps.

Falls may occur when people try to reach for objects on high shelves. What do people sometimes mistakenly use instead of a ladder?

Have you ever been hurt while playing in an active game? What causes collisions in games like soccer, baseball, or basketball? How might they be prevented?

Start your own record. List all the accidents that occur to you in the next two or three weeks. Notice how many are either a fall or a bump. Suggest a way you could have prevented each accident. How might such a safety record help make you more "safety-minded"?

Sum It Up

What are some safety guides for bicycle drivers?

What are some things you should check to see if your bicycle is in good repair?

How do many bicycle accidents occur?

What should you do in case of a fire in a house? In an apartment?

What can be more dangerous to people in a fire than the flames?

What are some safety guides that help prevent falls and bumps?

Do You Know?

Careless actions in school halls may lead to falls or bumps. What safety guide would you suggest to prevent a possible accident in each of the following cases:

Running in the halls

Failing to use handrails on stairs

Racing and jumping up the stairs, several at a time

Failing to keep to the right side of the hall when walking

Piling too many objects on the top shelf of a locker

What Should People Know About Drugs?

Suppose you are at a friend's house. You mention that you have a headache. Your friend offers you a pill.

Your friend says, "This really helped me when I had a headache."

Should you take the drug? Why or why not?

What should people know about safety with drugs?

Discuss these questions with your group. Then turn the page and read on. Compare your ideas with those on pages 250–253.

Drugs used as medicine can help prevent or treat an illness or deaden pain. Drugs change the way the body works.

Anything that can bring about changes in your body should be used cautiously. In fact, it is a good idea not to take any medicine at all for minor aches and pains. You can learn to "put up" with a little discomfort. By doing so, you will be staying safe.

Remember that no one knows for sure what effects any drug will have on any individual. Even doctors do not always know. Each person is different. A drug that helps one person may not help another. The drug might even produce harmful results called *side effects.*

Side Effects

A given drug might help you get rid of a headache. But the drug might also upset your stomach. Or the drug might make you dizzy or very drowsy.

Look carefully at the label on any over-the-counter drug. You will see warnings of side effects.

An *over-the-counter drug,* or OTC drug, is a *non-prescription* drug. You do not need a doctor's prescription to get it. It can be bought at a drugstore or food store. Aspirin, for example, is an over-the-counter drug. Most cough syrups are over-the-counter drugs. Drugs that a doctor must prescribe are *prescription,* or *Rx* drugs.

There is always uncertainty about how a drug may affect a person. This is true even with a prescription drug. Doctors who prescribe drugs generally ask their patients to let them know if there are any side effects.

You should follow the doctor's advice. Speak up if you think a medicine is making you uncomfortable. Tell your parents or whoever is taking care of you.

One important precaution should be remembered. Take a drug only as your parents or doctor instruct. Don't take any drug on your own. Because no one can be certain what effects any drug may have on him or her, there is some risk in taking any drug. So people should take medicines only when they are absolutely necessary. Then the directions should be followed exactly as given.

If anyone suggests you experiment with a drug, politely refuse. Don't be reassured if someone tells you the drug is harmless or will make you feel good. This might be true for them. But what might occur with another person?

One over-the-counter medicine for colds has this caution on it.

Alcohol Is a Drug

Do you know that drinks made with whiskey, gin, or vodka have a drug in them? If you answered "yes," you are right. The drug is *alcohol.* Beer and wine have alcohol in them too. But there is not nearly so much alcohol.

Like all drugs, alcohol brings about changes in people who drink it. Alcohol affects the way their bodies work. It affects their emotions too.

What happens when alcohol is taken into the body? The working of the brain slows down. This slows the working of the rest of the body.

Much depends on the amount of alcohol a person drinks. Even though its effects may not clearly show, alcohol keeps a person from thinking as clearly as usual. It may make a person clumsy. It may keep a person from talking distinctly. Also different people react differently to the same amount of alcohol. This is the case with all drugs. A person can never be sure exactly how alcohol will affect him or her. Alcohol may affect the same person differently at different times.

People behave in different ways after drinking too much. With heavy drinking, some people may act silly. Some may do foolish things. Others may become quarrelsome. Still others may become sleepy.

Alcohol is also a factor in accidents. Many traffic accidents involve drivers or pedestrians who have been drinking alcoholic beverages. Why?

It has been estimated that millions of adults in this country use alcoholic beverages in some form. Some of these people are moderate users. These users may drink small amounts of alcoholic beverages, such as wine, on special occasions. They may even drink it with a meal now and then.

Why Some People Start
to Drink Alcohol

It is served at home on special occasions.

They want to see what drinking is like.

They want to do what others are doing.

They think it makes them more "grown-up."

They think the drinks will make them forget their troubles.

Can you think of any other reasons?

252

Other people use alcoholic drinks more often or more heavily. Some can control their use. Others may sometimes have "alcohol problems." They may get sick, pass out, have accidents, get into fights, or even do violence to others.

Alcoholics

There are some people who are intoxicated often enough to prevent them from living normal lives. These people cannot control their heavy drinking. Family problems may result. Jobs may be lost. These people are known as *alcoholics.* A person who has this difficulty needs help. The help can be given by a doctor or by others who understand the problem.

Alcohol and Young People

There are things young people especially should know about alcohol. Alcohol affects a young person more than it does an adult. That is because a young body is usually smaller than an adult body. And all drug dosage is related to weight. Therefore, small amounts of alcohol cause faster and greater effects in young people than in adults. Too much alcohol taken at one time can even cause death.

Perhaps you wonder why some people drink alcoholic beverages and some don't. What are some reasons given on page 252 and at the right here?

Sum It Up

Why should people be very cautious in their use of any drug?

What should young people remember about drugs?

How does alcohol affect the brain?

What are some "alcohol problems" a heavy drinker may have at times?

How would you describe an alcoholic?

Why Some People Refuse to Drink Alcohol

They think alcoholic drinks may be harmful to their bodies.

They believe alcoholic drinks might lead to accidents.

They are afraid they might start drinking too heavily.

They think it is wrong to drink alcohol.

Can you think of any other reasons?

SAFETY AROUND US

You probably know there are laws against people driving cars when they have been drinking. If a car accident occurs, the police try to find out if anyone involved is intoxicated. Devices can be used to show whether enough alcohol is present in the blood to keep a driver from driving safely.

One such device, an *alcometer,* is shown below. It analyzes a person's breath to find out how much alcohol is in the blood. Other devices analyze the blood, urine, or saliva.

Why do you think such devices are used in the event of accidents?

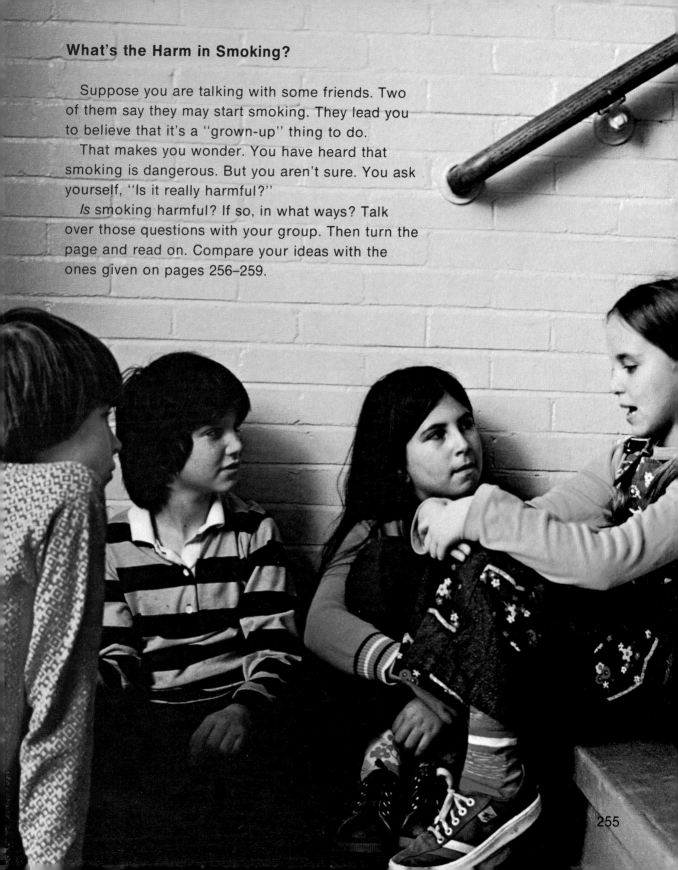

What's the Harm in Smoking?

Suppose you are talking with some friends. Two of them say they may start smoking. They lead you to believe that it's a "grown-up" thing to do.

That makes you wonder. You have heard that smoking is dangerous. But you aren't sure. You ask yourself, "Is it really harmful?"

Is smoking harmful? If so, in what ways? Talk over those questions with your group. Then turn the page and read on. Compare your ideas with the ones given on pages 256–259.

Maybe you think smoking is just harmful to older people. You may also think it couldn't harm you in your youth.

If so, read this statement from a leaflet called "Listen Smokers."[1]

You don't have to wait 20 years for cigarettes to affect you. It only takes 3 seconds. That's how long it takes for a cigarette to go to work.

In just 3 seconds, a cigarette makes your heart beat faster, shoots your blood pressure up, replaces oxygen in your blood with carbon monoxide, and leaves cancer-causing chemicals to spread through your body.

All this happens with every cigarette you smoke.

How Smoking Damages the Lungs

Just how does smoking hurt the lungs? The lungs have air tubes in them. These tubes branch out into smaller and smaller ones.

The inside walls of all these tubes are made of individual cells. The cells are packed closely together. Some of these cells have hairlike parts called *cilia.* Cilia constantly move back and forth. Normally they sweep dust particles and particles in smoke upward toward the throat. The dirt particles are swept into the back of the mouth. Then they are breathed or coughed out of the body.

[1]From "Listen Smokers," U.S. Department of Health, Education, and Welfare. DHEW Publication No. (CDC) 74-8731.

This is what happens when a cigarette is smoked. Microscopic particles of tar are carried into the lungs with smoke. The particles and smoke slow down the work of the cilia. Eventually the tar collects in the lungs. This tar contains hundreds of chemicals. Some of these chemicals can cause lung cancer. A person who smokes a pack of cigarettes a day puts a cup of tar into his or her lungs each year.

What happens when the cilia can no longer protect the lungs? The healthy lung cells are injured or destroyed. This damage is done by the particles that stay in the lungs. When normal lung cells are damaged, cancer cells may develop. Cancer cells crowd out or destroy normal cells. See the picture on this page. The growth of cancer cells can interfere with the work of the lungs.

You have no pain nerves in your lungs. So you have no warning that something is wrong. Lung cancer may start a long time before it is discovered.

The chances of getting lung cancer increase if a person smokes cigarettes. People who have never smoked show the lowest death rate from lung cancer. The more cigarettes a person smokes, the higher the lung-cancer death rate.

Lung cancer is hard to cure. Even with modern medical advances, only one out of every twenty lung-cancer victims can be saved.

Smoking and Other Lung Diseases

Other lung diseases are related to cigarette smoking. Substances in cigarette smoke irritate the nose, throat, and chest. These substances play a part in causing *emphysema,* a serious lung disease.

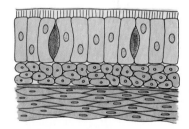

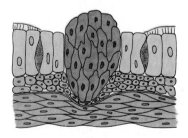

Lining of lung

Top. Normal cells
Bottom. Cancer cells shown in brown

Emphysema can result from damage done to the air sacs in the lungs. Two or three air sacs may join to become a large, irregular one. Stale air, full of carbon dioxide, now becomes trapped in the lungs. Proper amounts of fresh air, with oxygen, cannot get in. Then the whole body suffers. Breathing may eventually become very difficult as the disease worsens.

Chronic bronchitis is a disease that can be caused or made worse by cigarette smoking. The walls of the air tubes in the lungs become inflamed. Excess mucus is also formed. There is much coughing to bring up the mucus.

Smoking and Heart Disease

Cigarette smoking can cause the heart to overwork. When you smoke, your blood vessels constrict, or get smaller. Then the heart has to work harder to pump blood through them.

The death rate for *coronary heart disease* is about twice as high for smokers as for nonsmokers. What does this suggest about not smoking or about stopping smoking?

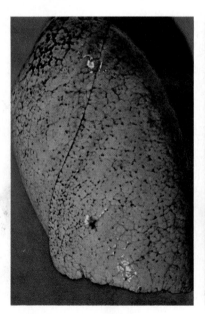
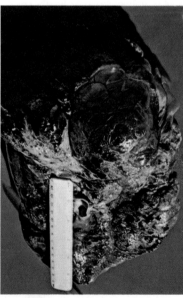

At the left is a normal lung of a middle-aged person. At the right is the lung of a middle-aged cigarette smoker. Inhaled smoke, containing gases and tar, has blackened the lung. What could happen to the blackened lung?

Reasons for Smoking

You may wonder why people smoke when it harms their health. Some people smoke because they think it is pleasurable. They say it relaxes them. Some adults began to smoke a long time ago. The harmful effects of cigarette smoking were not known for sure then.

Today, millions of people have given up cigarette smoking. They have looked at the research. Then they have decided to stop.

Some people find it very difficult to stop. Some smokers go to special clinics for help. People who try to stop smoking have made an important decision. They have decided that any pleasure they get from smoking isn't worth the risk to their health.

Another Kind of Smoking: Marijuana

People who smoke tobacco cigarettes are taking in a drug called *nicotine*.

Another kind of smoking is smoking *marijuana*. Like tobacco, marijuana has drugs in it. One drug is *THC*. That is short for a long chemical name. THC causes changes in the body. It can affect the emotions too.

All the effects of marijuana are still not completely understood. But it is known that marijuana can make some users feel confused or anxious. It can also affect vision. For example, a car driver may misjudge distances. So marijuana can be a factor in car accidents.

SMOKING POLLUTES YOU AND EVERYTHING ELSE

American Cancer Society

As with all drugs, marijuana affects different people in different ways. Why might this cause a person to be cautious about using marijuana?

Sum It Up

What are some reasons why smoking is dangerous to health?

Things to Do

1. Pick a holiday, such as Halloween, Christmas, or the Fourth of July. Prepare a list of safety guides that could help prevent accidents on these special days.

2. Create a line that rhymes with the one below to make a good safety guide.

If you drive a bike at night,

_____.

3. Discuss fire-safety guides used in your school, especially those for fire drills. Give some reasons for each guide.

4. You may have learned how to use electrical appliances safely when you were younger. Make a list of some safety precautions you remember.

5. Tell what you know about safety guides for swimming and boating.

6. Think of a game or sport you enjoy. Is it skating, fishing, or playing baseball? Tell or write about three safety guides to keep in mind when you take part in the game or sport.

7. Make a poster that gives a bicycle-safety rule.

8. Work with a group to act out the way to report a fire.

Special Research

1. Make a report on what to do in the event of an electrical storm, a hurricane, or a tornado.

2. Watch for articles in the daily newspapers about accidents to boys and girls. Bring these articles to school and be ready to discuss them. Tell how you think the accidents might have been prevented.

Bicycle Rider Injured

Racine, Wisconsin—A ten-year-old boy was struck by a car and suffered a broken leg and arm after trying to cross lanes at a busy intersection near his school. The boy, according to classmates who saw the accident, was pedaling his bicycle into another lane without signaling or checking traffic behind him. The driver of the car stopped immediately and covered the injured boy with a blanket while a passer-by called the police and an ambulance.

The boy was taken to a nearby hospital and is reported to be in fair condition.

More Things to Do

1. Bring in cigarette ads from news papers and magazines. Discuss how the ads try to get people to smoke certain brands. Discuss what sales points are on the cigarette packages. Do you think the claims are true?

Discuss what warning must be on every pack of cigarettes.

2. Look for printed articles about the effects of cigarette smoking on health. Bring in clippings that can be put in a class scrapbook or on the bulletin board.

3. Bring to class some ads about whiskey, gin, or vodka. Talk over what the ads say or show in pictures to get people to drink a certain brand. Discuss things that should be kept in mind when looking at such ads. For example, will any special brand of whiskey really make a person more popular or better in some sport?

Special Research

1. Investigate and report on the dangers of using hair sprays, paint thinners, or model-airplane glue in poorly ventilated places. What are some possible effects on the lungs? On other parts of the body?

2. Look for this book at the library: *Smoking and You* by Arnold Madison (Messner). Give a report on some information you find in it.

Can You Show What You Know?[1]

Page numbers show you where to look back in the chapter for information, if you need it.

1. List five safety rules for bicycle drivers. (238)

2. Demonstrate the proper hand signals for turning and stopping when you are driving a bicycle. (238)

3. Tell three things to check to see if a bicycle is in good repair. (240–241)

4. Tell what to do if you discover a fire in your house. (244)

5. Describe what people in an apartment should do if they discover fire in the building. (245)

6. Suggest five safety rules that might prevent falls and bumps. (248)

7. Tell what risk there can be in taking any drug. (250)

8. Explain what is meant by *side effects* of a drug. (250)

9. Tell some ways in which alcohol can cause changes in a person. (252)

10. Explain how alcoholic drinks can be a factor in causing accidents. (252)

11. List three harmful effects smoking can have on a person's health. (256–258)

12. Tell three ways in which marijuana may affect those who use it. (259)

[1]Behavioral objectives in the cognitive area are stated here directly to students themselves.

Review It

Page numbers tell you where to look back in the chapter for information, if you need it.

1. What are some common bicycle-safety violations? (238)

2. When a fire breaks out, what are two hazards more dangerous than the flames? (245)

3. Why should a person crawl on the floor to an exit door in case of fire? (245)

4. What are some careless actions that can cause bumps or falls? (248)

5. What is meant by an over-the-counter drug? (250)

6. What is a safe thing to do about very minor aches and pains? (250)

7. Why should medicines be taken only when they are absolutely necessary? (251)

8. What are some "alcohol problems" a heavy drinker may have? (253)

9. What is a special hazard for young people if they drink alcoholic beverages? (253)

10. What is one way to find out if a car driver has had enough alcoholic drinks to become intoxicated? (254)

11. What is an alcoholic? (253)

12. What happens when cancer cells start growing in the lungs? (257)

13. What do you know about the tar that is carried into the lungs with cigarette smoke? (257)

14. Why may a person have lung cancer for a long time before it is discovered? (257)

15. Why is lung cancer a dangerous disease? (257–258)

16. How does smoking affect the heart? (258)

17. How would you describe the disease emphysema? (258)

18. How would you describe chronic bronchitis? What can cause it or make it worse? (258)

19. What is the drug found in tobacco? In marijuana? (259)

20. Why are many people trying to break the smoking habit? (259)

Copy each sentence and fill in the missing word or words.

1. Drive your bicycle _____ the flow of traffic.

2. When you and others are driving bicycles together, drive _____ _____.

3. _____ your bicycle across busy intersections.

4. If you are in a building on fire, keep your _____ and _____ covered.

5. In escaping from a burning building, it is wise to _____ on the floor.

6. Once you are out of a burning building, do not _____ _____ into it.

7. Some falls occur because people stand on chairs instead of _____.

8. Always _____ a drawer after you have taken out what you want.

9. In checking a bicycle for safety, be sure the _____ is at the proper height.

10. _____ and _____ are hazards in fires as well as flames.

Copy each number on a piece of paper. After each number write the correct answer, *true* or *false.* Rewrite each false item to make it true.

11. A drug affects all people the same way.

12. A drug causes changes in the body.

13. Smoking is harmful only to adults.

14. There is tar in cigarette smoke.

15. Lung cancer can be caused by cigarette smoking.

16. It is difficult to cure lung cancer.

17. Emphysema can be caused by alcoholic drinks.

18. Cigarette smoking makes the heart beat more slowly.

19. There is a drug in cigarettes.

20. Alcohol is a drug.

Number of Answers   20

Number Right   _____

Score (Number Right X 5)   _____

What Do You Think?

What information in this chapter do you think will be useful to you? Write about it on a piece of paper.

SCHOOL & HOME

You have learned many things in this chapter that you may want to share with your family.

If you made a safety check of your bicycles, what would you check?

You and your family might want to have a fire drill at home. What could you show others about how to move through a smoke-filled room?

Or you might want to discuss why a person should take medicine only if it is needed. And you might discuss why directions should be followed carefully. What would you say about *side effects* or harmful results?

Do You *Use* What You Know?[1]

Page numbers after items tell where to look back for information, if you need it.

1. Have you felt angry recently? What did you do to try to get over such feelings? (20)

2. Have you recently felt left out of things? If so, what did you do about it? (18–22)

3. Have you felt that everything was going wrong lately? What did you do to get over the feeling? (22)

4. What interesting thing can you tell about yourself? (31)

5. Do you use your eyes to look for lovely things? What have you seen lately? (50)

6. What good TV-watching habits have you used recently? (83)

7. What do you do to keep from wasting water when you take a shower or bath? (102)

8. How did you trim your fingernails the last time you did it? How did you trim your toenails? (105)

9. Have you or anyone in your family had a small cut? What first aid did you use? (115)

10. Have you had a splinter recently? What did you do to get it out? (115)

11. Do you want to have strong, skillful muscles? If so, how are you trying to develop them? (139, 153)

12. Do you think your posture is good or poor? How might you improve it? (147, 148–149)

13. What would you do if you thought someone had broken a bone? (157)

14. Did you floss and brush your teeth this morning or last night? How did you do it? (164–165)

15. Have you bought any toothpaste lately? What should you look for on the container? (163)

[1]This End-of-Book review emphasizes application of health and safety information in daily life.

16. Jot down everything you ate yesterday at meals and for snacks. Did you have an adequate diet? How do you know? (184–187)

17. Have you or any family members bought any eggs lately? What did you do to be sure they were safe to use? (189)

18. How are you taking in air right now—through your nose or mouth? Which is better? (214–215)

19. Suppose a friend gets a cut that is bleeding a lot. What first aid can you give to stop the bleeding? (228)

20. What if you bruised yourself? What would you do about it? (228)

21. Have you been on a bicycle lately? What did you do to be a safe driver? (238–241)

22. What did you do in the school hall today to help prevent bumps or falls? (248)

23. Has your family had a fire drill at home lately? If so, what did everyone do? (244–245)

24. Have you thought about the effects of smoking on health? What did you decide? (256–259)

25. Suppose a friend said to you, "There's no harm in smoking when you are young. Only adults are harmed." What would you tell this person? (256)

26. Do you think it is safe or unsafe to take someone else's medicine? (251)

27. Suppose someone asked you to experiment with a drug. The person told you, "It makes you feel good, and it can't hurt you. It hasn't hurt me. I tried it. So have others I know." What would be your reaction? (250–251)

Books for Boys and Girls[1]

Books of Information

Adler, Irving and Ruth. *Taste, Touch. and Smell* (Day).

Balestrino, Philip. *The Skeleton Inside You* (T. Y. Crowell).

Bertol, Roland. *Charles Drew* (T. Y. Crowell).

Cadallader, Sharon. *Cooking Adventures for Kids* (Houghton).

Crook, Bette and Charles L. *Famous Firsts in Medicine* (Putnam).

Elgin, Kathleen. *The Human Body: The Skin* (Watts).

Kalina, Sigmund. *Your Blood and Its Cargo* (Lothrop).

Le Shan, Eda. *What Makes Me Feel This Way?* (Macmillan).

Madison, Arnold. *Smoking and You* (Messner).

Martin, M. W. *Let's Talk About the Wonderful World of Medicine* (Jonathan David).

Ravielli, Anthony. *Wonders of the Human Body* (Viking).

Zim, Herbert S. *Our Senses and How They Work* (Morrow).

Books to "Grow On"

Calhoun, Mary. *Depend on Katie John* (Harper).

Canfield, Dorothy. *Understood Betsy* (Holt).

Carlson, Natalie S. *Ann Aurelia and Dorothy* (Dell).

Cleaver, Vera, and Cleaver, Bill. *Grover* (Lippincott).

Conford, Ellen. *Me and the Terrible Two* (Little).

Gray, Genevieve. *Sore Loser* (Houghton).

Hodges, Margaret. *The Making of Joshua Cobb* (Farrar).

Rock, Gail. *The Thanksgiving Treasure* (Knopf).

Rogers, Pamela. *The Rare One* (Nelson).

Seredy, Kate. *The Good Master* (Viking).

Smith, Doris B. *A Taste of Blackberries* (T. Y. Crowell).

Stolz, Mary. *The Edge of Next Year* (Harper).

Vestley, Ann-Catherine. *Hello, Aurora* (T. Y. Crowell).

[1]See also page T40 for additional books.

Metric Chart

METRIC MEASURES   CUSTOMARY MEASURES

LENGTH

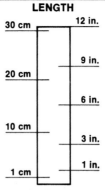

Metric		Customary	
10 millimeters (mm)	= 1 centimeter (cm)	12 inches (in.)	= 1 foot (ft.)
100 centimeters	= 1 meter (m)	3 feet	= 1 yard (yd.)
1000 meters	= 1 kilometer (km)	5280 feet	= 1 mile (mi.)

MASS (WEIGHT)

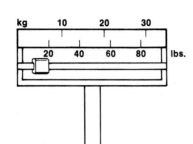

Metric		Customary	
1000 milligrams (mg)	= 1 gram (g)	16 ounces (oz.)	= 1 pound (lb.)
1000 grams	= 1 kilogram (kg)	2000 pounds	= 1 ton (t.)
1000 kilograms	= 1 metric ton (t)		

VOLUME

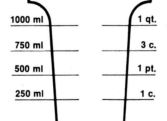

Metric		Customary	
1000 milliliters (ml)	= 1 liter (l)	8 fluid ounces (fl. oz.)	= 1 cup (c.)
1000 liters	= 1 kiloliter (kl)	2 cups	= 1 pint (pt.)
		2 pints	= 1 quart (qt.)
		4 quarts	= 1 gallon (gal.)

TEMPERATURE

CELSIUS   FAHRENHEIT

Water boils 100° —————— 212° Water boils

Body temperature 37° —————— 98.6° Body temperature

Water freezes 0° —————— 32° Water freezes

Glossary

Full Pronunciation Key

The pronunciation of each word is shown just after the word, in this way:
ab bre vi ate (ə brē′vē āt). The letters and signs used are pronounced as in the words at the right. The mark ′ is placed after a syllable with primary or heavy accent, as in the example above. The mark ′ after a syllable shows a secondary or lighter accent, as in **ab bre vi a tion** (ə brē′vē ā′shən).

Foreign Sound: H as in German ach. Pronounce k without closing the breath passage.

a	hat, cap	p	paper, cup
ā	age, face	r	run, try
ä	father, far	s	say, yes
		sh	she, rush
b	bad, rob	t	tell, it
ch	child, much	th	thin, both
d	did, red	ŦH	then, smooth
e	let, best	u	cup, butter
ē	equal, be	ủ	full, put
ėr	term, learn	ü	rule, move
f	fat, if	v	very, save
g	go, bag	w	will, woman
h	he, how	y	young, yet
i	it, pin	z	zero, breeze
ī	ice, five	zh	measure, seizure
j	jam, enjoy	ə	represents:
k	kind, seek		a in about
l	land, coal		e in taken
m	me, am		i in pencil
n	no, in		o in lemon
ng	long, bring		u in circus
o	hot, rock	ər	represents:
ō	open, go		er in mother
ô	order, all		ur in pursuit
oi	oil, voice		
ou	house, out		

This pronunciation key is adapted from the *Thorndike-Barnhart Intermediate Dictionary.*

al bi no (al bī′nō), person or animal that from birth has a pale, milky skin, very light hair, and pink eyes.

al co hol (al′kə hôl), the colorless liquid in gin, whiskey, wine, beer, and so on, that makes them intoxicating.

al co hol ic (al′kə hô′lik), person who has the habit of drinking too much intoxicating liquor.

al ler gy (al′ər jē), *pl.* **al ler gies,** unusual sensitiveness to certain substances, such as a particular kind of pollen, food, hair, or cloth. Hay fever, asthma, headaches, or hives are common signs of allergy.

an ti bod y (an′ti bod′ē), *pl.* **an ti bod ies,** substance produced in the blood or tissues of the body. It can destroy or weaken bacteria. Or it can make ineffective the poisons produced by bacteria.

a or ta (ā ôr′tə), *pl.* **a or tas** *or* **a or tae** (-tē), main artery of the body, leading out of the left side of the heart to smaller arteries all over the body, except for the lungs.

ar ter y (är′tər ē), *pl.* **ar ter ies,** one of the many blood vessels that carry blood away from the heart to all parts of the body.

ar thri tis (är thrī′tis), inflammation of a joint or joints of the body.

au di to ry ca nal (ô′də tôr′ē *or* ô′də tō′rē kə nal′), tube or passageway that leads from the outer ear to the middle ear.

au di to ry nerve (ô′də tôr′ē nėrv′), hearing nerve that carries messages of sound to the hearing center of the brain.

au ri cle (ôr′ə kəl), either of the two upper chambers of the heart that receive blood from the veins.

bac ter i a (bak tir′ē ə), tiny living plants that can usually be seen only through a microscope. Some harmful bacteria cause disease or tooth decay. Some helpful bacteria turn milk into cheese.

Beau mont (bô′mont), **William,** 1785-1853, American surgeon who made some important observations on digestion while watching a man's stomach at work.

bi cus pid (bī kus′pid), tooth having two cusps, or pointed ends, that tears and grinds food. An adult has eight bicuspids.

blood (blud), red liquid in the blood vessels; the liquid that flows from a cut.

blood ves sel (blud′ ves′əl), any tube in the body through which the blood circulates. An artery, vein, or capillary is a blood vessel.

bow el (bou′əl), tube in the body into which food passes from the stomach; one of the divisions of the intestines.

brain (brān), mass of nerve cells inside the skull or head of a person or animal. The brain controls almost all of the functions of the body. It enables us to learn, think, and remember.

brain stem (brān′ stem′), lower portion of the brain, where functions such as breathing and circulation are controlled.

bron chi al tube (brong′kē əl tüb′ *or* tyüb′), either of the two main branches of the windpipe leading into the lungs.

bron chi tis (brong kī′tis), inflammation of the mucous membrane that lines the bronchial tubes.

can cer (kan′sər), a very harmful growth in the body that tends to spread and destroy healthy tissues and organs.

cap il lar y (kap′ə ler′ē), *pl.* **cap il lar ies,** a blood vessel with a slender, hairlike opening. Capillaries join the end of an artery to the beginning of a vein.

car bo hy drate (kär′bō hī′drāt), substance made from carbon dioxide and water by green plants in sunlight, composed of carbon, oxygen, and hydrogen. Carbohydrates in food furnish heat and energy for the body.

car bon di ox ide (kär′bən dī ok′sīd), colorless, odorless gas present in air. It is a waste product formed by the body. You breathe out, or exhale, carbon dioxide that is in your lungs.

car ti lage (kär′tl ij), gristle; the firm, elastic, flexible substance forming parts of the skeleton.

cell (sel), basic building block of living matter. Animals and plants are made of cells.

ce men tum (sə men′təm), the hard, thin substance covering the roots of a tooth.

cer e bel lum (ser′ə bel′əm), the part of the brain that controls the automatic coordination of the muscles.

cer e bral cor tex (sə rē′brəl *or* ser′ə brəl kôr′teks), the outer layer of gray matter of the cerebrum.

ce re brum (sə rē′brəm *or* ser′ə brəm), the part of the brain that controls thought and voluntary muscular movements.

chem i cal (kem′ə kəl), any simple substance that is used to cause changes in other substances. Sulfuric acid, bicarbonate of soda, and borax are chemicals.

chyme (kīm), a pulpy, semiliquid mass into which food is changed by the action of the stomach. Chyme passes from the stomach into the small intestine.

cil i a (sil′ē ə), tiny, hairlike projections that grow on the surface of the respiratory mucous membranes.

coc cyx (kok′siks), a small triangular bone—usually several vertebrae fused together—forming the lower end of the spinal column in humans.

coch le a (kok′lē ə), a snail-shaped cavity of the inner ear, containing the nerve endings that transmit sound impulses along the auditory nerve.

cone (kōn), one of a group of cone-shaped cells of the retina of the eye that responds to light.

cor ne a (kôr′nē ə), the transparent "window" of the eye that covers the iris and the pupil.

cra ni um (krā′nē əm), part of the skull enclosing the brain.

cus pid (kus′pid), tooth having one cusp, or pointed end, and used especially for tearing food. An adult has four cuspids.

den tal car ies (den′tl ker′ēz *or* kar′ēz), decay of dental tissues; tooth decay.

den tin (den′tən), layer of hard, bony material beneath the enamel of a tooth. It forms the main part of a tooth.

der mis (dėr′mis), the layer of skin beneath the outer skin in which are located many blood vessels and nerve endings.

di a phragm (dī′ə fram), a partition of muscles and tendons separating the chest cavity from the abdominal cavity; midriff.

di ges tion (də jes′chən *or* dī jes′chən), the changing or breaking down of food in the mouth, stomach, and intestines so that the body can use it.

drug (drug), substance used as a medicine or in preparing medicines. Drugs are obtained from plants, molds, minerals, and so on, and are often made from chemicals. Aspirin is a drug.

duct (dukt), tube in the body for carrying a bodily fluid: *tear ducts.*

e lec tro car di o gram (i lek′trō kär′dē ə-gram), the tracing or record made by an electrocardiograph.

e lec tro car di o graph (i lek′trō kär′dē ə-graf), instrument that detects and records the electrical impulses produced by the action of the heart with each beat. It is used to diagnose diseases of the heart.

e lec tron mi cro scope (i lek′tron mī′krə skōp), microscope that uses beams of electrons instead of beams of light to enlarge images, and that has much higher power than any ordinary light microscope.

em phy se ma (em′fə sē′mə), respiratory disease in which the air sacs of the lungs become enlarged. The air sacs are less able to supply oxygen to the blood and remove carbon dioxide from it.

e nam el (i nam′əl), the hard, white substance that covers and protects the crown of a tooth.

en do crine gland (en′dō krən *or* en′dō-krīn gland′), any of various glands, such as the thyroid gland, that produce secretions which pass directly into the bloodstream or lymph instead of into a duct.

ep i der mis (ep′ə dėr′mis), the thin outer layer of the skin.

ep i glot tis (ep′ə glot′is), a thin triangular plate of cartilage that covers the entrance to the windpipe during swallowing, so that food and drink do not get into the lungs.

e soph a gus (ē sof′ə gəs), tube for the passage of food from the mouth to the stomach; it is also called the food tube.

Eus ta chi an tube (yü stā′kē ən *or* yü stā′shən tüb′ *or* tyüb′), a slender canal between the throat and the middle ear. It equalizes the air pressure on the two sides of the eardrum.

fats (fats), a class of nutrients essential in our diet; they build fatty tissues and serve as a source of energy.

Fer ri er (fer′i ər), **Sir David,** Scottish neurologist known for charting the brain.

---

a hat, **ā** age, **ä** far; **e** let, **ē** be, **ėr** term; **i** it, **ī** ice; **o** hot, **ō** go, **ô** order; **oi** oil, **ou** out; **u** cup, **ủ** put, **ü** rule; **ch** child; **ng** long; **sh** she; **th** thin; **ᵮH** then; **zh** measure; **ə** taken, mother

flu or ride (flü′ə rīd′), substance that can help prevent tooth decay. To do this, it is added to toothpaste, or it is put directly on the teeth by a dentist.

frac ture (frak′chər), break; crack: *The boy fell from a tree and fractured his arm.*

gall blad der (gôl′ blad′ər), pear-shaped sac attached to the liver in which bile is stored until needed for digestion.

gas tric juice (gas′trik jüs′), the digestive fluid secreted by glands in the lining of the stomach. It helps break down foods, particularly proteins.

germ (jèrm), a microscopic animal or plant, especially one which causes disease; microbe.

gland (gland), organ in the body which makes and gives out some substance which helps the body do its work. The liver and thyroid are glands.

growth plate (grōth′ plāt′), the middle section of growing bones, consisting of cartilage, which joins the ends and shafts of the long bones.

Har vey (här′vē), **William,** 1578-1657, English doctor who discovered the circulation of the blood.

heart (härt), a hollow organ made of muscle. It pumps the blood throughout the body.

he mo glo bin (hē′mə glō′bən *or* hem′ə glō′bən), the red substance in the red blood cells made up of iron and protein.

hor mone (hôr′mōn), chemical substance formed in the endocrine glands that enters the bloodstream and affects or controls the activity of some organ or tissue. Adrenaline and insulin are hormones.

im mu nize (im′yə nīz), protect from disease by inoculation or infection: *Vaccination immunizes people against smallpox.*

in ci sor (in sī′zər), tooth having a sharp edge for cutting; one of the front teeth. An adult has eight incisors.

in ner ear (in′ər ir′), innermost part of the ear. Sound waves traveling through the liquid in and around the snail-shaped part cause the nerve cells to send messages of sound to the brain. The inner ear also contains organs concerned with balance.

in tox i cate (in tok′sə kāt), make drunk: *Too much wine intoxicates people.*

in vol un tar y (in vol′ən ter′ē), not controlled by the will: *Breathing is involuntary.*

i ris (ī′ris), the colored part of the eye around the pupil. Muscles in the iris control the size of the pupil.

joint (joint), part in the body where two bones join, allowing motion, and the way those bones are fitted together.

kid ney (kid′nē), one of the pair of organs in the body that take liquid wastes and excess water out of the blood. The kidneys then pass on these wastes, called *urine,* to the urinary bladder.

Klee (klā′), **Paul,** 1879-1940, Swiss painter.

Laën nec (lā nek′), **Re né** (rə nā′), 1781–1826, French doctor who made the first stethoscope.

large in tes tine (lärj′ in tes′tən), lower part of the intestines into which the small intestine discharges digested food.

lar ynx (lar′ingks), upper end of the windpipe, where the vocal cords are and where the voice is produced.

lens (lenz), the part of the eye that directs light rays upon the retina.

lig a ment (lig′ə mənt), a band of strong tissue that connects bones or holds organs of the body in place.

liv er (liv′ər), large body organ that makes a digestive juice and helps the body use food. The liver also changes sugar into a different form and stores it.

LSD *(ly ser gic ac id di eth yl am ide)* (lī sėr′jik as′id dī eth′ə lam′īd), hallucinogenic compound of lysergic acid that has highly dangerous properties.

lung (lung), one of a pair of saclike, spongy body organs found in the chest. When you breathe in, the lungs take oxygen from the air. When you breathe out, they release carbon dioxide into the air.

Mal pi ghi (mäl pē′gē), **Mar cel lo** (mär chel′ō), 1628–1694, Italian doctor who discovered how blood gets from the arteries to the veins.

mar i jua na (mar′ə wä′na), the dried flowering tops and leaves of the Indian hemp plant. It is commonly called "pot."

mar row (mar′ō), the soft tissue that fills the hollow central part of most bones.

me dul la ob lon ga ta (mi dul′ə ob′long gä′tə *or* ob′long gā′tə), the lowest part of the brain stem, at the top end of the spinal cord. It contains the nerve centers that control breathing and other involuntary functions.

mem brane (mem′brān), thin, soft sheet or layer of animal tissue. It lines or covers some part of the body.

mid dle ear (mid′l ir′), a hollow space between the eardrum and the inner ear that contains three small bones. These bones carry sound waves from the eardrum to the inner ear.

min er al (min′ər əl), any substance that is neither plant nor animal, but which often occurs in tiny amounts in foods such as meats and vegetables. Minerals are important in the diet to provide material for body growth and repair and to help regulate body activities.

mo lar (mō′lər), tooth with a broad surface for grinding. Your back teeth are molars.

mo tor nerve (mō′tər nėrv′), bundle of nerve fibers that carry messages from the brain or spinal cord to the muscles.

mu cus (myü′kəs), a slimy substance that is made by and that moistens the linings of body cavities.

---

a hat, **ā** age, **ä** far; **e** let, **ē** bé, **ėr** term; **i** it, **ī** ice; **o** hot, **ō** go, **ô** order; **oi** oil, **ou** out; **u** cup, **ú** put, **ü** rule; **ch** child; **ng** long; **sh** she; **th** thin; **ŦH** then; **zh** measure; **ə** taken, mother

mus cle (mus′əl), tissue that can be tightened or loosened to make a part of the body move.

nerve (nėrv), fiber or bundle of fibers that carry messages between the brain or spinal cord and other parts of the body.

nerve end ing (nėrv′ en′ding), the end of a nerve fiber, where stimulation of the nerve occurs.

nic o tine (nik′ə tēn′), poison contained in the leaves, roots, and seeds of tobacco.

nu tri ent (nü′trē ənt *or* nyü′trē ənt), nourishing substance found in foods, having specific functions in maintaining the body. Vitamins and proteins are nutrients.

nu tri tion (nü trish′ən *or* nyü trish′ən), 1. food; nourishment. 2. series of processes by which food is used by animals and plants for growth, energy, and so on.

ol fac tor y (ol fak′tər ē), having to do with smelling; of smell. The nose is an olfactory organ.

oph thal mol o gist (of′thal mol′ə jist), doctor who specializes in the treatment of diseases, defects, and injuries of the eye.

op tic nerve (op′tik nėrv′), nerve that goes from the brain to the eyeball and ends in the retina.

op tom e trist (op tom′ə trist), a person who specializes in correcting eye defects by means of glasses and eye exercises.

or gan (or′gən), any part of the body that has a special job to do to help the body perform as it should. The eyes, stomach, and lungs are all organs.

os te o arth ri tis (os′tē ō ar thrī′tis), disease which destroys the joints.

out er ear (out′ər ir′), the visible curved flap of the ear and the short passageway that goes to the middle ear. The outer ear directs sound waves into the inner parts of the ear.

ox y gen (ok′sə jən), colorless, odorless gas that forms about one fifth of the air. Humans cannot live without oxygen.

pace mak er (pās′mā′kər), 1. area of specialized tissue in the heart, near the top of the wall of the right auricle, that sends out the rhythmic impulses which regulate the heart contractions. 2. an electronic device implanted in the chest wall to maintain or restore the normal heartbeat.

pan cre as (pan′krē əs), gland near the stomach that empties several secretions into the small intestine to aid digestion. Within the pancreas are cells called islets of Langerhans which secrete insulin.

pa pil la (pə pil′ə), *pl.* **pa pil lae** (-ē), a small nipplelike projection concerned with the senses of touch, taste, or smell: *the papillae on the tongue.*

pel vis (pel′vis), *pl.* **pel vis es,** the basin-shaped cavity formed by the hipbones and the end of the backbone.

per i stal sis (per′ə stäl′sis), movement in the wall of a hollow organ by which it propels its contents onward.

pig ment (pig′mənt), substance that occurs in and colors the tissues of an animal or plant. The color of a person's hair or skin is due to pigment in the body cells.

plaque (plak), thin film composed of saliva, bacteria, and food debris. It is constantly being formed on the surfaces of the teeth.

plas ma (plaz′mə), the clear, almost colorless, liquid part of blood or lymph, in which blood or lymph cells float. Plasma consists of water, salts, proteins, and other substances, and it makes up the largest part of the blood.

plate let (plāt′lit), one of many small disks which float in the blood plasma, and are involved in clotting of the blood.

pol lu tant (pə lüt′nt), a polluting, defiling, unclean agent or medium.

pol lu tion (pə lü′shən), polluting; defiling; uncleanness: air pollution.

pro tein (prō′tēn), one of the substances containing nitrogen which are a necessary part of the cells of animals and plants.

pulp (pulp), the soft inner part of a tooth, containing blood vessels and nerves.

pu pil (pyü′pəl), opening in the center of the iris of the eye. The pupil changes size to let more or less light into the eye.

red blood cells (red′ blud′ selz′), cells that with the white blood cells form a large part of blood. Red blood cells contain hemoglobin, which gives them their color.

ret i na (ret′n ə), layer of cells at the back of the eyeball that is sensitive to light and receives images of things looked at.

rick ets (rik′its), disease of childhood caused by a vitamin D and calcium deficiency. It results in softening, and sometimes bending, of the bones.

rod (rod), one of the microscopic sense organs in the retina of the eye that are sensitive to dim light.

sa crum (sā′krəm), bone at the lower end of the spine, which is formed by the joining of several vertebrae and which forms the back of the pelvis.

sa li va (sə lī′və), liquid that glands secrete into the mouth to keep it moist, aid in chewing, and start digestion.

sal i var y gland (sal′ə ver′ē gland′), any of the glands in the mouth that produce saliva.

scler a (sklir′ə), strong, white outer membrane covering the eyeball; the "white of the eye."

sem i cir cu lar ca nal (sem′i sėr′kyə lər kə nal′), any of the three curved, tubelike canals in the inner ear that help us keep our balance.

sen sor y nerve (sen′sər ē nėrv′), bundle of nerve fibers that carry messages from the senses to the brain or spinal cord.

skel e tal mus cle (skel′ə təl mus′əl), any of the more than 600 muscles that are attached to and cover the skeleton.

---

a hat, ā age, ä far; e let, ē be, ėr term; i it, ī ice; o hot, ō go, ô order; oi oil, ou out; u cup, ů put, ü rule; ch child; ng long; sh she; th thin; ᴛʜ then; zh measure; ə taken, mother

skel e ton (skel′ə tən), the bones of a body, fitted together.

small in tes tine (smôl′ in tes′tən), slender part of the intestines, extending from the stomach to the large intestine.

spi nal cord (spī′nl kôrd′), thick, whitish cord of nerve tissue in the human back.

spine (spīn), the backbone.

starch (stärch), a white, odorless, tasteless food substance; one of the carbohydrates. Potatoes contain much starch.

ster ile (ster′əl), free from living germs.

steth o scope (steth′ə skōp), instrument used by doctors to hear the sounds produced in the lungs, heart, and so forth.

stom ach (stum′ək), the large muscular bag in the body which receives, mixes the food, and digests some of it before passing it on into the intestines.

suf fo cate (suf′ə kāt), keep from breathing; hinder in breathing.

taste bud (tāst′ bud′), any of certain groups of cells in the lining of the tongue or mouth that are sense organs of taste.

ten don (ten′dən), a strong band or cord of tissue that joins a muscle to a bone.

tra che a (trā′kē ə). *See* **windpipe.**

trans fu sion (tran sfyü′zhən), transfer of blood from one person or animal to another.

ur i nar y blad der (yür′ə ner′ē blad′ər), sac that stores and discharges urine.

ur ine (yür′ən), the fluid that is excreted from the kidneys as a waste product.

vein (vān), one of the blood vessels or tubes that carry blood to the heart from all parts of the body.

ven tri cle (ven′trə kəl), either of the two lower chambers of the heart.

ver te bra (ver′tə brə), *pl.* **ver te brae** (ver′tə brē), any of the bones of the spine.

vil li (vil′ī), tiny hairlike parts growing out of the lining of the small intestine.

vi ta min (vī′tə min), any of certain special substances required for the normal growth and nourishment of the body.

vo cal cords (vō′kəl kôrdz′), two pairs of membranes in the larynx.

voice box (vois′ boks′). *See* **larynx.**

vol a tile chem i cal (vol′ə təl kem′ə kəl), substance which changes into vapor easily.

vol un tar y (vol′ən ter′ē), controlled by the will: *Talking is voluntary.*

white blood cells (hwīt′ blud′ selz′), cells that float in the blood and lymph. Some of them destroy disease germs.

wind pipe (wind′pīp′), passage by which air is carried from the throat to the lungs.

X ray (eks′ rā′), ray which penetrates substances that light cannot penetrate. X rays are used to locate bone breaks and tooth decay and to diagnose diseases.

---

a hat, ā age, ä far; e let, ē be, ėr term; i it, ī ice; o hot, ō go, ô order; oi oil, ou out; u cup, ů put, ü rule; ch child; ng long; sh she; th thin; ŦH then; zh measure; ə taken, mother

Index

Accidents (See also **Safety.**)
Alcohol and, 254
Bicycle, 242, 242 *(Illus.)*
Causes of, 238, 247–248
Preventing, 238, 248
Aging, 96–97
Air pollution, 100, 229, 259 *(Illus.)*
Air sacs, 215–217, 216 *(Illus.)*
Albino, 89
Alcohol, 181, 252, 253
Alcoholics, 253
Alcometer, 254, 254 *(Illus.)*
Anger, 12, 13, 14–15, 15 *(Illus.)*, 19–20, 19 *(Illus.)*
Antibodies, 207
Aorta, 202, 209–211 *(Illus.)*
Arteries, 90, 176 *(Illus.)*, 201 *(Illus.)*, 203 *(Illus.)*, 204, 204 *(Illus.)*, 208, 209–211 *(Illus.)*
Arthritis, 135
Artificial joints, 135, 135 *(Illus.)*
Audiometer, 58
Auditory canal, 52 *(Illus.)*, 53, 55–57 *(Illus.)*
Auditory nerve, 52 *(Illus.)*, 54, 55–57 *(Illus.)*
Auricles, 202–203, 203 *(Illus.)*

Backbone, 120–121 *(Illus.)*, 122, 122–123 *(Illus.)*, 128–129 *(Illus.)*
Bacteria, 163
Ball-and-socket joints (See **Joints.**)
Bathing, 101–102
Beaumont, William, 180–181, 180 *(Illus.)*
Bicycle safety, 237–242, 265
Bile, 172, 174, 178 *(Illus.)*
Bladder (See **Gall bladder, Urinary bladder.**)
Blind spot, 79

Blood
Alcohol in, 254
Antibodies in, 207
Circulation of, 201–205, 203 *(Illus.)*, 208
Clotting of, 100, 207
Formation of, in marrow, 132
Makeup of, 205–207, 205–206 *(Illus.)*
Oxygen and wastes in, 214, 218
Transfusions, 207
Blood cells, 132, 205–207, 205–206 *(Illus.)*
Blood types, 226
Blood vessels (See **Arteries, Capillaries, Veins.**)
Bones (See also **Skeleton.**)
Broken, 146, 157
Growth of, 119–121, 133, 133 *(Illus.)*
Joints, 127, 127 *(Illus.)*, 135, 135 *(Illus.)*
Marrow in, 130, 131 *(Illus.)*, 132
Of middle ear, 52 *(Illus.)*, 53, 55–57 *(Illus.)*
Shaft, 131
Types of, 119–130, 119–129 *(Illus.)*
Books to Read, 22, 42, 53, 72, 89, 132, 171, 207
Bowel movement, 175
Braille, 79 *(Illus.)*
Brain
Alcohol and, 252
Functions of, 68–72, 70–71 *(Illus.)*
Hearing and, 54, 70, 71 *(Illus.)*
Sight and, 42, 44, 48, 48 *(Illus.)*, 70, 71 *(Illus.)*
Skull, 119, 119–120 *(Illus.)*, 128–129 *(Illus.)*
Smell and, 63, 63 *(Illus.)*, 70, 71 *(Illus.)*
Structure of, 68–71 *(Illus.)*, 73–74 *(Illus.)*
Taste and, 61, 70, 71 *(Illus.)*
Touch and, 65, 70, 71 *(Illus.)*

Brain stem, 68, 68–69 *(Illus.),* 71 *(Illus.),* 72, 73–74 *(Illus.)*
Bread-Cereal Group, 186, 186 *(Illus.)*
Breathing (See **Respiratory system.**)
Broken bones, first aid for, 157
Bronchial tubes, 214, 215, 215 *(Illus.),* 220 *(Illus.),* 222 *(Illus.)*
Bronchitis (See **Chronic bronchitis.**)
Bruise, treating, 228
Brushing the teeth, 165, 165 *(Illus.)*
Bumps and falls, causes of, 247–248, 247 *(Illus.)*

Calluses, 107, 107 *(Illus.)*
Can You Show What You Know? 34, 80, 112, 154, 194, 230, 262
Cancer of lung, 227, 256–257, 257 *(Illus.)*
Capillaries, 90, 103, 103 *(Illus.),* 204, 204 *(Illus.),* 208, 218
Carbohydrates, 183
Carbon dioxide, 214, 218
Cardiac muscle, 139, 139 *(Illus.)*
Careers in health, 75, 180–181, 208, 212, 228
Caries, dental, 163
Cartilage, 52, 122, 122–124 *(Illus.),* 134, 135
Cells
  Blood, 132, 205–207, 205–206 *(Illus.)*
  Cancer, 257 *(Illus.)*
  Food and oxygen for, 183, 201, 214, 218
  Wastes removed from, 201, 214, 218
Cerebellum, 68, 68–71 *(Illus.),* 72, 73–74 *(Illus.)*
Cerebral cortex (See **Cerebrum.**)
Cerebrum, 68, 69 *(Illus.),* 70, 70–71 *(Illus.),* 73–74 *(Illus.)*

Chemical senses (See **Taste, Smell.**)
Choking, first aid for, 233
Chronic bronchitis, 258
Cigarette smoking, 215, 227, 255–258, 257–258 *(Illus.)*
Cilia, 256–257
Circulatory system, 201–207, 201 *(Illus.),* 203–204 *(Illus.),* 209–211 *(Illus.)*
Cleanliness, 101–103
Closed fracture, 146
Clot, 100, 207
Clothing, wearing proper, 103
Cochlea, 54, 55–57 *(Illus.)*
Compact bone, 130
Cones, 44, 45 *(Illus.),* 47 *(Illus.)*
Connecting ridges, 92, 93 *(Illus.),* 98 *(Illus.)*
Consumer health, 101, 111
Contact lenses, 49
Cookbooks, 183
Cornea, 43, 44, 45 *(Illus.)*
Corns, 108
Coronary heart disease, 258
Cut
  First aid for, 115, 228
  Healing of, 100, 100 *(Illus.),* 206–207
Cuticle, 107

Daily Food Guide, 133, 184–187, 184–187 *(Illus.),* 197
da Vinci, Leonardo, 150–151 *(Illus.)*
Dental caries, 163
Dental checkups, 163
Dermatone, 110
Dermis, 65, 90–92, 93 *(Illus.),* 94–95 *(Illus.)*
Diaphragm, 216, 217 *(Illus.)*
Differences, 26–28, 26–27 *(Illus.),* 37, 41

Digestion
Alcohol and, 180
Early experiments on, 180–181
Large intestine and, 175, 175 *(Illus.)*, 179
  (Illus.)
Mouth and, 167–168, 175 *(Illus.)*, 178
  (Illus.)
Small intestine and, 171, 172–173 *(Illus.)*,
  174, 175 *(Illus.)*, 178–179 *(Illus.)*, 182
  (Illus.)
Stomach and, 168, 169 *(Illus.)*, 175 *(Illus.)*,
  178 *(Illus.)*
Digestive juices, 171, 178 *(Illus.)*
Disclosing wafers, 166, 166 *(Illus.)*, 197
Disease, 43, 135, 206–207, 206 *(Illus.)*, 214,
  227, 256–258, 257–258 *(Illus.)*
Do You Know? 41, 54, 92, 99, 104, 202, 218,
  248
Doctors
First aid given by, 157
Medicines prescribed by, 250–251
Drew, Charles, 228, 228 *(Illus.)*
Drugs
Alcohol as, 252–253
Discussing with family, 265
OTC, 250, 251 *(Illus.)*
Rx, 250
Questions about, 236, 249–253
Transplants and, 182
Use of, 249–251

Eardrum, 53, 54, 55–57 *(Illus.)*
Ears (See also **Hearing.**)
Balance and, 41
How we hear, 52–54, 52 *(Illus.)*
Structure of, 52 *(Illus.)*, 53, 55–57 *(Illus.)*

ECG (See **Electrocardiograph.**)
Electrocardiograph, 213, 213 *(Illus.)*
Emotions
Alcohol and, 252
Dealing with, 17–24
Effects of, on body, 138, 149, 181, 218–219
Expressing, 12–13, 12–13 *(Illus.)*, 14–15,
  14–15 *(Illus.)*, 16
Hiding, 17–18
Emphysema, 227, 257–258
End-of-Book Test, 266–267
Enjoy It, 16, 30, 50, 98, 150–151, 188
Environmental health, 54, 100, 183, 215,
  218, 229, 259 *(Illus.)*
Epidermis, 65, 87–89, 87–88 *(Illus.)*, 93
  (Illus.), 94–95 *(Illus.)*
Epiglottis, 168, 214 *(Illus.)*, 215
Esophagus, 168, 168 *(Illus.)*, 175 *(Illus.)*,
  178 *(Illus.)*, 214 *(Illus.)*
Eustachian tube, 54, 55–57 *(Illus.)*
Excitement, 14–15
Exercise
Effects of, on body, 139, 148, 181, 218,
  224, 225
Types of, 152–153
Eyeball, 44, 44–45 *(Illus.)*
Eyes (See also **Vision.**)
How we see, 42–49, 48 *(Illus.)*
Structure of, 43–45 *(Illus.)*
Ways to correct defects in, 49, 49 *(Illus.)*

Fallacies, food, 189
Falls, causes of, 247–248, 247 *(Illus.)*
Family, talking things over with, 37, 83,
  115, 157, 197, 233, 265
Far-sightedness, 49, 49 *(Illus.)*

Fats, 183
Fatty layer in skin, 92, 93–95 *(Illus.)*, 99
Feelings (See **Emotions.**)
Ferrier, David, 75, 75 *(Illus.)*
Fingernails, 104, 105, 105 *(Illus.)*
Fingerprints, 92, 93 *(Illus.)*, 98 *(Illus.)*
Fire safety, 243–246, 246 *(Illus.)*
First aid
  Broken bone, 157
  Bruise, 228
  Choking, 233
  Cut, 115, 228
  Nosebleed, 228
  Splinter, 115
Fixed joints, 127
Flat bones, 130
Flat feet, 126, 126 *(Illus.)*
Flossing the teeth, 164, 164 *(Illus.)*, 197
Fluoride in toothpaste, 163
Food
  Digestion of, 167–176
  Fallacies, 189
  Importance of, to good posture, 148
  Use of, by the body, 158–197
Food groups, 133, 184–187, 184–187 *(Illus.)*, 197
Food tube (See **Esophagus.**)
Foods
  Daily Food Guide, 133, 184–187, 184–187 *(Illus.)*, 197
  Emotions and, 181
  Nutrients in, 183, 184–185
  Recipes for, 190–191
  Trying new, 193 *(Illus.)*
Footprints, 92
Fractures, types of, 146, 157

Freckles, 89

Gall, 172
Gall bladder, 174 *(Illus.)*, 178 *(Illus.)*
Gastric juices, 168
Germs, how destroyed, 43, 206, 206 *(Illus.)*, 207, 214
Glands
  Oil, 88, 90 *(Illus.)*, 91, 94–95 *(Illus.)*
  Pituitary, 73
  Salivary, 167, 167 *(Illus.)*
  Sweat, 90–91, 90 *(Illus.)*, 94–95 *(Illus.)*
  Tear, 43, 43 *(Illus.)*
Glasses, 49
Goose pimples, 91
Graft, skin, 110
Grooming, 101–103
Growth (See also **Emotions.**)
  Differences in, 28, 29, 29 *(Illus.)*
  Nutrients and, 183
Growth plate, 133, 133 *(Illus.)*

Hair
  Care of, 102
  In ears, 53
  Growth of, 109
  In nose, 214
  On skin, 87–88, 87–88 *(Illus.)*, 94–95 *(Illus.)*
Hair pits, 88, 91, 94–95 *(Illus.)*
Handicapped people, 58, 79
Hand signals, 238 *(Illus.)*
Handtalk, 78 *(Illus.)*
Hangnails, 107, 107 *(Illus.)*
Harvey, Dr. William, 208, 208 *(Illus.)*
Health Around Us, 25, 58, 110, 135, 182, 213, 223

Health Tests, 36, 82, 114, 156, 196, 232, 264, 266–267

Hearing
  Center in brain, 54, 70, 71 *(Illus.)*
  How noise affects, 54
  Loss of, 58
  Sense of, 51, 52–54, 52 *(Illus.)*
Hearing aids, 58, 58 *(Illus.)*
Heart
  Disease, 258
  Exercise and, 224
  Function of, 201–205, 203 *(Illus.)*
  Muscle, 139, 139 *(Illus.)*
  Overweight and, 224
  Sleep and, 225
  Smoking and, 258
  Structure of, 201 *(Illus.)*, 209–211 *(Illus.)*, 222 *(Illus.)*
  Transplant, 182 *(Illus.)*
Heartbeat, 202, 229
Heart-lung machine, 223, 223 *(Illus.)*
Height, 29 (See also **Growth.**)
Heimlich Maneuver for choking, 233, 233 *(Illus.)*
Hemoglobin, 89, 205
Hinge joints, 127, 127 *(Illus.)*
Hobbies, 25, 25 *(Illus.)*

Internal clocks, 41
Involuntary muscles, 139, 139 *(Illus.)*
Iris, 43, 43–44 *(Illus.)*

Jawbone, 119–120 *(Illus.)*, 122, 168 *(Illus.)*
Joints
  Artificial, 135, 135 *(Illus.)*
  Types of, 127, 127 *(Illus.)*

Kidneys, 176, 176 *(Illus.)*, 177 *(Illus.)*, 182 *(Illus.)*
Klee, Paul, 16

Laënnec, Dr. René, 212, 212 *(Illus.)*
Large intestine, 175, 175 *(Illus.)*, 179 *(Illus.)*
Larynx, 215, 215 *(Illus.)*, 219
Lens, 44, 45 *(Illus.)*, 48, 49, 49 *(Illus.)*
Ligaments, 134, 134 *(Illus.)*
Liver, 172, 174 *(Illus.)*, 178 *(Illus.)*, 182 *(Illus.)*
Long bones, 126, 130, 131 *(Illus.)*
Lungs
  Air pollution and, 229
  Air sacs in, 216 *(Illus.)*, 221 *(Illus.)*
  Breathing and, 215–217, 217 *(Illus.)*
  Cancer in, 227, 256–257, 257 *(Illus.)*
  Circulation and, 202–203, 203 *(Illus.)*
  Diseases of, 256–258, 257–258 *(Illus.)*
  Exchange in, 218–219
  Exercise and, 227
  Smoking and, 256–258
  Structure of, 220–222 *(Illus.)*
  Transplant of, 182
Lymphocyte, 205 *(Illus.)*

Malpighi, Dr. Marcello, 208, 208 *(Illus.)*
Marijuana, 259
Marrow, 130, 131 *(Illus.)*, 132
Meat Group, 185, 185 *(Illus.)*
Medical discoveries, 75, 180–181, 208, 212, 228
Medicines, 250–251, 265
Medulla oblongata, 68, 68–70 *(Illus.)*, 72, 73 *(Illus.)*
Mental health (See **Emotipns.**)

Milk Group, 187, 187 *(Illus.)*
Minerals, 183
Moles, 89
Motor nerves, 68
Mouth, 175 *(Illus.)*, 178 *(Illus.)*
Movable joints, 127
Mucus, 171, 214–215
Muscle sense, 41
Muscles
  In breathing, 217
  Cardiac, 139, 139 *(Illus.)*
  Contraction of, 137, 137 *(Illus.)*
  Exercise and, 139, 153 *(Illus.)*
  Eye, 44–45 *(Illus.)*, 49
  Facial, 136 *(Illus.)*
  Involuntary, 139, 139 *(Illus.)*
  Mouth, 168 *(Illus.)*
  Movement and, 134 *(Illus.)*, 137 *(Illus.)*
  Skeletal, 136–137, 138 *(Illus.)*, 140–145
   (Illus.), 150–151 *(Illus.)*
  In skin, 91, 94–95 *(Illus.)*
  Stomach, 168
  Smooth, 139, 139 *(Illus.)*
  Voluntary, 138, 138 *(Illus.)*

Nails, 104, 105, 107, 109
Near-sightedness, 49, 49 *(Illus.)*
Nerves
  Auditory, 52 *(Illus.)*, 54, 55–57 *(Illus.)*
  Motor, 68
  Olfactory, 63, 63 *(Illus.)*, 64 *(Illus.)*
  Optic, 44, 45–47 *(Illus.)*, 48
  Sensory, 68
  Spinal, 74 *(Illus.)*
  Taste, 61, 61–62 *(Illus.)*
  Touch, 65, 65–67 *(Illus.)*, 90 *(Illus.)*

Nervous system, 74, 216 (See also **Brain,**
  Nerves.)
Nicotine, 259
Noise, 54, 218
Nose, 63, 63–64 *(Illus.)*, 214–215, 214 *(Illus.)*
Nosebleed, first aid for, 228
Nutrients, 183, 184–185
Nutrition (See **Foods.**)

Oil glands, 88, 90 *(Illus.)*, 91, 94–95 *(Illus.)*
Olfactory nerve, 63, 63–64 *(Illus.)*
Open fracture, 146
Optacon, 79
Optic nerve, 44, 45–47 *(Illus.)*
Osteoarthritis, 135
OTC drugs, 250, 251 *(Illus.)*
Over-the-counter drugs, 250, 251 *(Illus.)*
Overweight, 224
Oxygen, 214, 218, 221

Pacemaker, 202
Pancreas, 172, 178 *(Illus.)*, 182 *(Illus.)*
Papillae, 60
Peristalsis, 168
Perspiration, 91
Pigment, 89
Pioneers in Medicine, 75, 180–181, 208,
  212, 228
Pituitary gland, 73
Plaque, 163, 164, 166, 166 *(Illus.)*, 197
Plasma, 205 *(Illus.)*, 207
Platelets, 205, 205 *(Illus.)*, 206–207
Pollution, 54, 100, 215, 218, 229, 259 *(Illus.)*
Pores, 90
Posture, 147, 147–149 *(Illus.)*
Prescription drugs, 250

Preview It, 10, 40, 86, 118, 160, 200, 236
Proteins, 183
Pulmonary artery, 209 *(Illus.)*
Pulse, 205
Pupil, 43, 43–44 *(Illus.)*

Recipes, 190–191
Red blood cells, 132, 205, 205 *(Illus.)*
Rejection of transplants, 182
Respiratory system, 214–219, 217 *(Illus.)*
   (See also **Lungs.**)
Retina, 44, 45–47 *(Illus.)*, 48, 49
Review It, 35, 81, 113, 155, 195, 230, 263
Rods, 44, 45 *(Illus.)*, 47 *(Illus.)*
Rx drugs (See **Prescription drugs.**)

Safety, 239–248, 265
Safety Around Us, 242, 246, 254
St. Martin, Alexis, 180–181
Saliva, 60, 167–168
Salivary glands, 167, 167 *(Illus.)*, 178 *(Illus.)*
School and Home, 37, 83, 115, 157, 197,
   233, 265
Sclera, 44, 45 *(Illus.)*
Self-image, 30, 31, 32 *(Illus.)*
Semicircular canals, 41, 52 *(Illus.)*, 54,
   55–57 *(Illus.)*
Senses, 41 (See also **Hearing, Smell,**
   Taste, Touch, Vision.)
Sensory nerves, 68
Shoes, posture and, 149
Side effects, 250, 265
Sight (See **Eyes, Vision.**)
Signing, 78 *(Illus.)*
Skeletal muscles, 136–137, 140–145 *(Illus.)*,
   150–151 *(Illus.)*

Skeleton, 119, 120–121 *(Illus.)*, 147 *(Illus.)*
   (See also **Bones.**)
Skin
   Aging and, 96–97
   Care of, 101–103, 102 *(Illus.)*, 106–107
      (Illus.), 108–109
   First aid for injuries to, 115, 228
   Functions of, 99–100
   Graft, 110, 110 *(Illus.)*
   Healing of cuts by, 100, 100 *(Illus.)*,
      206–207
   Ridges in, 92, 93 *(Illus.)*, 98 *(Illus.)*
   Structure of, 62–63 *(Illus.)*, 65, 65 *(Illus.)*,
      66–67 *(Illus.)*, 87–97, 87–88 *(Illus.)*, 93
      (Illus.), 94–95 *(Illus.)*
   Sunburn and, 103, 103 *(Illus.)*
   Tones, 96–97
Skin sense (See **Touch.**)
Skull, 68, 119–120 *(Illus.)*, 122
Sleep, 148
Small intestine, 171, 172–175 *(Illus.)*, 179
   (Illus.), 182 *(Illus.)*
Smell, 59, 63, 63–64 *(Illus.)*
Smoking, 215, 227, 255–259
Smooth muscle, 139, 139 *(Illus.)*
Something to Do, 18, 59, 101, 130, 183,
   244, 245
Sound waves, 51–52
Special Research, 33, 79, 111, 193, 229,
   260, 261
Spinal cord, 68, 69 *(Illus.)*, 74, 74 *(Illus.)*,
   122
Spine (See **Backbone.**)
Splinter, first aid for, 115
Spongy bone, 130
Stethoscope, 212, 224

Stomach
  Blood supply to, 170 *(Illus.)*
  Digestion and, 168, 169 *(Illus.)*, 175 *(Illus.)*,
    178 *(Illus.)*
  Effects of alcohol on, 181
  Effects of emotions on, 181
  X ray of, 173 *(Illus.)*
Striped muscles, 138, 138 *(Illus.)*
Sum It Up, 20, 24, 29, 49, 54, 63, 72, 89, 92,
  100, 103, 132, 134, 139, 163, 176, 187, 207,
  219, 248, 253, 259
Sunburn, avoiding, 103, 103 *(Illus.)*
Sweat glands, 90–91, 90 *(Illus.)*, 94–95
  (Illus.)

Tar, in cigarettes, 257
Taste, sense of, 59–61, 60–62 *(Illus.)*, 167
Taste buds, 59, 60, 61, 61 *(Illus.)*
Tear glands, 43, 43 *(Illus.)*
Teeth
  Care of, 163–166, 164–166 *(Illus.)*, 197
  Digestion and, 161
  Shapes of, 161, 161–162 *(Illus.)*
Television, guides for watching, 83
Tell It, 106, 189, 224
Tendons, 134, 134 *(Illus.)*
Things to Do, 32–33, 78–79, 111, 152–153,
  190–193, 228–229, 260–261
Tobacco (See **Smoking.**)
Toenails, care of, 105, 105 *(Illus.)*
Tongue, 59, 60, 60–62 *(Illus.)*
Tooth decay, 163
Touch, sense of, 65, 65–67 *(Illus.)*
Trachea, 168, 168 *(Illus.)*, 214, 214–215
  (Illus.)
Transfusions, 207, 226

Transplants, 182
True skin (See **Dermis.**)

Ureter, 176 *(Illus.)*, 177 *(Illus.)*
Urinary bladder, 176, 176 *(Illus.)*
Urine, 100, 176

Valves, heart, 203 *(Illus.)*
Vegetable-Fruit Group, 184
Veins, 90, 176 *(Illus.)*, 201 *(Illus.)*, 203
  (Illus.), 204, 204 *(Illus.)*, 208, 209–211
  (Illus.)
Ventricles, 202–203, 203 *(Illus.)*
Vertebrae, 122, 122–123 *(Illus.)*, 128–129
  (Illus.)
Vibrating, 51, 51 *(Illus.)*, 52, 53
Villi, 172, 172 *(Illus.)*
Vision center, 42, 44, 48, 48 *(Illus.)*, 70, 71
  (Illus.)
Vitamins, 100, 183
Vocal cords, 51, 219, 219 *(Illus.)*
Voice box (See **Larynx.**)
Voluntary muscle, 138, 138 *(Illus.)*

Warts, 106, 106 *(Illus.)*
Water, conserving, 183
Weight, 29
What Do You Think? 28, 36, 82, 91, 114,
  156, 196, 232, 264
White blood cells, 132, 205, 205 *(Illus.)*,
  206, 206 *(Illus.)*
Windpipe (See **Trachea.**)
Worry, dealing with feelings of, 14–15
Write It, 31, 76, 108–109, 146, 226–227

X ray, 173, 173 *(Illus.)*

About the Book

This book is a part of the Scott, Foresman Health series. It grows out of the preceding popular *Health and Growth* series which has already been used by several million children. Learner and teacher feedback on *Health and Growth* has pointed the way to this new highly teachable series.

This book has been designed especially to meet the health and safety needs, interests, and concerns of children from ten to eleven or so.

These youngsters are showing interest in their bodies and how they work. Research in child growth and development and in children's health concerns indicates there is peak interest at this age in learning "all about the body." Scott, Foresman's own learner research verifies this interest.

This book, then, satisfies the major health and safety queries—and the minor, intriguing ones —of students who are "going on eleven" or so.

Vivid full-color drawings show, often in minute detail, the structure of various parts of the body. These drawings, made by well-known medical illustrators, help enrich the text and clarify concepts about the body's structure and function.

Problems of mental and emotional health also are dealt with, as young people this age work at coping with strong feelings such as anger, loneliness, and being "different." Mental health is a featured strand in the book. Boys and girls can learn how body, mind, and emotions together make them what they are. They can also discover the study of themselves as a most fascinating pursuit.

Interspersed throughout each chapter are special features such as health-related poems and works of art and student's own writings on pertinent health topics.

Tests and quick reviews abound and help students check their own progress. And a notable feature of each chapter ending is the "School & Home" page which motivates sharing health information at home and applying it in daily living.

Marginal notes to students and "Things to Do" sections at chapter endings also offer a variety of activities, reading lists, demonstrations, and experiments.

To facilitate successful use of this book by the students for whom it is particularly intended, much attention has been given to making the text highly readable. Classroom tryouts prior to publication indicated that this book can easily be read by youngsters the age for which it was designed.

Acknowledgments

For illustrations and photographs on these pages: Cover—Robert Amft. 14–15, 17, 25, 43, 44, 45, 46–47, 49, 55–57, 62, 64, 65, 66–67, 68, 69, 71, 73, 74—Copyright © 1971, 1974 by Scott, Foresman and Company. 79—Courtesy of the Hadley School for the Blind, Winnetka, Illinois. 88—Copyright © 1972, 1974 by Scott, Foresman and Company. 90, 93, 94–95, 96–97—Copyright © 1971, 1974 by Scott, Foresman and Company. 98 (Bottom)—Photographs from Federal Bureau of Investigation, U.S. Department of Justice, Washington, D.C. 100—Copyright © 1971, 1974 by Scott, Foresman and Company. 106, 107 (Left)—Copyright © Carroll H. Weiss, RBP, 1976. 110—Information on dermatome, courtesy of Stryker Corporation, Kalamazoo, Michigan. 120–121, 122, 123, 124, 125, 126, 127, 128–129, 131, 133, 134, 137, 138–139, 140–145—Copyright © 1971, 1974 by Scott, Foresman and Company. 147, 153—Copyright © 1972, 1974 by Scott, Foresman and Company. 161, 162—Copyright © 1971, 1974 by Scott, Foresman and Company. 166—Slides courtesy of Dr. Norman H. Olsen, Northwestern University Dental School, Chicago, Illinois. 167, 168, 169, 170, 172—Copyright © 1971, 1974 by Scott, Foresman and Company. 173—X ray from X-ray Department, Children's Memorial Hospital, Chicago, Illinois. 174, 175, 176, 177, 178–179, 201—Copyright © 1971, 1974 by Scott, Foresman and Company. 205—Copyright © 1972, 1974 by Scott, Foresman and Company. 206—Courtesy Dr. James G. Hirsch, The Rockefeller University. 209–211—Copyright © 1971, 1974 by Scott, Foresman and Company. 213—Electrocardiogram being transmitted by telephone from hospital bedside to the Reingold ECG Center, Northwestern University Medical School, Chicago, Illinois. 214, 215, 216—Copyright © 1971, 1974 by Scott, Foresman and Company. 219—Copyright © 1972, 1974 by Scott, Foresman and Company. 220–222—Copyright © 1971, 1974 by Scott, Foresman and Company. 223—Courtesy Artificial Organs Division, Travenol Laboratories, Inc., Deerfield, Illinois. 228—Courtesy T. Y. Crowell Publisher (Copyright © 1970). Illustrated by Jo Polseno. 238, 239—Copyright © 1971, 1974 by Scott, Foresman and Company. 240–241—Reprinted courtesy of Bicycle Manufacturers Association of America. 246—Courtesy of WGN, Chicago, Illinois. 257—Copyright © 1971, 1974 by Scott, Foresman and Company. 258—Photographs courtesy of Hinsdale Sanitarium and Hospital, Hinsdale, Illinois. 259—Courtesy of American Cancer Society.